Humanism
and the Humanities
in the Twenty-first
Century

Humanism
and the Humanities
in the Twenty-first
Century

Edited by
William S. Haney II and Peter Malekin

Lewisburg
Bucknell University Press
London: Associated University Presses

Associated University Presses
440 Forsgate Drive
Cranbury, NJ 08512

Associated University Presses
16 Barter Street
London WC1A 2AH, England

Associated University Presses
P.O. Box 338, Port Credit
Mississauga, Ontario
Canada L5G 4L8

The paper used in this publication meets the requirements of the American National Standard for Permanence of Paper for Printed Library Materials Z39.48-1984.

Library of Congress Cataloging-in-Publication Data

Humanism and the humanities in the twenty-first century / edited by William S. Haney II and Peter Malekin.
        p.   cm.
    Includes bibliographical references and index.
    ISBN 0-8387-5497-X (alk. paper)
    1. Humanism.   2. Humanities—Philosophy.   I. Haney, William S.
II. Malekin, Peter.
    B821.H659   2001
    001.3—dc21   2001035055

PRINTED IN THE UNITED STATES OF AMERICA

Contents

Introduction

WILLIAM S. HANEY II AND PETER MALEKIN

THIS BOOK IS ABOUT THE FUTURE, ABOUT OUR PRESENT THAT IS shaping the future, about where we are, what we are doing, where we are going. Its scope is therefore much wider than the humanities and the past of literary humanism. The humanities are dying, or so it would seem, and giving way to doctrinaire socioeconomic theory, most of it untestable, and to technologies that are transforming and possibly destroying the environmental support systems that sustain our lives. To say that the world is in crisis is a value judgment, but to some of us it certainly looks like it. To this crisis the past is not totally relevant, since what it meant to be human in the seventeenth century, let alone remoter periods, is not what it means to be human today. Parameters, expectations, possibilities of freedom diverge, and so too do possibilities of enslavement or subjection. Authority, however, remains authoritarian, even when disguised as media persuasion or political correctness. Moreover, as Foucault allows, all authority generates its own opposition, and the official cultures of the modern West are by no means the total cultures. The undersurge movements loosely called New Age think in terms very different from those of official science, religion, and ethics, and they are accompanied by a varied collection of alternative spiritualities, lifestyles, and therapeutic and mental methodologies. The official culture on the whole prefers to pretend that they do not exist.

In this world it is by no means clear that the humanities deserve to survive. But what happens if they do not? And what might we have lost by their death? And if they are to live on, how must they change to receive a new lease of life? The contributors to this book face these and related questions from their own very different viewpoints, for the book is intended not as a monolithic answer, focusing on one "theme," which implies one set for the formulation of the problem and entails a limited range of answers, but rather as a kind of exploding firework, entertaining perhaps, but also stimulating in suggesting ways of viewing the situation that receive little space in conventional official or academic discourse. Its range of reference extends from the sciences to critical theory, from the historical perspective of humanist scholarship to Eastern philosophy, from the advocacy of ethical engagement to the view that ethics are not the fundamental concern of the arts.

The first section of the book groups chapters that question the nature of consciousness. Assumptions on this matter constitute a series of metaphysics underlying all views of the humanities, including those of modern theory, historicism, and traditional criticism dominated by ethical concern. The foundations on which we build deserve examination.

In the opening chapter, William Haney examines scientific and philosophical attempts to understand consciousness, the relation between consciousness and modernist/postmodernist conceptions of language and identity, and the future that a reintegration of consciousness and culture would create for humanism and the humanities. Saussure, Barthes, Derrida, Foucault, Lacan, Lyotard, and others have all contributed in different ways to the decentering of text, author, and human identity. But consciousness as ever-present witnessing awareness always already underlies all of our thoughts, emotions, sensations, memories, and perceptions, making it not only integral to human experience but also unavoidable. The tension in critical theory between materialism-metaphysics, theory-praxis, modernism-postmodernism recurs in the field of consciousness studies, in which approaches to consciousness range from reductionism and functionalism to phenomenology and mysterianism. Crick's reductivist notion of consciousness as "just a bunch of neurons" contrasts with the neurophenomenology of Chalmers and Varela, who interpret consciousness not psychologically as distinct from the Freudian or Jungian unconscious but rather ontologically as distinct from entirely nonconscious experience. In his proposal for a cooperation between phenomenology and cognitive science, theory and praxis, Varela opens a possible way toward a reintegration of consciousness and culture while simultaneously differentiating between the three value spheres of art, morals, and science. This reintegration/differentiation, which prevents the monological domination of any one sphere, such as science, over the other two, can be enriched by the insights of Advaita (nondual) Vedanta. The post-modern reduction of all values to mere interpretative contexts, in which consciousness is not situated but erased as part of the so-called "myth of the given," has in an age of consciousness studies become untenable and anachronistic. For Vedanta, the witnessing Seer, simple, ever-present and spontaneous, is that consciousness beyond attributes into which arises all of our experience, and back to which we move with greater recognition through the suggestive power of literature.

Peter Malekin also sees the question of consciousness as funda-mental but approaches it from a very different angle. The potential destruction of the biosphere, the self-destruction of humanity, and the destruction of human freedom by the development of a global so-called "free" market economy cannot be halted by education as currently pursued, with its emphasis on objective "fact" uninte-grated with a search for human wholeness, whether attainable or not. If, in this situation, the sciences outface the arts and divinity, then the fault lies with the latter. The possibility of alternative ways of knowing and alternative modes of consciousness is broached through a consideration of Plotinus, with some reference to Eastern thought, a consideration of the limitations of scientific epistemol-ogy, and a review of issues raised by David Jasper. We need to rise above the anthropomorphism of the current sciences and arts and the sharp subject-object divide inherited by science from European religion, philosophy, and theology. Recognizing the potential for developing human consciousness beyond its present limitations, Malekin advocates the development of something like Feyerabend's open society, with it ethic of intellectual open-mindedness and so-cial tolerance. In the meantime, economics urgently needs a human and ecofriendly face and science needs balancing by human and hu-mane considerations. It is time once again to question ruthlessly our categories of thought; the nature of the good life; the nature, basis, and limits of authority, including the authority of "experts"; the ef-ficacy and point of our so-called democratic institutions; and the purpose, function, and limitations of religion, science, and national economics. These are life questions, not mere theory, and they need to become—again—central to the arts and humanities.

David Jasper's chapter on the death of God takes up divinity and the human. The death of God is the divine *via negativa* that makes language possible and participation in it is thinking God in a way

that overcomes the restrictions of dogma, whether in theology or
the postmodern philosophy of language, while retaining the rigor of
intellectual discourse. Divinity in this sense is the realization of the
freedom of the human mind which is central to all the humanities.
One of the consequences of David Jasper's position is the creation
of an opening for direct participation in the divine, more than apo-
phatic theology as intellectual system, nearer the *via negativa*, the
negative way or method of the mystics. In this respect it links the
postclassical and medieval with the modern, and also links East and
West. The use of relative negation to point to transcendent reality is
indeed more common in the East than the West, and the way to direct participation in That (the ultimate Reality for which no name
is apt) is as much a part of Eastern traditions as it is of Platonism
or Eastern Orthodox theology. Nonetheless, David Jasper's formulation arises out of our world and is a decidedly Western, twentieth-
century theology. Moreover, it constitutes by implication a rethinking of language different from the more textually oriented move
toward Midrash in the later work of Derrida.

The chapters by Daniel Meyer-Dinkgräfe and Frederick de
Armas constitute a bridge from the discussions of consciousness in
the opening papers to the specific foci of the later ones. Daniel
Meyer-Dinkgräfe analyzes acting theory and the contemporary
teaching of theater to bring out the possibility of transforming the
linear conflicts of drama through the culturing of audience consciousness. The influence of Eastern philosophy on the theory and
practice of so many leading directors in the twentieth century is
discussed and carried further by a consideration of major ideas
from the *Natyashastra*, and pointers are set up for a completely new
departure in modern theater. The paper instances a multicultural
humanism in the modern world.

Starting from *Don Quixote* and Botticelli's *Primavera*, Frederick
de Armas explores the power of the arts to transform consciousness
through rapture and image, linking the aesthetic with what Rudolf
Otto called "numinous awe." The contradictions within text and
image are certainly there and are the contradictions of humanity itself. Political and social conflicts are not suppressed in art, but there
is in human consciousness something that can rise above them, ac-
tualizing a *discordia concors*. In our contemporary world it is this
actualization that is the function of the humanities and humanism
in its widest sense.

In the final section, Daniel Schwarz takes up the need for literature to resonate with human experience and challenges the idea of
the lack of immediacy posited by modern critical theories. He emphasizes our ethical responsibility to heed the witnessing voice of
narrative, especially voices on the political edge. Elie Wiesel's
Night, an autobiographical novel of the Holocaust, exemplifies the
call on human agency and ethical commitment, the will to survive
and witness, to resist deconstruction by enacting the *power of language*. Humanism, canonicity, ethics, and even the author emerge
in harmony with the pluralism and multiple possibilities of readings, texts, and cultures. Schwarz's reading of *Heart of Darkness*
invites a *de-deconstruction* of binary pairs used to undermine humanistic criticism. Through a series of questions, Schwarz's pluralistic approach stresses "the inseparability of ethical, aesthetic,
political, and contextual issues," which range from Conrad's time
of personal crisis and Marlow's self-discovery to the Belgians' exploitation of the Congo and the intellectual history of modernism.
In all readings, the words must ultimately resonate with our personal experience and renew our understanding of the witnessing
voice of narrative.

In the final chapter, Robert Torrance's historical survey discrimi-
nates the many meanings borne by "the humanities" and "humanism" from Roman and Greek times on through the Middle Ages
and Renaissance until today, pointing out the recurring concern of
humanism not only with this world but also with the religious and
spiritual endeavors of humanity. Torrance thus reinforces the link,
established in the opening chapters, between literary humanism and
the religious and spiritual concerns of human beings. The occa-
sional fatuousness and pomposity of some humanists is acknowledged, but the central engagement of the tradition with the driving
innovative force of a specifically human consciousness is seen as
stretching down to our own time in the work of humanist scholars
and humanist scientists alike. Humanism is a modern antidote to
inhumanity, mechanization of consciousness, and those dogmas of
political correctness that reduce the multicultural to splintered fac-
tions. Torrance is therefore also concerned with transcending the
limitation of current thinking, though in his view this would take
place more through a change in ideas and attitudes than through an
enhancement of human consciousness itself. Torrance's humanism

is tough-thinking, rational, hardheaded, and defensible in contemporary terms.

The epilogue is a science fiction conversation by Brian Aldiss. The intrusion of science and technology has been the major factor in what we regard as an imbalance between the arts and the sciences. Fiction is traditionally one of the central concerns of the humanities. Science fiction in particular is the only form of literature to explore rigorously the epistemological limits of science and its human consequences. (It has done this at least since H. G. Wells, and the epistemological issues are very fully investigated in classics like Stanislaw Lem's *Solaris*, with its long parallel between science and religion, and its discussion of the limits imposed on communication through the very limitations of consciousness itself.) Brian Aldiss has himself produced work that succeeds in rendering previously alien forms of consciousness. The opening chapters by Haney and Malekin stress, from different viewpoints, the link between body and mind, so that alteration in the one produces alteration in the other. Meyer-Dinkgräfe and de Armas also point to the influence of the physical on the mental in different specific instances. Malekin points out that a change in physiology is also a change in consciousness. For Brian Aldiss the abstract statement is experiencable fact. If this book seems like an abstract academic discussion, then Brian Aldiss's humans of the future bring it down to earth, for the unexpected disclosure of the ending is the result of the genetic and surgical manipulation that is happening now. We had better decide, and quickly, whether this is what we want.

Humanism
and the Humanities
in the Twenty-First
Century

Part I
The Nature of Consciousness

The Science of Mind, Consciousness, and Literary Studies

WILLIAM S. HANEY II

INTRODUCTION

IN PROCLAIMING THE DEATH OF MAN, GOD, AND MEANING, POST-modernists have called into question the universalism of a liberal humanism. But in the twenty-first century, theories of the self will undoubtedly continue to play an important role in literary and cultural studies. As Howard Mancing puts it, the "vast interdisciplinary activity centered around cognitive science has enormous implications for literary theory and criticism and it will be ignored at our great peril as it continues to form the prevailing mode of discourse of the physical, biological, social, and human sciences in the twenty-first century" (1999, 167). Since romanticism the metaphors of the self have steadily devolved outward from the notion of a deep interior. Defined as the soul and the seat of inspiration, creativity, passion, and genius, the romantic self gave way in modernism to a rational and fully predictable self that functions like a machine, and in postmodernism to a fragmentary, relational self devoid of essence or autonomy. As Kenneth Gergen says, "With the spread of postmodern consciousness, we see the demise of personal definition, reason, authority, commitment, trust, the sense of authenticity, and faith in progress" (1991, 228). But given the current boom of research into consciousness in fields ranging from philosophy and cognitive science to quantum physics, the story of the self in Western culture is far from over. Research in the burgeoning field of consciousness studies indicates that the self is regaining its status of unity, irreducibility, and autonomy. Recent studies suggest that when viewed not psychologically (as distinct from the Freudian or Jungian unconscious) but rather ontologically (as distinct from the nonconscious), consciousness is not an epiphenomenon, not reduc-

17

ible to the structure and functions of the physical domain, not a cultural construct (Wallace 1970; Farrow and Herbert 1982). Consciousness in this ontological sense has significant implications for humanism and the humanities in the twenty-first century.

In their introduction to the inaugural issue of the *Journal of Consciousness Studies*, a journal devoted to controversies on the self in science and the humanities, the editors highlight the need for research into consciousness through "systematic investigative methods" that would "replace the naive, commonsensical Aristotelian-Cartesian" approach (J. A. Goguen et al., 1994, 8), while pointing out that these methodologies need not be developed "entirely *de novo*." "For while development of appropriate procedures has not been the major concern of western culture, Eastern cultures, for a variety of reasons, have traditionally given more attention to the problem." Many Eastern methodologies along with their associated physiological and experiential claims have recently begun to be discussed in scientific literature. As the editors of *JCS* suggest, "If we come to believe that we are all 'just a bunch of neurons,' then it is fanciful to assume that concepts like the sanctity of human life will survive unaltered. Alternately, if the sort of idealist cosmology espoused by the perennial and contemplative traditions is found to have some scientific basis, then the transformative claims of the meditation procedures associated with these [Eastern] traditions will have to be taken seriously."

My concern here will be mainly with the relevance of Western research into consciousness for the humanities. One effect of a post-structuralist postmodernism (as opposed to a reconstructive postmodernism suggested by Suzi Gablik [1991], Danah Zohar [1994]; and others) has been to blur the distinction between high and popular cultures and in so doing to eliminate the notions of a unified self and universal truth. If perennial notions of the self are found to have a valid empirical basis, then postmodernist claims about consciousness will have to be reconsidered and the bias against humanism reevaluated. Already we see emerging a powerful alternative to the postmodernist view of the self as no more than a social construction or the product of material forces.

I begin this chapter with an overview of the concepts of the self in literary theory and trace their development from premodernity through modernity to postmodernity. I then review contemporary views on consciousness and its recent history from William James to the current controversies on the "hard problem" of consciousness (why mental processing is accompanied by conscious awareness in the first place). On the basis of these developments I speculate on the phenomenology of consciousness in the postmodern condition. In the final sections I compare Eastern and Western, reductive and nonreductive theories of consciousness in light of the difference between mind/body dualism (in the West) and consciousness/matter dualism (in the East)—where matter includes both mind and body. Throughout this chapter I propose a nonreductive theory of consciousness and emphasize the importance to the field of literary and cultural studies of a full understanding not only of the intellect and mind but also of pure consciousness itself. Other theorists who have recently defended humanism include John Ellis (1997) and Wendell Harris (1996); my approach adds the dimensions of consciousness and perennial psychology. As Ellis observes, "Enlightenment thinkers realize that humane values can prevail only if we identify ourselves as human beings first and foremost" (112). As I will propose here, consciousness is innate to all human beings and the basis of our common humanity.

THE SELF IN CRITICAL THEORY

As the prevailing cultural paradigm, postmodernism over the past few decades has made the antihumanist, anti-idealist claim that man (including the author) and unitary meaning are dead—if they were ever more than an illusion to begin with. Ferdinand de Saussure, Jacques Lacan, Roland Barthes, Michel Foucault, Jean Baudrillard, Jean-Francois Lyotard, Jacques Derrida, and others propose that language and consciousness are not what they appear to be. For Saussure, language as an arbitrary system of signs precedes being and also assumes a vital role in its construction. Barthes, Derrida, and others claim that this conclusion holds regardless of the way we approach the concept of self, whether through phenomenology or deconstruction. Hence, if the self is a linguistic construct and language has no tangible reality "out there," no actual referent, then what reality can we ascribe the self?

Louis Althusser, with his influential concept of ideology as the "imaginary representation" of real social relations in the world, argues that individuals are socially constructed subjects (1969, 56), subjugated by "ideological state apparatuses" (54). The "individ-ual *is interpellated* [hailed] *as a (free) subject* [by ideology] *in order that he shall submit freely to the commandments of the Sub-ject, i.e. in order that he shall (freely) accept his subjection. . . . . There are no subjects except by and for their subjection*" (62, Al-thusser's emphasis). For Barthes, who defines textuality as an inter-play of codes without origin, the author is dead: "Writing is that neutral, composite, oblique space where our subject slips away, the negative where all identity is lost, starting with the very identity of the body writing" (1977, 142). Even in claiming that "the birth of the reader must be at the cost of the death of the Author" (148), Barthes gives priority to the sign and its codes over the reader. Sim-ilarly, in asking "What Is an Author?" Foucault defines the author not as a unified consciousness but as comprised of "author-func-tions" or socially determined roles. "The author does not precede the works, he is a certain functional principle by which, in our cul-ture, one limits, excludes, and chooses" (1989, 274). Foucault thus rejects the "philosophies of consciousness" in favor of structural-ism. In volume 1 of *The History of Sexuality* (1990), he finds the Freudian-Marxist notion of the repressed libido too existentialist and instead explains human sexuality in terms of the pressure to conform exerted by the discourses on sex as they developed through the course of history.

While Barthes and Foucault decenter the reader in the text, Lacan, in his "meta-theory" of psychoanalysis, decenters the self from within, arguing that the unconscious is "structured like a lan-guage" (Eagleton 1983, 157). The identity of the self is constituted by relations, like the relation between the sign and referent, subject and world, with the subject dispersed along a chain of signifiers in its desire to regain the imaginary fullness of a whole identity, the pre-oedipal unity of signifier and signified, self and world, child and mother (Lacan 1989, 301–20). For Lacan, the loss of unity and the primary repression of the desire for the lost mother marks our entry into the Symbolic Order, which constitutes our self-identity. The speaking subject is thus defined in terms of lack. Terry Eagleton refers to this as a state of "poststructuralist anxiety" (1983, 116).

Whereas Saussure divides the sign from the referent, Derrida di-vides the sign within itself through the play of *différance*, and thereby further undermines the notion of a transcendental signified or integrated self. For Derrida, "there is nothing outside the text"

(1976, 158). Reference becomes self-reference, as meaning is created not through a directedness to things or concepts but rather through intertextual play, a play of the world structured within a linguistic system of differences. In deconstructing logocentrism and the Western metaphysics of presence, Derrida argues that the subject is a function of language—of "a retention and protention of differences, a spacing and temporalizing, a play of traces" (1973, 146). He calls into question the notion of a presence or self-presence of consciousness prior to language and the play of traces. In his critique of Husserl, for whom consciousness is a "self-presence, a self perception of presence," Derrida holds that "the power of synthesis and of the incessant gathering-up of traces is always accorded to the 'living present' " (1973, 147). Like J. Hillis Miller, Paul de Man, and other post-structuralists, Derrida regards the self as a social construction that is different in different societies.

Modernity adopted the view that reason, unity, and singularity are "good" and disunity and fragmentation are "bad." Deconstructive postmodernity, or what Harris calls "hermetic poststructuralism" (1996, 65–66), conversely rejects unity, singularity, and reason in favor of disunity, fragmentation, irrationality, and undecidability. Postmodernists like Lyotard and Baudrillard claim there can be many viewpoints, all subjective, and many truths, all relative. At the decentered core of postmodernity is the fragmentary self, consciousness splintered by social forces and a multiplicity of conflicting voices. The political and philosophical grand narratives of emancipation and enlightenment give way to splintering micronarratives. Hence the postmodern condition often exhibits an aura of exhaustion or "used-upness," with the earlier optimism of linear progress replaced by the despair of relativism and no future. The sense of nothingness outside the "language game" described by Wittgenstein has led some postmodernists to predict "the end of philosophy." Nietzsche had already declared that "God is dead" (1974, 181), and that "facts are precisely what there is not, only interpretations" (1968, 267). But, remarkably, many of the principles of deconstructive postmodernism—undecidability and infinite freeplay, multiple perspectives and the saturation of the subject by relative voices—do not necessarily contradict and in fact often complement the principles of humanism and perennial psychology. This complementarity also appears between Eastern and Western theories of consciousness.

Premodernity, Modernity, Postmodernity:
Interior and Exterior Domains

The move from the premodern view of the self to the modern has resulted in the current division between the interior and exterior realms of experience. The Great Chain of Being of the premodern era, reaching from matter to body to mind to spirit, has been superseded by the modern differentiation of what Ken Wilber refers to as the spheres of cultural value: namely, art, morals, and science (1998a, 1–36). This differentiation has meant that scientists, artists, and scholars can pursue truth in their diverse fields unimpeded by repressive domination by the other spheres. This is the positive side of modernity. The negative side is that differentiation in modernity has gone to the extreme of scientific imperialism, resulting in dissociation, alienation, and fragmentation. In the premodern era the inner and outer domains were not so much integrated as undifferentiated, and in the modern era the dignity of differentiation has turned into the soulless dissociation of monological science.

Wilber, who has written extensively on Eastern and Western philosophy, notes that modern empirical science has until recently rejected an epistemological pluralism that would allow for a correspondence between levels of knowing (sensory, mental, archetypal, and mystical) and levels of being (body, mind, and spirit) (1998b). He sees the need for a differentiation and a reintegration of the spheres of knowledge. Huston Smith, who agrees with this view, discerns that "reality is graded, and with it, cognition" (*Forgotten Truth*; quoted in Wilber 1998b, 35)—a truth also stated in the Upanishads. Wilber condenses the four levels of knowing into three: the eye of flesh (the "It" of empiricism), the eye of mind (the "We" of rationalism), and the eye of contemplation (the "I" of mysticism) (1998b, 59–70). Instead of differentiating and then reintegrating these forms of knowing, science asserts the dominance of the It of empiricism or the eye of flesh. The It perspective, which is monological, represses the We perspective, which is dialogical, and the I perspective, which is translogical. Colin McGinn, in *Ethics, Evil and Fiction*, also argues with regard to science that we should be wary of selecting "one sort of knowledge as setting the standard for all the rest; this is apt to be arbitrary and tendentious, not founded on the application of impartial criteria of epistemic value" (1997, 35–36). Because moral facts and events, unlike physical facts and events, do not cause our belief in them does not, for McGinn, preclude the possibility of ethical knowledge—which he considers a key element of aesthetics. He asserts that "humans enjoy a natural, spontaneous knowledge of ethical truth, which is part of their innate endowment" (45).

Like Wilber, Margaret Wertheim traces the move from a premodern spatial dualism composed of a physical space and a spiritual space, to a modern monism in which physical space takes over, and ultimately to a postmodern cyberspace, which is being "touted as a new realm for the 'self' " (1999, 41). The erasure of spiritual space began in the Renaissance with perspective art, when physical vision supplanted "spiritual vision" (108), and continued with the growth of science and the discovery that the physical universe is infinite. Attempts to integrate science and culture are increasing, however, particularly in the field of consciousness studies. The encounter between the physical and spiritual generates a transcendental naturalism or a naturalistic transcendentalism, which is best described in terms of consciousness and aesthetic experience.

In contemplating a beautiful object, whether visual or verbal, one may have the experience of freedom from all activity, including the desire or will to do anything but continue in this state of contemplation. The aesthetic object suspends our grasping for anything in the regretted past or anticipated future, opening a clearing for the awareness in the timeless present. This stasis results not from the expressed content of the work of art but rather from the response it evokes through the power of suggestion. Although rarely discussed in Western theory, this contemplative response is known in Indian literary theory as *rasadhvani*, the flavor of the subtle sentiments leading toward "liberation" or *moksha* suggested by a work (Krishnamoorthy 1968, 26). Entering the timeless present suggested by a work of art can bring transpersonal revelations or translogical connections: a flash of truth or a moment of eternity. Although science posits only one kind of empiricism and thus only one kind of truth—the sensory or material associated with physical space—we generally experience three (interrelated) kinds of empiricism: sensory, mental, and contemplative. All three are posited by the theory of *rasadhvani* and by the *Mundaka Upanishad* (Radhakrishnan 1992), and are largely accepted by Eastern cultures. Great works of art comprise an interrelationship among them: the expressed form and content belong to sensory and mental empiricism, while the suggestion of a timeless freedom belongs to the contemplative.

Historically, in the West, the principle of falsifiability, the criterion of scientific validity, has been applied only to sensory empiricism and denied to the other two. In Eastern cultures, on the other hand, falsifiability has been applied to mental and contemplative empiricism and today, through Eastern influence, this principle is also being applied in the Western philosophy of science. That is, as in sensory empiricism, so in mental and contemplative empiricism one can apply the three strands of valid knowledge: injunction (doing something), apprehension (getting results), and confirmation (testing these results)—or exemplar, data, and falsifiability (Wilber 1998b, 137–75). McGinn points out that not only ethical and aesthetic knowledge but also logic and mathematics "are not causally responsible for our knowledge of them" (1997, 40). He observes, following John Locke and Bertrand Russell, that "scientific knowledge is conjectural and inherently stretches our natural capacities, but moral knowledge has certainty and universality, and hence admits of demonstration" (41).

Scholars outside the humanities are beginning to apply the criteria of science in the study of art. V. S. Ramachandran and William Hirstein, in "The Science of Art: A Neurological Theory of Aesthetic Experience" (1999), explore the relation between aesthetic experience and consciousness. Although "The Science of Art" is reductive to the extent that it links consciousness to the physiology of the brain, unlike post-structuralism it also seeks universal rules and principles. Ramachandran and Hirstein believe that any theory of art should have three components: a logic of art, an evolutionary rationale, and an understanding of the brain circuitry involved (15). They propose eight principles for a total of what they call "eight laws of aesthetic experience" (49–50) (peak shift, isolation, perceptual grouping, extraction of contrast, perceptual problem solving, abhorrence of unique vantage point, visual 'puns' or metaphors, and symmetry). Though criticized by peer commentators in the sciences and humanities for oversimplifying aesthetic experience, they nonetheless offer an alternative to the linguistic determinism and cultural relativism of a deconstructive postmodernism. They are among a growing number of scientists who emphasize the phenomenological dimension of great art. Even though they see art in physiologically reductionist terms, they acknowledge that no simple

metric or quantification such as galvanic skin response or Birk-
hoff's aesthetic ratio (Goguen 1999, 13) can fully account for aesthetic experience.

Although science and culture are beginning a process of reintegration, Wilber traces three failed reactions against the domination
of monological science: idealism, romanticism, and postmodernism. But as I will suggest, even within postmodernism we can find
the beginnings of a differentiation that successfully reintegrates art,
morals and science, one based on a transcendental naturalism of
aesthetic experience. Of the three reactions to modernity, romanticism was the first to understand that dissolution was a disease in
need of a cure. But the romantics, in Wilber's view, made the mistake of trying to de-differentiate the spheres of knowledge rather
than trans-differentiate them in a way that would avoid the failure
of dissolution. Instead of advancing through modernity, they
wanted to go backward, confusing pre-differentiation with trans-
differentiation (Wilber 1998b, 90–101). Idealism, on the other
hand, came the closest to reestablishing the validity of interior
knowledge against the flattening influence of science. Immanuel
Kant, Johann Fichte, Georg Hegel, and Friedrich Schelling understood that the prerational modes of knowledge existing before
modernity may appear to be transrational, but are really only nonra-
tional and therefore cannot constitute a ground for valid knowledge.
Having fallen into the world, Spirit began a process of ascent to
return to itself, that is, to becoming self-reflexively aware. Unfortunately, the idealists did not have a practical and effective way to
realize the transpersonal and translogical insights of their contemplative vision. They lacked, for instance, the practice of yoga
through which Vedanta provides a way to realize the identity of
Atman, or the koans through which Zen meditation provides a way
to enlightenment. These techniques have been tested for falsifiability through injunction, apprehension, and confirmation and thus
proved to be valid means of gaining knowledge.

Postmodernism, the third reaction, attempts the most radical cure
for the dissolution or flattening of the value spheres by monological
science. While modernity killed two value spheres, aesthetics and
morals, postmodernity killed all three, including that of science. By
rendering all three spheres equally defunct, postmodernity rejects
all foundationalism, essentialism, and transcendentalism. That is, it
rejects the myth of the given. All values are replaced by interpreta-

tion, which becomes the foundation or essential feature of the universe. The modernist view of the world, in which language is representational, "the mirror of nature," gives way to the linguistic turn of semiotics, structuralism, and post-structuralism: a shift from modernity to postmodernity. Language becomes opaque and meaning no longer points objectively but becomes undecidable, a network of dialogical and intersubjective contexts. Signifiers are grounded not in natural referents or signifieds but in nothing but power, ideology, prejudice, gender, race, and colonialism. Hence, the sliding chains of signifiers in postmodernity constitute sliding material contexts only, or chains of data alienated from the values of inner life. Modernity at first differentiated the diverse spheres or contexts of knowledge, only to dissolve them into one—displacing the individual and collective interior domains with the exterior domain of sensory empiricism. Postmodernity, in turn, flattened the distinction between the interior and exterior, substituting an infinity of sliding contexts in which the individual's intentionality as a source of meaning is not situated but erased.

Yet in spite of the attempt to reduce the translogical/transpersonal mind to a form of sensory knowing, the interior domain is still with us. Even the mediated data of sensory empiricism in science must finally become unmediated experience at the moment of apprehension, otherwise there would only be mediation without experience.

It may help to clarify the nature of the interior domains as the basis of contemplative empiricism, as in aesthetic experience (*rasadhvani*), if we return for a moment to the idealist tradition. As Jonathan Shear notes on the topic of self-knowledge, Descartes, Hume, and Kant held that this knowledge provided the basis "of all human understanding," but they found that to understand the self was problematic (1998, 673). Descartes concluded on the basis of common sense that everyone has a "clear intuitive knowledge of the self as *single*, *simple* and *continuing*," which he expressed through the phrase *cogito ergo sum*, or in modern parlance, "I am conscious, therefore I exist" (Shear's emphasis). Hume, on the other hand, looked within but could find nothing corresponding to Descartes's single, continuing self, which he regarded as nonsense. Kant, however, found that Descartes and Hume were both right. He argued, as Shear puts it, that "we *have to have*" a unified self as posited by Descartes, but that as Hume indicated "there is *no possi-*

bility whatsoever of experiencing it, or indeed of knowing it as anything but an *abstract vacuous cipher*" (Shear's emphasis).

Kant thus agreed with Hume that we have no overall sense of unity of the self based on the content of our experiences, but he also argued that such an overall unity, which he called "the transcendental unity of apperception," must be presupposed as the underlying principle of all human understanding (674). He reasoned that because experience is extended in time and space, it consists of separate parts; but to exist as a single experience, it must have a single experiencer, which for Kant means that a single, simple, and continuing self is the essential precondition for any experience. But Kant also agreed with Hume that we have no concept of or any way of knowing this simple, unified self. As Shear states, one of Kant's "major conclusions about the self is that it cannot have any experiential quality of its own at all. That is, it has to be a 'pure, original unchanging consciousness,' a 'bare consciousness' with 'no distinguishing features' of its own" (675). This implies that the self is knowable only as a "blank abstraction," necessary to all experience yet unexperienceable and unknowable in itself, a paradox that, as Kant said, "mocks and torments" even the wisest philosopher. He thus describes the self as a "qualityless pure consciousness"; it has "no distinguishing quality of its own," but as the witness or seer it underlies all of our manifold experience (675–66). It is the observer of our changing mental content, but is itself devoid of empirical content. Hence, even as our bodies and personalities mutate over time, we still identify them as belonging to us, to the self as a qualityless, unchanging witness.

This ungraspable nature of the self, which cannot be known by observing it but only by being it, is the reason for its divination in premodernity and also the apparent ease with which its erasure has been accepted in postmodernity. No solution to the problem of modernity can effectively ignore this unified transpersonal, translogical self. As a remedy to postmodern fragmentation, the transpersonal self is not difficult to find; if anything, it is unavoidable. As discussed in the final section below in terms of Eastern thought, the self as qualityless pure consciousness, the witnessing awareness devoid of empirical content, is always already here behind every thought, feeling, and perception. It is the ever-present witness of the mind, body, and socially constructed self.

Paradoxically, postmodernism serves as a kind of Derridean pha-

rmakon for the self, both a poison and a remedy. That is, it denies
the self and simultaneously suggests a way to reach it. To begin
with, postmodernity flattens the world to mere surfaces, eliminating
values, depth, and the need to search for meaning below the surface. Meaning is determined by its contexts, and contexts are infinite and ultimately unmasterable. Similarly, the qualityless self of
Kant and Eastern cultures is also a kind of surface phenomenon,
one that extends beyond conceptual content such as language. But
for Derrida, even though meaning is undecidable, it is nevertheless
a linguistic undecidability. He is not able to "pole-vault" beyond
language as a system of difference into the realm of pure witness.
In his essay "Edmund Jabès and the Question of the Book," Derrida claims that in Judaism one does not find God or Being intu-
itively or directly, as through the Book: "Being never is, never
shows *itself*, is never *present* . . . outside difference" (1978, 74; his
emphasis). Harold Coward notes that in Derrida the real is experienced only "when the opposites of language are maintained in dynamic tension . . . through a continual deconstruction of first one
and then the other" (Coward & Foshay 1992, 210). Derrida attempts to undermine the Western logocentric tradition by arguing
that we never reach a moment of presence or pure consciousness,
but only its trace in the linguistic flickering of presence and absence
held in tension.

Nonetheless, the gaps between the pairs of opposites in the pen-
dulum swing of deconstruction, as the traces of presence, need to
be understood in terms of the witnessing experience of such mo-
ments of (non)presence. These gaps evoke Kant's "qualityless pure
consciousness," the witnessing awareness that has "no distinguishing quality of its own" (Shear 1998, 675–76). Derrida argues that
the silence between words, as between the words of God's voice,
is pregnant with desire and intentional meaning. He gives sensory
attributes to that which belongs to contemplative empiricism. But if
the gap or silence between words is by definition empty of empirical content, then to experience silence suggests the ever-present
witnessing awareness of the nondual mystics, from Plotinus and
Eckhart in the West to Shankara and Nagarjuna in the East. As Kant
pointed out, moreover, we have no concept or way of knowing this
unified witnessing self. We cannot think the gap; we can only be it.
The deconstructive movement of difference attempts to undermine
the unity of presence; but in designating empirical gaps and pro-

moting our continual experience of them in the oscillation between pairs of opposites, it simultaneously suggests the silence of pure awareness—the simple, qualityless, ever-present witness of all empirical difference and its gaps. Otherwise, for whom would the mediation of difference be an object of experience? Would it be another mediation in an endless series, with no experiencer ever at hand? Even in postmodernity, then, literary and cultural studies and the human sciences suggest that the various domains of knowing can remain distinct yet complementary, integrated on the basis of consciousness.

THE EXISTENCE OF CONSCIOUSNESS

The attempt to reintegrate the value spheres has received a boost from consciousness studies as a discipline, even though the opposition found in the humanities between materialism and metaphysics can also be found in the scientific literature on consciousness. In *The Astonishing Hypothesis*, Francis Crick, Nobel Laureate, defines consciousness reductively by eliminating the notion of conscious experience altogether in favor of a neurobiological account. "Consciousness is associated with certain neural activities" (1994a, 251), probably related to "visual awareness" (252). On the other hand, the physicist Roger Penrose, in *The Emperor's New Mind* and *Shadows of the Mind*, invokes the mechanism of quantum coherence in an attempt to explain the unified nature of conscious experience. He defines consciousness as something separate, more than the sum of the parts, "some sort of global capacity which allows us to take into account the whole of a situation at once" (1994a, 20). Because quantum mechanics is incomplete, however, he thinks we can't really look to it for an explanation of consciousness; we need to go beyond it (21). Nevertheless, quantum mechanics tells us, he says, what we need to look for in a theory of consciousness: "we need to look for large-scale quantum states."

In his book *The Large, the Small and the Human Mind*, Penrose continues his argument on the noncomputability of consciousness and the need to go beyond our monological sensory worldview to better understand the relation between the subjective and physical realms. Of great interest to him are what he calls the three worlds or three mysteries and the relationships between them: the physical

world, the mental world, and the Platonic or mathematical world.
"The more we understand about the physical world," he says, "and
the deeper we probe into the laws of nature, the more it seems as
though the physical world almost evaporates and we are left only
with mathematics" (1997, 3). In an interview he says that physical
matter we now understand "as much more of a mathematical thing
. . . much more of a mental substance" (1994a, 24). He thus attempts to integrate the monological (sensory) perspective of
science with the dialogical and translogical (rational and contemplative) perspectives. He finds problematic the notion that the mental world emerges out of the physical world, that our feelings, sense
of color, and happiness could arise out of physics, with its concern
for particles, massive objects, energy, space, and time (1997, 94).
In terms of the differentiation of the domains of knowledge, it is
anachronistic and indeed untenable for postmodernist and Marxist
critics to hold it on faith that consciousness is entirely a materialist
product.

The physicist Jean Burns, in "Volition and Physical Laws,"
points out that volition, an aspect of consciousness and the basis of
ethical choice, "is not a part of presently known physical laws and
it is not even known whether it exists—no physics experiments
have ever established its presence" (1999, 27). Burns defines free
will in philosophical terms as "an influence on physical events
which corresponds with mental intention and causes a physical
change which would not otherwise occur in identical physical circumstances" (29). But whether volition and consciousness are considered physical or nonphysical, she demonstrates that the physical
effects of volition cannot be explained by "presently known physical laws because these laws encompass only determinism and quantum randomness" (32), which are not what is indicated by
consciousness or volition.

The astrophysicist Undo Uus, in "The Libertarian Imperative,"
also argues that free will, defined "as the ability to select one actuality from several possibilities," is "incompatible with causal determinism" (1999, 51). Linking free will with consciousness, he says
that "the empirically grounded science of phenomenal consciousness is possible only if the physical world as conceptualized by
modern materialistic science is causally open," a view that at present does not prevail and that requires "denying the causal complete-
ness of physics" (50). Science has discovered no laws that account

for ethics and free will, which are thus either illusions or not physi-
cally determined. To characterize phenomenal consciousness as an
epiphenomenon, a product of the physical, would be to exclude the
possibility of ethics and volition. These are not explainable by any
known conceptual discourse or determined by any presently known
laws of physics.

Penrose observes that even though it cannot be said that any of
the three worlds simply emerges out of the others, the physical
world seems to obey mathematical laws in an extremely precise
way (1997, 95). He notes that "there is a small part of the Platonic
world which encompasses our physical world" (97). This observation in physics has radical implications for the post-structuralist notion that language precedes meaning and that the self is a linguistic
construct. Saussure's claim that language is an arbitrary system of
differences together with Derrida's movement of *différance* cannot
account for the way the Platonic world of mathematics seems to
encompass the physical world. As Shear explains in terms of philosophy:

> The discovery and articulation of mathematical structures has led time
> and again directly to the discovery of previously unperceived and unsus-
> pected structures and phenomena of nature. And many of these pre-
> viously unsuspected structures and phenomena have turned out to be
> identifiable and even perceivable (laser light, atomic lattices, telecom-
> munication phenomena, moons and rings orbiting planets, etc.) com-
> pletely independently of the abstract mathematical considerations that
> originally led to their discovery. That is, it is clear that our mathemati-
> cally oriented physical sciences have regularly uncovered objective
> structures and phenomena which exist and function independently of
> both our perceptions and our theorizing. (1990, 190)

Contrary to post-structuralist claims about the lack of a natural connection between sign and thing, the language of mathematics indicates that referents accessible to conscious experience do seem to
exist prior to and independently of the language system. Derrida's
decentering of metaphysics and logocentrism is thus problematized
by mathematical laws.

While physicists such as Penrose (1994a, 1994b, 1997), Paul Davies (1983), Nick Herbert (1985), Fritjof Capra (1977), John Hagelin (1987) and theorists such as Katherine Hayles (1984) have
observed the parallels between consciousness and quantum physics,

it has also been suggested that quantum theory has a need for consciousness, not the other way around. Euan Squires states that "the main reason why quantum theory is relevant to consciousness is that the theory cannot be completely defined without introducing some features of consciousness" (1994, 201). Whereas books on classical mechanics deal with "what is and the way things are," books on quantum mechanics deal with "what is observed" (202). The significance of quantum theory for research into consciousness does not involve any ability on the part of theory to explain consciousness, but rather the role of consciousness in providing "a concept of what it means to 'know' " (203). The hermeneutic circle here is that we can't explain consciousness in terms of physics because we can't fully understand physics without consciousness. Arguably, the same circle would apply in a deconstructive understanding, which deals with "what is observed" in the act of reading, and therefore cannot do without firsthand conscious experience. For deconstructive postmodernism to deny consciousness is a performative contradiction. Any theory of what it means to "know" would depend on the light of awareness, unless we associate epistemology with a state of darkness.

The History of Consciousness

Consciousness has been defined in many ways throughout the history of Western philosophy, from Plato and Plotinus to Descartes, Kant, the German Enlightenment, Hegel, Husserl, Heidegger, Sartre, and Derrida. As Güven Güzeldere observes, Sartre and others have used two possible meanings of consciousness: "the state or faculty of being conscious, as a condition and concomitant of all thought, feeling and volition [as distinct psychologically from the Freudian/Jungian unconscious]"; and "the state of being conscious, regarded as the normal condition of healthy waking life [as distinct ontologically from the nonconscious]" (1995a, 34). The former sense corresponds with Descartes's usage of consciousness as "consciousness of," the awareness of our mental states, a transitive usage that also implies intention. The latter is something more basic, an intransitive usage that implies a state of consciousness by itself, as in the experience of nonintentional, pure consciousness in the tradition of Eastern cultures. Güzeldere notes that consciousness can also be defined in terms of its two faces, "two major, equally attractive, pre-theoretic intuitions" (35). The first is "consciousness is as consciousness does," and the second "consciousness is as consciousness seems" (36). The former intuition is causal and associated with third-person observation (theory), and the latter is phenomenal and associated with direct, first-person experience (praxis). While post-structuralist postmodernists would deconstruct phenomenal intuition, there is a growing consensus in consciousness studies that the two aspects of conscious experience are not mutually exclusive but complementary.

The modern Western history of the study of consciousness begins with the early work of William James. As psychology broke from philosophy and started to develop into a scientific discipline in its own right, one of its first offspring was introspectionism, a study of the phenomenology of the human mind (Güzeldere 1995a, 38–49). James began by saying that introspection was so obvious it hardly needed to be defined. When we look inwards, *Every one agrees that we there discover states of consciousness*" (1950, 185; James's emphasis) Later he denounced consciousness, saying it "is the name of a non-entity" (1971, 4). Gradually, in its bid to become classified among the natural sciences, psychology was shaped by positivism, and behaviorism replaced the study of introspection. In this shift psychology moved from phenomenal intuition, or first-person experience, which did not seem to fit with scientific methodology, to causal intuition or third-party observation, with the emphasis on publicly observable behavior. Reducing first-person experience to observable behavior came about largely due to professional anxiety among psychologists. As Julian Jaynes aptly notes, "Off the printed page, behaviorism was only a refusal to talk about consciousness" (1976, 15).

Cognitivism, the next phase in psychology, was inspired by computational models. Consciousness is here defined in terms of information processing, as in computer science. The taboo on the study of consciousness began to disappear, but not until the current boom of neuropsychological research, which started in the 1970s, did consciousness begin to reclaim the spotlight. As Güzeldere notes, "In cognitivism, cognition needed defense over behaviorism no longer, but consciousness over cognition still did" (1995a, 43). Because information-processing models were so successful in explaining functions such as memory, learning, and problem solving—almost everything except consciousness—the unexplained phenomenon of consciousness began to call for greater attention. The various models of consciousness in cognitive psychology, including models of the unconscious in Freud and cognitivism, always seemed to leave something out. To remedy this, new research paradigms on consciousness started being developed to take into account the subjective, experiential aspect of mental phenomena.

Contemporary paradigms of consciousness have had to deal with a puzzle: the epistemic factor that consciousness can be approached from different points of view, first-person phenomenological or third-person physicalist. The latter we know only through external reports, while the former we know intimately through the phenomenology of aromas, sights, sounds, tastes, and other contacts that enrich our daily lives—known as *qualia* (see Chalmers 1996, 249–75). This puzzle includes the fact that in our study of consciousness the object and the means of study are the same. The dilemma here parallels that of the deconstructive attempt to undermine logocentrism by means of a language inextricably invested in metaphysics. But if phenomenology seeks the basis of experience in the light of consciousness, deconstruction would apparently place it in the dark.

The experience of *qualia* constitutes an individual's mode of being, or in Thomas Nagel's famous phrase, "what it is like to be" that individual (1974, 435–50). In an effort to explain this phenomenon, scientists have formulated two aspects of the study of consciousness: the "easy problems of consciousness," how the brain processes sensory stimulation and integrates information used when we report on subjective states; and the "hard problem: Why is all this processing accompanied by an experienced inner life?" (Chalmers 1996, xi–xii)

THE HARD PROBLEM OF CONSCIOUSNESS

In "Facing Up to the Problem of Consciousness," David Chalmers elaborates on the hard problem and how it stems from the inability of cognitive science to explain consciousness nonreductively:

What makes the hard problem hard and almost unique is that it goes beyond problems about the performance of functions. To see this, note that even when we have explained the performance of all the cognitive and behavioral functions in the vicinity of experience—perceptual discrimination, categorization, internal access, verbal report—there may still remain a further unanswered question: *Why is the performance of these functions accompanied by experience?* . . . This further question is the key question in the problem of consciousness. Why doesn't all this information-processing go on "in the dark," free of any inner feel? (1995, 203; Chalmers's emphasis)

Chalmers suggests that a full theory of consciousness would explain why and how the information globally accessible to us rises into conscious experience. He finds that current strategies for solving the hard problem and formulating a full theory have proved inadequate. Deconstruction, as if content to operate "in the dark," would reduce the self to a function of difference.

For Chalmers and an increasing number of others philosophers, no purely physical or functional account can explain mental phenomena. The result is an "explanatory gap" between these mainly reductive accounts and consciousness itself (1996, 47). Chalmers proposes what he calls a psychophysical theory of consciousness that would bridge the explanatory gap between the mental and physical without being reductive. This theory, which he calls a "naturalistic dualism" (1996, 168–71), postulates properties that exist above and beyond those described in physics. Physics characterizes entities only in their extrinsic relations, leaving out their intrinsic properties. While some scientists have argued that the intrinsic or phenomenal doesn't exist, Chalmers notes that this creates the problem of a world of "primitive differences" in a "causal flux" with no properties being causally related. "If physics is pure information," he says, "there will be nothing to distinguish instantiations of the two information spaces" (1996, 303). Phenomenal properties, however, can ground these information spaces. "We might say that phenomenal properties are the internal aspect of information" (1995, 217). This is one way that quantum physics has a need for consciousness, as Squires suggests. The phenomenal approach to the hard problem of consciousness, then, though stretching the limits of our present understanding of physics, has supporters in a variety of disciplines.

In "Neurophenomenology: A Methodological Remedy for the Hard Problem," Francisco Varela defends Chalmers's basic point that subjective, first-person experience is irreducible (1996). He also argues in favor of cooperation or "mutual constraints" between the two basic approaches to the field of phenomena: the experiential and the cognitive sciences. This cooperation would allay the fears among psychologists working in the experiential about the rigor of their scientific research. In developing his theoretical model, Varela distinguishes four basic approaches to consciousness in the ongoing resurgence of interest in mental phenomena: reductionism, functionalism, mysterianism, and phenomenology. Reductionists (like F. Crick, P. S. Churchland, and C. Kock) try to eliminate phenomenal experience in favor of neurobiological accounts; functionalists (D. Dennett, B. Baars, and G. Edelman) try to assimilate conscious experience to behavior or function; mysterians (like T. Nagel and C. McGinn) find the hard problem unsolvable due to the limitations in our means of understanding mental phenomena; and phenomenologists (Penrose, Chalmers, Varela, Searle, and Shear) define firsthand consciousness as irreducible. This last group, emphasized here, seems to offer the greatest hope in the twenty-first century for understanding consciousness—and ultimately, one suspects, for human survival.

In the sustained evolution of phenomenology—which unlike most theories has thrived uninterruptedly on a global scale since its inception—Varela attempts a rigorous methodology and pragmatics based on the style of thinking known as "phenomenological reduction" inaugurated by Edmund Husserl. Rejecting our habitual attitude toward things as existing independently of the subject, phenomenological reduction puts things "in brackets" in order to examine them reflexively as being posited or intended by consciousness. Although phenomenology has been criticized as a form of transcendental idealism, Husserl's famous dictum, "Back to the things themselves" (Varela, 1996, 336), represents a return to the primacy of firsthand experience. Based on the experience of openness, phenomenology is not an authoritarian theory, as some critics have argued (Eagleton 1983, 57). This label would better characterize the closure of a third-person objectification, although even this finally comes down to a theorist giving a firsthand epistemic account.

Through a neurophenomenological approach, which integrates

phenomenal experience and cognitive science, Varela hopes to avoid some common misconceptions about phenomenology. The first takes phenomenology as merely uncritical introspectionism. But introspection involves "seeing inside," while phenomenological reduction gives us insight into the phenomenal world. As Wilber would say, it differentiates and then reintegrates. Varela notes that this reflexive phenomenal move goes beyond the duality of subject-object and "opens into a field of phenomena where it becomes less and less obvious how to distinguish between subject and object (this is what Husserl called the 'fundamental correlation')" (1996, 339). Penrose confirms this point in his theory of the three worlds, with mathematical laws found at the basis of the physical world. In another misunderstanding, intuition is taken for something "fluffy," a "will-o'-the-wisp inspiration." Varela refutes this misconception with an example from mathematics: "ultimately the weight of a [mathematical] proof is its convincing nature, the immediacy of the evidence which is imposed on us, beyond the logical chains of symbolic reasoning." The decisiveness of intuitive evidence stems less from argument than from a convincing clarity.

Rather than deconstruct binary oppositions such as reason-intuition, subject-object, phenomenology finds their fundamental correlation in consciousness. Consciousness transcends the split between the subjective and objective through its phenomenal link to the external world. In Husserlian language, consciousness in this sense is "transcendental." That is, rather than being restricted to private, internal events, it encompasses the external world, which, though apparently nonconscious, may possibly (as Chalmers believes) embody phenomenal properties. In spite of the Derridean notion of difference, consciousness seems to follow certain structural principles that lead it beyond duality. There is intuitive and empirical evidence for this move—as well as the record of Eastern cultures. Although post-structuralists question conscious experience for being strictly personal, Varela notes that this "does not mean it is private, in the sense of some kind of isolated subject that is parachuted down on a pre-given objective world" (1996, 340). This phenomenal experience radically differs from Anglo-American empiricism with its concern for private inspection. Instead, consciousness is linked to the phenomenal world, and in its transcendental state comprises the basis for the empathetic web of human existence, or what Husserl and Jürgen Habermas call intersubjectivity.

Ultimately, Varela's working hypothesis for neurophenomenology calls for reciprocal restraints between firsthand accounts of the structure of conscious experience (praxis) and the accounts of cognitive science (theory). Phenomenological accounts turn out to be important for two reasons: first, without them the direct quality of our experience disappears or becomes a mystery; and second, they monitor empirical observations indispensable to modern science (1996, 343). The interconnection between human experience and cognitive science (which can be said to include critical theory) may also help to open up new aspects of firsthand experience not readily available before (like those recorded in Eastern cultures).

THE PHENOMENOLOGY OF CONSCIOUSNESS

Even though consciousness can only be known firsthand, people tend to agree on certain external accounts of its characteristics. We all know, for example, that "what it is like to be" conscious involves the experience of *qualia,* or empirical phenomenological qualities, and that our thoughts can freely range across the boundaries of space and time. Colin McGinn investigates the lack of extension and other spatial properties in consciousness first postulated by Descartes (1991). He notes that once we acknowledge the nonspatial character of consciousness, the notion of mental causation, or "how conscious events cause physical changes in the body," becomes problematic (1995, 223). As mentioned earlier, Burns and Uus have pointed out that consciousness as the basis of ethical choice is not accounted for by any presently known physical laws. For McGinn, this nonspatiality involves radical implications for the origin of consciousness. Although critical theorists complacently define the self as a social construction, a product of material forces, science and philosophy have yet to find the real source of consciousness.

McGinn relates consciousness to the theory of the big bang. In the consensual view, space was created during the big bang, before which it was nonexistent. But McGinn asks, how can space come from nonspace? (1995, 224). He suggests that the big bang may not have been the beginning of all existence. In terms of consciousness, the brain seems to reverse the effect of the big bang through the nonspatial dimension of thought, erasing the spatial rather than creating it: "This suggests the following heady speculation: that the origin of consciousness somehow draws upon those properties of the universe that antedate and explain the occurrence of the big bang. If we need a pre-spatial level of reality to account for the big bang, then it may be this very level that is exploited in the generation of consciousness." McGinn recognizes that we are spatial beings par excellence, that the brain has spatial properties, and that thoughts appear to be spatial because of their link to the spatial framework of our perceptions. But he asserts that this appearance does not nullify the nonspatial conception of consciousness—the experience that consciousness is not a thing.

The difficulty we have in fathoming the nature of consciousness and formulating a theory about it, McGinn concludes, stems from the lack of an adequate fit between consciousness, which is nonspatial, and thoughts, which through our visual perceptions are tied to the notion of time and space. "We can form thoughts *about* consciousness states, but we cannot articulate the natural constitution of what we are thinking about. It is the spatial bias of our thinking that stands in our way (along perhaps with other impediments)" (1995, 229; McGinn's emphasis). As Wertheim notes, the dominance of physical space over the past three and a half centuries has made it difficult for spiritual space to be appreciated (1999, 31).

C. J. S. Clark (1995) argues that the awareness of visual percepts linked to space makes our thoughts appear spatial, when in fact they are nonspatial. The spatial dimension is not inherent in the mind but originates from outside. He observes that even the brain is not entirely spatial, that "there is a perfectly good place for the nonspatial in physics" (231). Clark is among the many mathematicians who find that conscious experience, while related to the structure of brain processes, is fundamentally separate from it. He accounts for the nonlocality of the brain associated with consciousness through "quantum logic" (239), an approach that takes into consideration the total quantum state of the brain. Clark's account of nonlocality resembles Penrose's notion of the mind's global capacity—his view that "matter itself is now much more of a mental substance" (1994a, 24).

Related to nonlocality is the generation problem (generating consciousness out of matter) addressed by McGinn and also by Chalmers and Nagel. For Nagel, emergence is impossible and reduction is nonsense. Chalmers proposes that consciousness emerges from or is somehow linked to the physical, but is not reducible to or dependent for its functional description on it. As mentioned earlier, he also suggests that consciousness may be inherent in information and thus a basic feature of the "material" world. Bluntly stated, as William Seager observes, what is at issue here is panpsychism, the doctrine that "all matter, or all nature, is itself psychical, or has a psychical aspect" (*OED*; in Seager 1995, 279). Although objections to panpsychism go back to James (see his notion of "the combination problem," 1950, 160), Seager emphasizes how quantum theory highlights "the ineradicable incompleteness of a purely physical picture of the world" (283). This perception of incompleteness seems plausible from a phenomenal (intuitive) perspective even without quantum mechanics. When confronted with the generation problem in 1874, for example, W. K. Clifford argued that the theory of evolution does not account for an event in the line of physical development where consciousness emerged (quoted in Seager 1995, 280). Seager thus concludes that "one can postulate with at least bare intelligibility that consciousness is a fundamental feature of the universe" (282).

EAST/WEST

Western philosophy of mind has traditionally made a basic distinction between dualists and monists. Dualists include substance dualists, who think the mind and body are two separates kinds of substance, and property dualists, who think the mental and physical are merely two properties of the same substance—as in the case of the psychophysiology of a human being. Like dualists, monists also come in two categories: idealists, who believe the world is ultimately mental, and materialists, who believe it is ultimately material. Most researchers in the philosophy of mind are monists of the materialist bent who try to get rid of the mental by rejecting dualism. But the problem materialists have is that after describing the material facts of the world they are still left with a lot of unexplained mental phenomena. The materialist Crick, for instance, defines consciousness reductively through a neurobiological account: "Consciousness is associated with certain neural activities" (1994a, 251), probably related to "visual awareness" (252). But the quantitative and objective description of neuron firings does not explain our qualitative, subjective experience. As Searle says, "How, to put it naively, does the brain get us over the hump from electrochemistry to feeling?" (1997, 28).

K. Ramakrishna Rao, in "The Two Faces of Consciousness," defines several possible meanings of consciousness and then places them into two categories: "object awareness" and "subject awareness" (1998, 309). As their names imply, "object awareness" predicates awareness on an object, while "subject awareness" is the awareness of awareness itself or one of its aspects. Object awareness is the phenomenal or intentional domain of consciousness, and subject awareness is the transcendental or nonintentional domain. Further, object awareness, as the intentional aspect of consciousness, is associated with the West, and subject awareness, as the nonintentional aspect, with the East. Because different cultures have different notions of consciousness, one's preference here usually depends on one's cultural background. As Rao puts it, "in the Western tradition the dominant perspective is one of *rational* understanding of what consciousness is. In the Eastern tradition the approach is one of developing practical methods for *transforming* consciousness in specific ways for specific purposes" (310; emphasis added).

In terms of Advaita (nondual) Vedanta, the philosophical tradition founded by Shankara, one of India's most influential philosophers, the indeterminate, transcendent Absolute (Brahman) comprises the "content" of the nondualistic experience of pure consciousness (Atman). Though without attributes, Brahman is traditionally characterized as *sat* (infinite being), *chit* (consciousness), *ananda* (bliss). Brahman is the truth of the universe, and Atman is the truth of the self. "All this is, verily, *Brahman*. This self [Atman] is *Brahman*. This same self has four quarters" (*Mandukya Upanishad*, verse 2; Radhakrishnan ed. 1992, 695). The four quarters refer to the three ordinary states of consciousness—waking, sleeping, dreaming—and a fourth, *turiya*: a state of pure consciousness without qualities or content. As the ever-present witness (Atman), *turiya* underlies all mental phenomena manifested in the three ordinary states of consciousness.

Unlike Western epistemology, in which knowledge is based on language, the *Mundaka Upanishad* distinguishes "two kinds of knowledge [that] are to be known, as, indeed, the knowers of *Brahman* declare—the higher as well as the lower. . . . Of these, the lower is the *Rg Veda* [plus the other three Vedas and assorted Vedic texts] . . . . And the higher is that by which the Undecaying [Brahman] is apprehended [directly]" (I.1.4; Radhakrishnan 1992, 672). Lower knowledge corresponds to the three ordinary states of consciousness and to sensory and mental empiricism, and higher knowledge to the fourth state of pure consciousness (*turiya*) and to contemplative empiricism. Advaita (nondual) Vedanta refers to these two aspects or modes of Brahman as *saguna* and *nirguna*. As Eliot Deutsch explains, "*Nirguna* Brahman—Brahman without qualities—is just that transcendent indeterminate state of being about which ultimately nothing can be affirmed. *Saguna* Brahman—Brahman with qualities—is Brahman as interpreted and affirmed by the mind from its necessarily limited standpoint" (1973, 12). Since higher knowledge or consciousness (*nirguna*) is latent within the lower (*saguna*), the different knowledge spheres of modernity can be said to be distinct on one level yet integrated on another. To flatten this differentiation monologically into empirical science or discursive reason would be to deny the higher level of knowledge, just as to nondifferentiate by collapsing everything to the metaphysical would be to deny legitimacy to the full evolutionary range of human experience. Hence the two kinds of knowledge are complementary. As exterior and interior domains, they can be integrated through aesthetic experience (*rasadhvani*), in which the sensory and mental dimensions of a work lead the awareness back to itself as timeless witness through the contemplation of the beauty of art. In this way the naturalistic transcendentalism of art constitutes a unity of opposites.

As Deutsch observes in his lucid account of Shankara's Vedanta, "The central concern of Advaita Vedanta is to establish the oneness of Reality and to lead the human being to a realization of it" (1973, 47). This realization occurs through the "experience" of consciousness in its unified or irreducible state as witness or seer: single, simple, and continuing. Atman, however, is beyond "experience" in the usual sense of a division of subject and object found in the three ordinary states of consciousness. It is "self-shining," "spaceless," and "not-different from Brahman" (48–49). In the words of Shankara, "the knowledge of the Atman is self-revealed and is not dependent upon perception and other means of knowledge" (*Brahmasutrabhasya*; quoted in Deutsch, 49). A work of art or literature does not create this state but only helps one to recognize it as an ever-present reality. Aesthetic experience facilitates our letting go of the boundary between the subject and object.

In " 'I' = Awareness," Arthur Deikman further distinguishes awareness as the ground of experience (Atman) and the objects of awareness—thoughts, sensations, images, moods, emotions, and memories (1996). The difference here, as we have seen, is between a psychological interpretation of consciousness (as distinct from the Freudian or Jungian unconscious) and an ontological interpretation of consciousness (as distinct from nonconscious experience). Most psychology texts deal with the contents of awareness, the sensations of the body, and memories of our social identities, and not with "awareness as a phenomenon in its own right" (352). While the pronoun "I" usually signifies the ego, Deikman intends the "I" of awareness to signify the witnessing faculty and not an object of observation as in ordinary experience. It is "the experiencer, prior to all conscious content" (350). "Experiencing" the "I" or Atman solves the problem of infinite regress, since "we know the internal observer not by observing it but *by being it*" (355; Deikman's emphasis). As the ever-present witness it is unavoidable, yet our recognition of it is heightened during aesthetic experience. The ultimate reality of the world or a text is not something perceived, but rather the witnessing awareness or the seer. Because it is neither this nor that, you cannot see the seer; you can only be it. The self as witness does not have to be searched for; it is always present and constantly functioning in our spontaneous awareness of everything around us. All the events of the past and future occur for the witness now in the present, which is all we ever know. Timeless, spaceless, causeless, beginningless, and endless, the witness that we always already are is the radical emptiness into which arise all manifestations of thoughts, sensations, emotions, and perceptions. The recognition of this ever-present witness—to varying degrees of fullness—is what aesthetic experience brings us through its suggestive power (*rasadhvani*) as we transcend the subject and object duality in our identification, for example, with a fictional character.

In a recent exchange between Henry W. Sullivan and Howard Mancing in the journal *Cervantes* (1999), Sullivan argues that a fictional character, while not a real person, can still be the subject of psychoanalysis, as in a Lacanian analysis of *Don Quixote de la Mancha*. To support this argument Sullivan proposes a distinction between body and "organism," the latter defined in Lacanian terms as a linguistic and psychological being. He claims that the human biological animal (body) is not the same thing as a human linguistic and psychological being (organism), and thus questions the assumption that the "real person" means exclusively a human biological mammal "who has, or had, a historical existence" (1998, 12). In this way Sullivan makes a case for "the virtual psychic reality of personae in literature whose life extends beyond the time of their literary creation into an indefinite future posterity." The organism—defined through the Lacanian notions of the Imaginary, the Symbolic order, and the Real through which the subject is constructed—constitutes the essence of fictional personae, serving to " 'debiologize' the human subject" (14). With the concept of organism Sullivan also intends to undermine the mind/body dualism that cognitive scientists increasingly find untenable.

Mancing, however, questions Sullivan's definition of organism as a concept distinct from body and accuses him of positing "an absolute (Cartesian) mind-body dualism as the cornerstone of psychoanalytic theory" (1999, 158). He does not accept the notion of an organism as a culturally constructed virtual psyche, condemning it as a reaffirmation of Cartesian dualism; instead he espouses reductive concepts in cognitive science such as the "embodied mind," "the body in the mind," and "the mind-brain" (162). He quotes Richard Restak's assertion that consciousness is "a very special *emergent* property of the human brain . . . made possible by a sufficient number of parallel interacting modules" (163; emphasis in the original). Sullivan, however, is amazed by Mancing's misunderstanding of his use of organism, which he intended to overturn an absolute Cartesian dualism. Organism as a "third term" was meant to provide a "solvent" to binary dualisms by replacing them with the notion of a mind/body distinction. Hence the title of Sullivan's response to Mancing: "Don Quixote and the 'Third Term' as Solvent of Binary Dualisms" (1999).

For Sullivan, then, a "mind/body *distinction* is not the same as a mind/body *dualism*," for the "mind is *inseparable* from the brain, but *distinct* from it" (1999, 192; Sullivan's emphasis). He attempts to deconstruct binary thinking by identifying the third term responsible for creating dualisms in the first place. Yet however much Sullivan and Mancing may agree or disagree about their definitions of dualism in the context of cognitive science, they both differ from the notion of dualism in Eastern thought, in which the mind and body are both material. In the tradition of Samkhya-Yoga, which like Vedanta belongs to the six systems of Indian philosophy, the structure of reality consists of twenty-five components in a firm dualism.

As Lloyd Pflueger explains, in Samkhya-Yoga "there are two irreducible, innate, and independent realities in our universe of experience: 1. consciousness itself (*purusha*); 2. primordial materiality (*prakrti*)" (1998, 48). In these copresent and coeternal realities, primordial materiality (*prakrti*) contains twenty-three components, including intellect (*buddhi*, *mahat*), ego (*ahamkara*), and mind (*manas*). The intellect, ego, and mind, together with thought, feeling, and perception are, as Pflueger notes, "all seen as merely different forms of nonconscious matter. . . . This is not the garden variety of mind/body dualism encountered in Western philosophy! Here both body and mind are seen as unequivocally material. Even so, Samkhya-Yoga cannot reduce the universe of experience to the nonconscious permutations of matter alone" (49). As in Vedanta, the material content of experience related to the intellect, ego, and mind is "only half the equation of experience—[for] our experience necessarily involves the element of consciousness." That is, in addition to the twenty-four material components of experience, there is also *purusha* [or Atman in Advaita Vedanta], "the principle of consciousness itself."

From this perspective, the Western mind/body dualism is really a monism, for the mind and body comprise the material building blocks of experience as distinct from the witnessing faculty (*purusha* or Atman) that "illuminates" this experience (Pflueger 1998, 50). Samkhya-Yoga dualism thus consists on the one hand of *purusha* or consciousness itself, and on the other hand of *prakrti* or matter, which includes all "psychological faculties: intellect, ego, mind, sense capacities, and action capacities; and subtle elements, gross elements, and material objects" (51). *Purusha* is contentless pure consciousness "without which even mental processes *know* nothing" (Pflueger's emphasis). The mistake of the intellect is to identify the intellect, ego, and mind with consciousness. Even though the intellect seems to know, the knowing or witnessing faculty belongs to consciousness alone. As a material linguistic construct, the intellect has no light to shine on experience and cannot answer Chalmers's question, "Why doesn't all this information processing go on 'in the dark,' free of any inner feel?" (1996, 203).

The answer lies with consciousness, the immaterial witness of language and all other objects of awareness. No subject/object duality obtains in consciousness, which is not a process of knowing, as in self-consciousness, but a state of being, as in knowingness. As Pflueger puts it, "Consciousness is eternally free of . . . objects, infinite, immaterial, and awake. The sensations and judgments assembled by the intellect are mere permutations of matter, *prakrti*, without consciousness of any kind" (55).

For Vedanta and Samkhya-Yoga, which combine theory and direct experience, consciousness is not apprehended by faith or any other mental construction. It is not a material product like the notion of organism in Sullivan or mind in Mancing and cognitive science. Sullivan's third term is thus only a synonym for the other two terms in a nondual or monist materialism: mind-body. When Sullivan accuses Mancing of collapsing the mind-body distinction on the side of body instead of accepting the notion of organism, he is merely accusing him of unintentionally recognizing what Samkhya-Yoga already posits: that mind and body, or mind-body in its various permutations, belong to the material realm. The concept of organism does not save the distinction except insofar as mind and body are different aspects of the same material process. By disassociating mind from its (mis)identification with pure consciousness, which can be achieved only through direct experience, Eastern thought would transform human suffering into a freedom from bondage to the material realm. As an innate experience, pure consciousness entails liberation from "all concepts, all thinking, all words, all feeling, all memory, and all perception" (Pflueger 1998, 69–70).

It is important to remember, then, that Eastern thought distinguishes between consciousness and mind, whereas Western thought identifies the two. The Eastern tradition regards consciousness as completely noncorporeal, the witnessing aspect of awareness, and mind, which is a form of matter, albeit subtle, as related to the content of consciousness. The mind is the link between the phenomenal world of sense impressions and the realm of qualityless pure consciousness, defined as the experience of awareness itself without intentional content. As Rao explains, the Western definition of consciousness in terms of intentionality means that consciousness is always "*of* or *about* something" (1998, 313; Rao's emphasis). John Searle also holds that intentionality, which requires that consciousness be of something—an object—is the essence of mind or consciousness (1997), as does Edmund Husserl. Understanding consciousness in terms of intentionality and its identity with the mind is central to a phenomenology that does not accommodate pure consciousness.

As Rao puts it, "whereas the Western perspective is focused on the phenomenal manifestation of consciousness, the Eastern tradition pays special attention to the transcendental aspects of consciousness through its concern with pure consciousness" (1998, 317). The Western tradition, in positing an identity between consciousness and mind, considers intentionality the defining characteristic of consciousness. It thus lacks any practical means of applying an understanding of consciousness toward improving the human condition. In contrast, the Eastern tradition distinguishes between mind and consciousness, posits the existence of qualityless pure consciousness or awareness as such, and has developed methods such as yoga and meditation for realizing pure consciousness and thereby achieving tangible benefits and specific goals.

In deconstructive postmodernism, of course, being, presence, and consciousness are flattened out of existence by an external viewpoint. The notion of an "experiencer prior to all conscious content" falls prey to Derrida's distinction between speech and writing. Traditional humanism favors the "phonocentric," which permits a first-person experience of the unity of voice and meaning. Derrida's third-person theory of *différance*, on the other hand, extends the freeplay of the graphic text over the entire field of signs, including speech. But as Harris has aptly demonstrated, Derrida relies heavily on (among other fallacies) equivocation and the ambiguities that make it possible (1996, 54–58). In terms of the possibility of preverbal meaning, Eastern philosophy provides a language theory that accounts for the experience of meaning in relation to different levels of consciousness corresponding to the two kinds of knowledge in the *Mundaka Upanishad* (Ramachandran 1989). This theory, which is beyond the scope of this chapter, explains how meaning changes from ordinary consciousness to the nonordinary state of pure consciousness (*turiya*), which subsumes the difference of signthing, sound-meaning, consciousness-information (Haney 1993, 1–65). Robert Forman, moreover, points out that no one "has ever explained how language and its background are actually part of a mystical experience" (1994, 41)—part of witnessing awareness.

Harold Coward (1980, 1990) provides a lucid description of the different levels of language and consciousness and argues forcefully against the leveling influence of a deconstructive postmodernism.

CONCLUSION

The post-Saussurean theories of language that allegedly undermine the unity of self and text through the notion of difference relate at best to the ordinary states of consciousness; they do not fathom the ever-present witness (*turiya*). But even for the ordinary waking and dream states—whose content consists of *qualia*—third-person accounts are hardly indisputable. Although deconstructive postmodernism may apply to mental phenomena, it does not apply to witnessing awareness as a state of being. One might therefore suggest that rather than being dead, man is but momentarily out of focus or lost from sight. The revival of humanism and the humanities may only take a shift in our perspective away from a monological theory toward a greater comprehensiveness of theory and practice.

The conjunction of theory and praxis in Eastern cultures can provide a model for the cooperation that Varela proposes between phenomenology and cognitive science (1996). This model may help us shift our perspective toward a new humanism through which all knowledge domains—sensory, mental, and contemplative—are seen as distinct yet integrated, with no one sphere dominating the others, as in the post-structuralist domination of the subject. Since consciousness remains a mystery to sensory and mental empiricism, it is hard to see how deconstruction, or any critical theory for that matter, can effectively call into question something still beyond our consensual, third-person understanding. Could it be that critical theory has reached a closure on the humanities, shut the doors of perception even as other disciplines advance in their explorations on the final frontier of consciousness? Through a greater openness to and recognition of consciousness in its irreducible condition, the humanities would be better poised to participate in a renaissance of the self and a reenchantment of humanity.

WORKS CITED

Althusser, Louis. 1969. *For Marx.* Trans. Ben Brewster. Harmondsworth: Penguin.

Barthes, Roland. 1977. *Image-Music-Text.* Ed. and trans. Stephen Heath. New York:

Hill and Wang.

Bloom, Harold. 1997. *Omens of Millennium.* London: Fourth Estate.

Burns, Jean E. 1999. "Volition and Physical Laws." *Journal of Consciousness Studies* 6 (10): 27–47.

Capra, Fritjof. 1977. *The Tao of Physics.* New York: Bantam.

Chalmers, David. 1995. "Facing Up to the Problem of Consciousness." *Journal of Consciousness Studies.* 2 (3): 200–19.

———. 1996. *The Conscious Mind.* New York: Oxford University Press.

Clarke, C. J. S. 1995. "The Nonlocality of Mind." *Journal of Consciousness Studies* 2 (3): 231–40.

Coward, Harold. 1980. *The Sphota Theory of Language.* Columbia, Mo.: South Asia Books.

———. 1990. *Derrida and Indian Philosophy.* New York: State University of New York Press.

Coward, Harold, and Toby Foshay, eds. 1992. *Derrida and Negative Theology.* Albany: State University of New York Press.

Crick, Francis. 1994a. *The Astonishing Hypothesis.* London: Simon and Schuster.

———. 1994b. "Interview: The Astonishing Hypothesis." By Jane Clark. *Journal of Consciousness Studies* 1 (1): 10–17.

Davies, Paul. 1983. *God and the New Physics.* New York: Simon and Schuster.

Deikman, Arthur. 1996. " 'I' = Awareness." *Journal of Consciousness Studies* 3 (4): 350–56.

Derrida, Jacques. 1973. *Speech and Phenomena: And Other Essays on Husserl's Theory of Signs.* Trans. David B. Allison. Evanston: Northwestern University Press.

———. 1976. *Of Grammatology.* Trans. Gayatri Spivak. Baltimore: Johns Hopkins University Press.

———. 1978. "Edmund Jabès and the Question of the Book." In *Writing and Difference,* trans. Alan Bass. Chicago: University of Chicago Press.

Deutsch, Eliot. 1973. *Advaita Vedanta.* Honolulu: University of Hawaii Press.

Editors. 1994. "Editors' Introduction." *Journal of Consciousness Studies* 1 (1): 4–9.

Eagleton, Terry. 1983. *Literary Theory: An Introduction.* Oxford: Basil Blackwell.

Ellis, John M. 1997. *Literature Lost: Social Agendas and the Corruption of the Humanities.* New Haven: Yale University Press.

Farrow, J. T., and R. Herbert. 1982. "Breath Suspension during the Transcendental Meditation Technique." *Psychosomatic Medicine* 44 (2): 133–53.

Forman, Robert. 1994. " 'Of Capsules and Carts:' Mysticism, Language and the *Via Negativa." Journal of Consciousness Studies* 1 (1): 38–49.

Foucault, Michel. 1989. "What Is an Author?" In *Contemporary Literary Theory: Literary and Cultural Studies,* ed. Robert Con Davis and Ronald Schleifer. New York: Longman.

———. 1990. *The History of Sex: Volume 1: An Introduction.* Trans. Robert Hurely. New York: Vintage.

Gablik, Suzi. 1991. *The Reenactment of Art.* New York: Thames and Hudson.

Gergen, Kenneth. 1991. *The Saturated Self: Dilemma of Identity in Contemporary Life.* New York: Basic Books.

Goguen, Joseph A. 1999. "Editorial Introduction." *Journal of Consciousness Studies* 6 (6–7): 5–14.

Güzeldere, Güven. 1995a. "Consciousness: What It Is, How to Study It, What to Learn from Its History." *Journal of Consciousness Studies* 2 (1): 30–51.

———. 1995b. "Problems of Consciousness: A Perspective on Contemporary Issues, Current Debates." *Journal of Consciousness Studies* 2 (2): 112–42.

Habermas, Jürgen. 1987. *The Theory of Communicative Action, Volume 2. Lifeworld and System: A Critique of Functionalist Reason.* Trans. Thomas McCarthey. Boston: Beacon Press.

Hagelin, John. 1987. "Is Consciousness the Unified Field?" A Field Theorist's Perspective. *Modern Science and Vedic Science* 1 (1): 29–87.

Haney, William. 1993. *Literary Theory and Sanskrit Poetics: Language, Consciousness and Meaning.* Lewiston, N.Y.: Edwin Mellen Press.

Harris, Wendell V. 1996. *Literary Meaning: Reclaiming the Study of Literature.* New York: New York University Press.

Hayles, Katherine N. 1984. *The Cosmic Web: Scientific Field Models and Literary Strategies in the 20th Century.* Ithaca: Cornell University Press.

Heidegger, Martin. 1962. *Being and Time.* Trans. J. MacQuarrie and E. Robinson. New York: Harper and Row.

Herbert, Nick. 1985. *Quantum Reality: Beyond the New Physics.* Garden City, N.Y.: Anchor Press/Doubleday.

James, William. 1950. *The Principles of Psychology.* New York: Dover.

———. 1971. "Does 'Consciousness' Exist?" In *Eassays in Radical Empiricism,* ed. R. B. Perry. New York: Dutton.

Jaynes, Julian. 1976. *The Origin of Consciousness and the Breakdown of the Bicameral Mind.* Boston: Houghton Mifflin.

Krishnamoorthy, K. 1968. *Some Thoughts on Indian Aesthetics and Literary Criticism.* Prasaranga, India: University of Mysore Press.

Lacan, Jacques. 1989. "Seminar on 'The Purloined Letter.' " Trans. Jeffrey Mehlman. In *Contemporary Literary Criticism,* ed. R. C. Davis and R. Schleifer. New York: Longman.

Mancing, Howard. 1999. "Against Dualisms: A Response to Henry Sullivan." *Cervantes: Bulletin of the Cervantes Society of America* 19 (1): 158–76.

McGinn, Colin. 1991. *The Problem of Consciousness.* Oxford: Blackwell.

————. 1995. "Consciousness and Space." *Journal of Consciousness Studies* 2 (3): 220–30.

————. 1997. *Ethics, Evil, and Fiction.* Oxford: Oxford University Press.

Nagel, Thomas. 1974. "What Is It Like to Be a Bat?" *Philosophical Review* 83 (4): 435–50.

————. 1986. *A View from Nowhere.* Oxford: Oxford University Press.

Nietzsche, F. 1968. *The Will to Power.* Trans. Walter Kaufmann and R. J. Hollingdale. New York: Vintage Press.

————. 1974. *The Gay Science.* Trans. Walter Kaufmann. New York: Vintage Press.

Penrose, Roger. 1994a. "Interviews with Jane Clark." *Journal of Consciousness Studies* 1 (1): 17–24.

————. 1994b. *Shadows of the Mind.* Oxford: Oxford Univeresity Press.

————. 1997. *The Large, the Small and the Human Mind: With Abner Shimony, Nancy Cartwright and Stephen Hawking.* Ed. Malcolm Longair. Cambridge: Cambridge University Press.

Pflueger, Lloyd W. 1998. "Descriminating the Innate Capacity: Salvation Mysticism of Classical Samkhya-Yoga." *The Innate Capacity: Mysticism, Psychology, and Philosophy.* Ed. Robert K. C. Forman. New York and Oxford: Oxford University Press.

Radhakrishnan, S., ed. and trans. 1992. *The Principal Upanishads. Centenary Edition.* Delhi: Oxford University Press.

Ramachandran, S., ed. and trans. 1989. *The Principal Upanishads.* New Delhi: Oxford University Press.

Ramachandran, V. S., and William Herstein. 1999. "The Science of Art: A Neurological Theory of Aesthetic Experience." *Journal of Consciousness Studies* 6 (6–7); 15–51.

Rao, K. Ramakrishna. 1998. "Two Faces of Consciousness: A Look at Eastern and Western Perspectives." *Journal of Consciousness Studies* 5 (3): 309–27.

Seager, William. 1995. "Consciousness, Information and Panpsychism." *Journal of Consciousness Studies* 2 (3): 272–88.

Searle, John. 1997. *The Mystery of Consciousness.* London: Granta Books.

Shear, Jonathan. 1990. *The Inner Dimension: Philosophy and the Experience of Consciousness.* New York: Peter Lang.

————. 1998. "Experiential Clarification of the Problem of Self." *Journal of Consciousness Studies* 5 (5–6): 673–86.

Squires, Euan. 1994. "Quantum Theory and the Need for Consciousness." 1 (2): 201–4.

Sullivan, Henry W. 1998. "Don Quixote de la Mancha: Analyzable or Unanalyzable?" *Cervantes: Bulletin of the Cervantes Society of America* 18 (1): 4–23.

————. 1999. "Don Quixote and the 'Third Term' as Solvent of Binary Dualisms: A Response to Howard Mancing." *Cervantes: Bulletin of the Cervantes Society of America* 19 (1): 177–97.

Uus, Undo. 1999. "The Libertarian Imperative." 6 (10): 48–64.

Varela, Francisco. 1996. "Neurophenomenology: A Methodological Remedy for the Hard Problem. *Journal of Consciousness Studies* 3 (4): 330–49.

Wallace, R. K. 1970. "Physiological Effects of Transcendental Meditation." *Science* 167: 1751–54.

Wertheim, Margaret. 1999. *The Pearly Gates of Cyberspace: A History of Space from Dante to the Internet.* New York: W. W. Norton.

Wilber, Ken. 1998a. *The Eye of Spirit: An Integral Vision of a World Gone Slightly Mad.* Boston: Shambhala.

———. 1998b. *The Marriage of Sense and Soul: Integrating Science and Religion.* Dublin: Newleaf.

Zohar, Danah, and Ian Marshall. 1994. *The Quantum Society: Mind, Physics and a New Social Vision.* London: Flamingo.

What Price Humanity?

PETER MALEKIN

THINGS NOW AND THINGS TO COME

HUMAN BEINGS ARE DESTROYING THE BIOSPHERE AS FAST AS CAN reasonably be expected. After all, their power, though great, remains limited, and while certain modern technologies are very promising it is too early to say how profound or extensive their impact will be. Of an estimated ten million species, one is reputedly becoming extinct every half hour—and the estimate of ten million is the lowest conceivable. At this rather slow rate it would take 570 years, 283 days, 7 hours, and 30 minutes to kill off the lot (570 years, 283 days, and 8 hours if we include ourselves). There is, however, hope that this rate may be increased exponentially, although there is also a danger that some of the other species may survive while we exterminate ourselves.[1]

Catastrophe theory anticipates that a system such as the biosphere can change state in an instant after a steady accumulation of minor changes. At the moment we are inducing many such changes. Familiar factors, such as the worldwide disruption of weather patterns, the puncturing of the ozone layer, the apparent beginning of the end of the Gulf Stream, and others suggest that we have indeed begun to succeed in producing global warming. Pollution of the ground water has proceeded apace throughout the world (some twenty years ago, for instance, the only fresh water acquifer under Riyadh was just becoming polluted: now water is pumped from a desalination plant through a vulnerable pipeline). While combustion engines now individually pollute less, there are more and more of them, and the private car will soon spread to China and India, with their joint populations of some two billion. The dead lakes of Scandinavia bear ample witness to our own (British) contribution to air pollution. Meanwhile, the startling progress of modern agriculture has increased demand for water by leaps and bounds (fifteen feet of water submerge the cropping areas of Imperial Valley in California every year and agriculture in East Anglia is catching up fast). Human overpopulation is everywhere, not least in England, the Netherlands, and adjacent areas of the European coastline. Shifts in climate could lead to water shortages and the decimation of human populations, but such an eventuality is by no means certain.

True, other factors could also slow progress. Strains of bacteria resistant to all developed antibiotics can apparently transfer their learned resistance genetically to related strains, and older diseases from TB to diptheria are already resisting treatment, while globally new diseases from Aids to Ebola fever are cropping up, so that humanity might be culled by a plague or two.[2] In addition, the complicated infrastructures of nations and conurbations invite disruption—much of Sweden was briefly plunged into darkness some years ago when a fault in one electrical box cut off the national power supply. Disruption to food and water supplies, trucked and piped in, would lead to migrations and violence that no modern army, trained to fight other modern armies, could stop. Overcrowding in any case tends to produce violence; the road rage of today will be followed by the sidewalk rage of tomorrow, possibly directed against the car (most centers of population in England are currently towns fit for cars to live in, or at least car-dedicated with pedestrians coming second—if you want proof, try pushing children round London in a stroller using public transport, or try crossing with them at a major crossing with one-man cars streaming past you).

While the honor for the current state of affairs could be attributed solely to science and the prodigious increase of human knowledge to which it has led, this would be simplistic and unjust. Early men with stone tools managed to exterminate whole species quite satisfactorily, London was black with seacoal in the Elizabethan period, child apprentices making lead statues or sweeping chimneys were dying of cancer in the eighteenth century. Plagues, famines, and massacres are the regular fodder of history. Climatic change is also nothing new. We are doing nothing that we have not done before, apart from putting the odd man on the moon, but we are, thanks be to technology, now doing it better and faster. Even science, despite dizzying achievement, does not live in a vacuum, and credit must be shared more equally among the religions, economic systems, and cultural institutions of mankind—and indeed rests with every one of us, for we individually live to forward the progress we have made.

One institution in question is the Western educational system, and one dyadic factor within it is what is now called the sciences, and used to be called natural philosophy, and what used to be called the humanities and is now more often called the arts. If humanity has no future then neither does any art or any science, but if as a species we have a future, the kind of future will decide what—if any—survival is likely for the arts and humanities. The survival of the species is not of course the same thing as the survival of humanity. We have always been an inhumane species, and might become more so. The question of the survival of humanity depends on what is meant by humanity. It also depends on what is entailed by the idea of survival, for that idea subsumes assumptions about the nature of time, and also about the relation between time and consciousness as well as between the objective universe and consciousness. Time is not necessarily simply the arrow in the box of Newtonian physics or the multiple arrows of relativity theory. Nor is the human mind simply trapped in a fixed objectivity of time; time can be and is experienced differently. Moreover the concept of a fixed objective universe to which the mind merely responds is culturally induced and decidedly open to question. Since these issues are as germane to the sciences as the arts, natural philosophy is a better term for the sciences than "science" (*scientia*), with its bogus claims to absolute knowledge. (If science is *scientia,* what are the non-*scientias*? The humanities perhaps?)

The sciences, especially perhaps the fringe sciences that impinge directly on the human—medicine, biology, archaeology, paleontology—have a strongly anthropomorphic value system, indeed a system that might be called neoanthropomorphic in that it models the world in terms of the interests and assumptions of twentieth-century Western culture. Americans now have their heads frozen in order to be revived to enjoy the splendors of this life in the world to come—at a later date. According to Egyptologists, the ancient Egyptians did much the same on a more primitive level, producing mutilated mummies to enable at least the chosen few to enjoy this life somewhere else in a postmortem state, despite the inconveniences of death and judgment (the latter not allowed for in the frozen head scenario). The pursuit of knowledge about the Egyptians owes much to archaeology and specifically the digging up of tombs, to be sharply distinguished from grave robbing in that the profit sought is knowledge of a kind considered valuable by modern intellectual man, rather than the production of curios, artifacts, or "mummy" for medicinal purposes valued by other kinds of women or men.

The current attitude to alternative life forms is similarly anthropomorphic. Professor Dawkins, the distinguished spokesman of modern science, in a radio interview justified the torment of laboratory animals in that it led to human knowledge, something the animals themselves would have recognized as valuable had they been capable of it. English law takes a similar view. You can be tried for tormenting an animal unless you do so for profit, as a modern farmer, or for knowledge, as a modern scientist. To *enjoy* the suffering is obscene, to inflict it is not. The human need to know is paramount and justifies any means to that end—with the one sacrosanct exception of inflicting torment on human beings themselves, at least in theory. Records of the findings of medical experiments in the Nazi death camps were burnt, but every now and then accounts of human experimentation by others leak out, like the recent exposure of the deliberate infection of Negroes in the U.S. with syphilis (and indirectly their spouses and children) or the much earlier scandals such as the dosing of Italian children with bacteria. The same is true of the defense experiments perpetrated by democratic governments on their own populations, such as the experimental release of biological pathogens in London and San Francisco (the enthusiasm of Western governments for genetic engineering of course has nothing to do with its potential for targeted biological warfare). Many cases presumably do not leak out. They are hushed up.

Human beings are animals, one species among many, and all animals as animals are equal, but some animals are more equal than others. The justification for this is our supreme intelligence—obvious ability, measured in our terms by us. The ability is, of course, to achieve things that we consider valuable and pursue methods of operation useful to our ends. The final end is knowledge, especially knowledge enabling us to make predictions about and to alter the material world. We have come full circle.

The ability to know is part of consciousness itself, currently often held to be a by-product of purely physical systems. This by-product develops out of evolution, which works through natural selection (an oddly purposeful term) for the survival of the fittest—of the fittest to survive, were it not that knowledge has superseded survival in the value system. Survival is through adaptation, but adaptation suggests a relatively external change, whether in behavior and mode of life or even in physiology. The adapted entity is, however, not the entity that preceded adaptation, and neither presumably is its consciousness. Whether physiology produces or mediates consciousness, a change in physiology goes together with a change in consciousness. Even a change in lifestyle produces a change in consciousness. The ancient Egyptians would not have come up with the concept of evolution, not because they did not "know" what we "know," but because their knowing was of a different kind. In fact, they knew certain things that modern science does not know (they had a knowledge of postmortem states and could use what we call "art" to stimulate levels of the human nervous system that are a closed book, or rather a nonexistent book, to contemporary science). Evolution is a concept based on ourselves and seen in terms of "higher" animals, approximating our own species, and interpreted through the spectacles of our modern society, a society shaped by and shaping us. The science of which it is one aspect is similarly a cultural and social entity, not some absolute existent in its own right: a system with great virtues, but not the extinction of all other modes of knowing. The only protection against the hubris of science is the recognition of its complementarity.

To know is to have power over. To have power over is in some degree to possess. Most knowing and most possessing are symptoms of insufficiency, weakness, incompleteness, insecurity. Science itself is now largely owned by our modern consumer society. Research is mostly commercial and government-directed toward prestige and profit, and is largely valued for bestowing military and economic advantage. The conduct of affairs is heavily influenced by "experts." Like Strindberg's "all right-thinking people" in *A Dream Play*, experts are self-appointed; "peer-assessment" is a mechanism that encourages conformity and, as a number of scientists themselves have pointed out, can lead to mediocrity in that ideas completely at variance with establishment thinking, or examination of the assumptions behind that thinking, are not encouraged.

The link between the expert and the commercial is very close. When Professor Fagan in the States returned a research grant of six hundred thousand dollars on the basis that the research he was to carry out on genetic engineering was in fact dangerous and liable to misuse, he then attended a session of the Codex Alimentarius Commission dealing with food labeling to try to ensure that all genetically engineered food was clearly labeled as such (personal conversation 1994). When he arrived there, he discovered that all the other scientific experts in attendance were funded by the genetic engineering food corporations. The official decision, "objectively" taken, was to ensure, insofar as possible, that the consumer consumed what he was told to consume by the "experts" and the requirement to label for the "free" market economy was waived.

The parallel category to "expert" is "charlatan," and those who offend the establishment tend to be expeditiously ejected from the one and deposited in the other. The fate of Jacques Benveniste of INSERM is a case in point, and Rupert Sheldrake provides another (Sir John Maddox, editor of *Nature*, reviewed Sheldrake's work in 1981 under the heading "A Book for Burning?" 1981, 245). This kind of phenomenon is not peculiar to Western or modern society. Indian gurus are also "experts" liable to sudden demotions and having a peer interest in retaining their status—and the status quo. In an earlier period in Europe it was the theologians, the men of God, who were the prime claimants to a similar position, as they still are in Islamic countries. Their arguments were concluded by the loser's being subjected to anything from ritualistic humiliation to torment and death. In our enlightened age we simply cut off failed experts' funding and leave them free to seek employment as janitors.[3]

Networks of interest groups are of course part of every society, but the extent of their current power is a slight on representative democracy, which is dying. The important question is, representative of what? The honing of techniques of persuasion and the control of media by financial interest groups are contributory causes of democracy's malfunction. Human beings are manipulated through weakness, laziness, greed, and fear. A salient feature in all this is the power of money, an imaginary entity, whose power comes precisely from its being imaginary. Its grip on the communal imagination means that we all string along in its wake.

Education should be part of an answer, but clearly not simply scientific education, which would give a view of the world as partial as Islamic education, or Marxist education, or the stricter forms of

Hindu or Christian education, or any other form of political correctness. The arts, once called "liberal," were supposed to generate
strong, fearless, and independent minds, and did so up to a point,
for some, but the basis of the arts, like the basis of democracy, was
a unified culture with an enforced and dominant value system. In
our present world there is no consensus about fundamentals, no set
of assumptions that can safely be taken for granted, and no single
cultural tradition that can be regarded as central in the way "high
culture" used to be. The resultant relativism and disorientation
present an opportunity for liberation, but in conjunction with the
noise, ceaseless activity, and insidiously intrusive persuasion of our
technological culture they hinder the pursuit of some point of rest
within us from which to survey the hectic external scene. Education, like everything else, needs to be rethought.

The humanities were once so called to distinguish them from the
divine science of theology (another *scientia*). They consisted of the
study of the civilized languages, ancient Greek and Latin, which
gave access to the world that fell with the Roman Empire and *was*,
in some ways, more civilized than the ages that succeeded even
down to the present. To Greek and Latin were added New Testament Greek and Hebrew, which gave direct access to the Scriptures
held to embody absolute truth. In combination they equipped a perfect gentleman for this world and the next. Literature was part of
the linguistic tradition and rhetoric a major means of studying it,
while philosophy accessed the highest (and most abstract) level of
civilization.

This way of thinking is no longer valid. Theology may be about
the divine, but it is a product of the human, and no body of writing
can be unquestionably accepted as *the* embodiment of absolute
truth. The dichotomy between humanities and divinity, part of the
basic dichotomizing of Western civilization (temporal versus divine, body versus mind, matter versus spirit, reason versus feeling,
even male divine versus female material), is no longer tenable. Yet
just as the humanities were needed to temper and civilize theology,
so a balancing factor is now required to humanize technology, or
we will all move into a world where no bird sings and the self-open-
ing doors slide shut behind us, leaving nothing but metal, glass, and
the whir of air-conditioning. This is a paradise, no doubt, but it is a
paradise I would not share. It privileges only the linear ratiocinative
understanding, omits a sense of the living numinous, replacing it

by the required gasp of admiration at scientific thought (despite the metaphysical crudity of science), and downplays feeling to a mere accessory, to be satisfied, if at all, in a series of kicks. Life simply as kicks becomes a line of hamburgers stretching to infinity, good for business but not the digestion. The search for knowledge becomes the search for objective fact, devoid of the pursuit of human wholeness, whether attainable or not. Knowledge devoid of feeling becomes the scientific curiosity demonstrated by Nero when he ripped up his mother's womb to see where he had been conceived.

Some equivalent of the humanities is needed. But in rethinking the humanities, we must also rethink divinity, science, economics. Our theologies, our arts, and our sciences need to move beyond themselves. Our philosophy needs to free itself from the limitations of logic-chopping around the skirts of science and return to consideration of a much fuller range of human experience and much more important questions. Our modes of mental operation need reform. Kosko (1993) boasts that science has displaced religion and philosophy, and he is right. Is this the result of the splendor of science, or the feebleness of religion and philosophy? And if the latter, where does that feebleness lie and what might be done to remedy it? Perhaps we could start, with all due reverence of course, by taking a look at notions of theism and bouncing them off something that is not nontheistic, but not theistic in the ordinary sense.

BEYOND THEISM?

The Unity is without shape, even shape Intellectual.

Generative of all, the Unity is none of all; neither thing nor quantity nor quality nor intellect nor soul; not in motion, not at rest, not in place, not in time: it is the self-defined, unique in form or, better, formless, existing before Form was, or Movement or Rest, all of which are attachments of Being. . . .

In knowing, soul or mind abandons its unity . . . knowing is taking account of things; that accounting is multiple; the mind thus plunging into number and multiplicity departs from unity.

Our way then takes us beyond knowing; there may be no wandering from unity; knowing and knowable must all be left aside; every object of thought, even the beautiful, we must pass by, for all that is beautiful is later than This and derives from This as from the sun all the light of the day. (Plotinus 1991, incorporating Dillon's note, 6.9.3–4, pp. 539–40)

This passage in Plotinus presupposes a model of the mind, and of the relationship between mind and matter, completely at variance with modern scientific orthodoxy and the orthodoxies of ratiocinative scholarship. It points to a path, a mode of human development, and the statements it makes are experiential and experience-directed and many of them negative, entailing a breaking of the limitations of the condition of mind that we now consider to be normative. It therefore has implications that in modern Western categories we would tend to label metaphysical, ontological, and epistemological. It does not fit within the delimitations of contemporary discourses: not psychology, not theology, not religion, not philosophy, not science as we understand these things. The only modern things about Plotinus's writings are argument from an articulated experiential base and the highlighting of a need for what we would call "curriculum redevelopment" in the modern world (though that is usually taken to entail new instances of the same, not anything more radical). Whether the passage is theistic or not depends on your definition of theism. Whether it is religious or not depends on your definition of religion. Whether it speaks of God or not depends on your definition of God. Whether it presents a perhaps feasible mode of development depends on your model of the mind and assumed epistemology.

There is tremendous variation in conceptualizations of the divine. In Plotinus's conceptualization it figures as the One, or that which is beyond number, for Plotinus explicitly makes the point that the One is not a numerical unit and cannot strictly be described as a unity. "This we cannot but name The Unity, indicating it to each other by a designation that points to the concept of its partlessness while we are in reality striving to bring our own minds to unity" (Plotinus 1991, 6. 9. 5, p. 541). In addition, this comment foregrounds a concept of epistemology as a theory of the knower as well as the known, a point to which I will return. It also places the One as the Absolute, described in the *Brihad-aranyaka Upanishad* by negatives, *neti, neti*, "not this, not this" (2.3.6; Radhakrishnan 1992, 194), and therefore neither personal nor impersonal and not knowable as an object. The last point of course also entails questions of language and hermeneutics, the gap between sign and signified, to which I will also return.

The divine can equally be envisaged as a manifest unity, with or without a transcendent aspect. It can be an impersonal force, with or without intelligence, a blind or seeing will. It can be personal, and either male or female or subsuming both sexes and genders, or subsuming sex and gender as such. Indian icons of the god and consort combine together in hermaphroditic form (the *ardhanareeshwara*) in the temple of Madurai in South India (Chidbhavananda 1971, 140–41). This is one possible projection, if you take the Hindu view that the gods are in fact one god, a view again found in Plotinus.

The gods may be plural in number rather than one, either as a family of separate entities, beings, or as the many facets of one being. Or of course there may be no God or gods at all. This is in practice the dominant view today, at its crudest associated with fundamentalist scientism, though often given more cogent and reasoned expression. Bertrand Russell states it in a counterargument to claims of purpose as part of the design argument for the existence of a personal and specifically a Christian God: "So far as scientific evidence goes, the universe has crawled by slow stages to a somewhat pitiful result on this earth, and is going to crawl by still more pitiful stages to a condition of universal death. If this is to be taken as evidence of purpose, I can only say that the purpose is one that does not appeal to me. I see no reason therefore to believe in any sort of God, however vague and however attenuated" (quoted by Ayer 1973, 220). Science is thus and inevitably dragged into the arguments about the existence and nature of God or gods.

All the positions outlined carry with them a metaphysic in the sense of theories of the relation between mind and matter together with various assumptions, usually unspoken assumptions, about the nature and structure of time and space and the material universe. They also carry a wide variety of associated epistemologies, theories of knowledge and its reliability or limitations, as well as psychologies or models of the mind, implicit from the outset in the mere idea of relating mind to matter.

The epistemological issues are bound up with the truth status of the various religious traditions of the world, some twenty thousand in number, as well as the truth status of the sciences and the kind of reliability accorded to scientific theory. Both science and religion are somewhat vague terms. The social sciences, for instance, are radically different from hard-core material sciences like physics, and these in turn differ markedly from sciences like paleontology. Equally, religions claim authority from a variety of sources: oral tradition, written documents, revelation, established custom and authorities, experience, or, more speciously, from reason (reasoning). All these sources of religious authority are open to question and all or almost all are subject to change. Oral tradition and written texts alike are constantly reinterpreted according to need, circumstance, and fashion. Power structures and accepted authority are similarly revised.

Revelation is ambiguous in nature, including direct dictation by a god or gods (as in the case of the Koran or the oracles of Delphi), looser notions of inspiration, or notions of direct cognition, as, for the Hindu, the Vedas record direct cognitions by particular *rishis* of the sound substrate, the Word if you like, underlying space-time (in consequence the Vedas are regarded as eternal, and also subject to addition at any time through new cognitions). Textual status as a source of authority can be questioned in various ways. The Vedas, for instance, are not accepted by the Buddhists, who regard the claims of Vedic cognition as bogus. Similarly, the idea of a text as in some sense dictated by God depends on the prior assumption of a personal God who communicates through human language. To justify the idea of such a god on the basis of a text making this assertion is therefore to argue in a circle. Consequently, the normal riposte to rejection of a text as the Word of God is not to argue but to murder the objector or to attempt to murder him or at least reduce him to silence—the Moslem reaction to Salman Rushdie is a case in point, even though Rushdie does not reject the status of the whole Koran, but merely raises the question of its status. Experience can include anything from the general experience of life in a particular culture (usually interpreted by an assumed hermeneutic, unconsciously taken for granted and not formulated for questioning) to specific emotional or nonemotional experience resulting from conversion, fortuitous grace, or austere discipline (Forman 1998; James 1961).

Finally, the arguments that a particular religion is susceptible to rational proof are convincing only to those who already adhere to that religion, or are predisposed to take its worldview seriously. As in the case of textual status, the final argument is usually murder— the pagan Sambian nation of Old Prussia, for instance, was simply wiped out for refusing to abandon polytheism and accept Christianity (Jones 1997, 173). Moreover, the acceptance of discursive rationality as decisive is a culturally conditioned value judgment, and value judgments—like moral systems—are not finally provable. In addition, reasoning inevitably involves some prior assumed propositions that are not open to proof, and reason always operates *on* something, a mass of experience that is itself culturally as well as individually conditioned. Virtually all religions can be defended rationally, given appropriate assumptions; none can be proved true by that means alone or to universal satisfaction.

In science the position is not totally dissimilar. The most obvious difference is that the technological applications of science are more tangible and more reliable than those of religion. Salvation, enlightenment, the joys of conversion in those religions that include conversion processes are all subjective experiences not easily susceptible to objective verification or reliable corroboration, whereas a tank, a refrigerator, or an airplane are materially there and tend to work pretty reliably.

The truth status of science is, however, a different and far less certain matter. Popper was particularly perturbed by the case of Newton: virtually no scientific theory covers all the available observations, as Thomas Kuhn also noted (1970), but Newton's theory of gravity was, as Popper pointed out, as well established as any theory could well be. Yet it was wrong. The whole causative explanation and conceptualization was displaced by relativity theory. Nonetheless, the macro applications of Newton's mathematical formulae are still employed and valued. In other words, a theory may not correspond with what is the case, and in that sense be untrue, yet it may work very well in practice nonetheless. (Much the same was of course sometimes said of Christianity in the eighteenth century.) Popper in consequence postulated a constantly closer scientific approximation to a hidden truth whose existence had to be accepted a priori on the basis of common sense—again, a familiar Western religious way of thinking. Popper concluded that in the experimental sciences one contrary instance could disprove the truth of a theory, even though no amount of positive corroboration could prove it true. In other words, he accepted Hume's strictures on the validity of inductive reasoning. Yet he nonetheless granted science a truth value beyond that of any other human endeavor (Popper 1979, 63–84).

It is this general way of thinking that leads scientists to speak so ambivalently about the truth status of science. On occasion they speak of their theories as tools; you may find a spade very useful to dig with, but you do not usually say, "O spade, thou art truth!" However, in practice they easily glide from the tool to the truth approach, and popularly science is regarded as simply true, despite anomalies in observations and the dubious assumptions involved in the concepts of objectivity, objective observation, and the formulation of theory.

A number of the difficulties are brought out by A. J. Ayer and by Paul Feyerabend. Ayer, commenting on Darwinian theory in the context of the problem of knowledge of the past, gives an amusing instance of one recurring difficulty with theories:

> The critic Edmund Gosse related in his book *Father and Son* that his father, a member of the sect of Plymouh Brethren, held firmly to Archbishop Ussher's calculation, on the basis of biblical evidence, that the world had been created in the year 4004 B.C. In face of the abundant scientific evidence of a considerably earlier date, he reasoned that God had endowed the world with delusive appearances of much greater antiquity in order to test men's faith. Once more this is not a position that can be refuted. The hypothesis that everything is and will continue to be as if the world had existed for many millions of years will fit the available facts just as well as the hypothesis that the world has existed for many millions of years. (Ayer 1973, 135–36)

If we are to reject Gosse senior we must do so on grounds that may appear reasonable to us, but we cannot justifiably claim that we are being rational and he is not.

Nor is the matter even as simple as this, for Ayer assumes that observation will always reveal the same thing, the "facts." In the case cited he may be right. What, however, would he do with the claim of Patanjali in the *Yoga Sutras* that a trained yogi perceives as one nondiscursive totality the past and future of anything and everything (3.16ff.)?[4] The claim involves a completely different way of conceptualizing and perceiving time and the objective world from the one we regard as normal and exclusively correct. Feyerabend has indeed argued more generally that observation and perception are learned skills, and consequently not only is scientific observation theory-dependent, but perception itself cannot take place without culturally imbibed norms, norms that could in our culture be formulated as a theory. In other words, cultures largely

create the worlds they live in. Personally I agree. I remember my
next-door neighbor in Durham speaking with utter incredulity of a
forest dweller in the remote parts of Sweden who claimed she had
seen a troll in the forest. I did not like to point out that I did not see
any reason why the woman should not have seen a troll, though her
observation would be subject to all the epistemological doubts surrounding any other observations. Perception is one thing, its explanation is another, but to dismiss out of hand all that does not fit with
one's own worldview is simply prejudice.

In his "Postscript on Relativism" in *Against Method,* Feyerabend
deals with these points in a language recognized by our culture.
After asserting that culture and nature, or culture and being, cannot
be disentangled one from the other, he continues:

> Now considering that scientists use different and often contradictory
> methods of research . . . that most of these methods are successful and
> that numerous non-scientific ways of life not only survived but pro-
> tected and enriched their inhabitants we have to conclude that Being
> responds differently, *and positively*, to many different approaches.
> Being is like a person who shows a friendly face to a friendly visitor,
> becomes angry at an angry gesture, remains unmoved by a bore without
> giving any hint as to the principles that make Him (Her? It? Them?) act
> the way they do in different circumstances. What we find when living,
> experimenting, doing research is therefore not a single scenario called
> "the world" or "being" or "reality" but a variety of responses, each of
> them constituting a special (and not always well-defined) reality for
> those who have called it forth. (1993, 270)

This is an interesting formulation in that it distinguishes being from
realities, making it a potentiality in itself hidden in the manner of
the religious transcendent, but giving rise to graspable objectivities
in response to human approaches. However, Feyerabend points out
that his view is not ordinary philosophical relativism, since "not
every approach succeeds" (*ibid.*). Humans presumably also emerge
from this potentiality, though no such implication is worked out,
and they become in some measure agents of creation. Within a
given framework they formulate their worlds.

Feyerabend's whole formulation has numerous potential affilia-
tions, for instance with Schrödinger's cat and the idea in quantum
theory that observation even on the macro level actualizes one only

from a vast variety of potential waves of probability (Davies 1983, 114–15); with the statement in the *Gita* that Krishna responds to human beings in forms appropriate to the ways in which they approach him; with Shankara's formulations of maya, the snake superimposed on the rope of the Absolute, Brahman. It allows room for the diversity of human experience, the experiential content of Tibetan Buddhism, for instance, or the realm of the shamans virtually the world over. Above all, it makes a vital allowance for the role of consciousness in experience, cognition, perception, and formulation. The assumption that everybody exists in identical consciousness within an identical world is crass, as is the assumption that human worlds have nothing at all in common.

The provision for the role of consciousness is further developed by Feyerabend himself in his discussion of Thomas Kuhn's Robert and Maurine Rothschild Distinguished Lecture of 19 November 1991:

[Kuhn asserts that] "the Archimedian platform, outside history, outside of time and space, is gone beyond recall." Yes, and no. It is gone as a structure that can be described and yet shown to be independent of any description. It is not gone as an unknown background of our existence which affects us but in a way which forever hides its essence. Nor is Archimedianism gone as a possible approach. It would be the politically correct approach in a theocracy, for example. . . . (1993, 271)

[Feyerabend then takes up Kuhn's discussion of the relation of science to reality; Kuhn] challenges the traditional notion of truth as correspondence to reality. "I am not suggesting, let me emphasize, that there is a reality which science fails to get at. My point is, rather, that no sense can be made of the notion of a reality as it has ordinarily functioned in the philosophy of science." Here I agree with the proviso that more metaphysical notions of reality (such as those proposed by Pseudo Dionysius Areopagita) have not yet been disposed of.

Let me repeat that cultures call forth a certain reality and these realities themselves are never well defined. Cultures change, they interact with other cultures and the indefiniteness resulting therefrom is reflected in their worlds. This is what makes intercultural understanding and scientific change possible: potentially every culture is all cultures. (1993, 272)

Feyerabend comments that if cultures were clearly defined and if scientific terminology had been nailed down, then "only miracles or revelation could reform our cosmology" (*ibid*). Taken in connection with Eastern thought, this position begins to approach the idea of *samsara*, the flux of relativity that constitutes the worlds. Taken in connection with Western thought, it opens up at least the possibility of a plurality of worlds in a sense wider than the plural material universes mooted in scientific speculation and developed by scientists in works of fiction, such as *Timescape* by Gregory Benford, a professor of physics. The metaphysical world of Dionysius the Areopagite is static in comparison with *samsara*, but multilayered compared with the monomaterialism of science.

Feyerabend's inclusion of the aside on Dionysius is extremely important in three respects. *Historically,* Dionysius's interpretation of Christianity provided the original stimulus of all the traditions of Christian mysticism, including the Spanish. He lay behind the tradition of mystical theology in the Eastern Orthodox Church and through the *via negativa* linked Plato with Christianity via Plotinus. Though Christian and a lesser figure, he has a considerable amount in common with Plotinus, and he has enough in common with Shankara and Hindu and Buddhist thought in general to make comparison and relatedness possible. He also has at least something in common with Ibn Arabi's school of Sufism in Islam, and the Islamic mystical traditions were also directly influenced by Plotinus himself. *Theologically,* Dionysius takes account both of the divine names and divine ineffability and explicitly recognizes a non-subject-object experience of God as well as a personal experience within the subject-object category. He thus makes possible, for instance, Eckhart's account of the soul being carried back into and being lost in the godhead, just as he prepares the way for the account by St. Simeon the New Theologian of the mind, naked of all thought, that is similarly merged into and lost in the godhead. *Most important of all,* he begins to open up within the Christian tradition the potentialities of human consciousness.

Plotinus goes further in two respects. Being nondenominational and not religious, he formulates the culminating experience-cum-non-experience of the *via negativa* ("pure consciousness" devoid of empirical content) in terms of the nature of the human mind as such, and he allows for the maintenance of this culminating experience together with the everyday subject-object operation of the mind, thus allowing for a transformatory development of human consciousness beyond what is currently regarded as normal or possible. This development has very far-reaching implications for the experience of the subject-object relationship, the experience of time, and the development of noetic rather than discursive intelligence (noetic implying direct holistic cognition ontologically prior to space-time). This again links especially with Hindu and Buddhist tradition. Dionysius does not go nearly so far, but he goes far enough to lay a foundation and open up a world.

In positing a development of consciousness, Plotinus provides an epistemology and method of investigation that are alternatives to those of the modern sciences. The main claim of science to a unique epistemological status is its predictive ability plus the explanatory range of its theories. Explanation is, however, not an objective discovery but an achievement of integration within subjective theory. It is thus truer to say that Newton invented the law of gravity, up to a point combining Galileo's formulation of laws of motion with observed planetary orbits, than that he discovered it.

As already pointed out, Popper acknowledged Hume's demonstration of the fallibility of inductive knowledge. In consequence he posits corroboration as the key to scientific knowledge (1980, 33). An alternative view claims probability rather than certainty for scientific findings. Feyerabend goes further by pointing out that probability is a culturally conditioned notion. Feyerabend also notes that scientists are plagued by human failings (like a desire for high salaries, plenty of research funding, and eminent status) and that they are subject to the cabals and factioning that feature so strongly in religious history, or any other history come to that.

Feyerabend, however, goes even further, venturing into the politics of culture in the broadest sense. He points out that the criteria for testing science are created by science, so that it constitutes an epistemological closed shop. Science is thus incapable of testing fairly the merits, for instance, of scientific medicine as opposed to the merits of other and older medical systems. He also believes that its values are distorted, in that they do not allow for human or natural need. Scientific theoreticians and the rationalist defenders of science "extol the 'rationality' and 'objectivity' of science without realizing that a procedure whose main aim is to get rid of all human elements is bound to lead to inhuman actions. . . . They distinguish between the good that science can do 'in principle' and the bad things it actually does. That can hardly give us comfort. All religions are good 'in principle'—but unfortunately this abstract Good has only rarely prevented their practitioners from behaving like bastards" (Fayerabend 1987, 299). Leaving aside the issue of whether this account makes religion as methodologically inhuman (inhumane) as science, it is clear that for Feyerabend science thus becomes what Doris Lessing called it, "the most recent religion" on this earth (1972, 120).

On the mundane level, the best answer to all these difficulties is an open and free society. Feyerabend asserts that "a free society is a society in which all traditions are given equal rights, equal access to education and other positions of power" (1993, 228). By this standard there is no free society on earth. It is surely time we created one.

From the conventional point of view, Plotinus is even more way out than Feyerabend. Plotinus posits alternative modes of consciousness taking the mind beyond the limitations of the space-time world and beyond discursive knowledge. Like Patanjali, Plotinus holds that noetic cognition, subject uniting with object, is certain; the noetic can function or not function, but when it does function it is never mistaken 1.1.9.11. While this does not dispose of the need for discursive thought in a discursive world, it does make such thought secondary and its results partial. Consciousness is thus integral to knowledge and ultimately transformable into truth, in the sense of timeless and spaceless infinitude. The pursuit of knowledge becomes the pursuit of truth when the mind is transformed to become its source. The essence of education thus becomes for Plotinus not the acquisition of knowledge but the self-transformation of the knower.

This approach presents its own difficulties, in that until the mind has become ultimate reality there is no certainty that such a state is possible, and that until such a state is arrived at all formulations are inevitably extrapolations of partial experiences. It also demands a particular course of life and a dedication greater than that of the scientist in his pursuit of truth. Also it points to the ultimate inadequacy of linguistic and other formulations: the net of the finite cannot catch the fish of infinitude. Obviously no one could or should be pressured into adopting such an approach, but knowledge of its existence and of the means of pursuing it should be readily available in Feyerabend's open society.

For such an open society tolerance is essential. The greatest achievement of the Enlightenment was the introduction of a limited measure of tolerance within Western civilization, but it has remained decidedly limited. Tolerance, of course, also introduces problems of its own, and I would agree with Feyerabend that the only practical recourse is to something akin to a modified version of what has been called the Utilitarian calculus, though this will clearly not work in quantitative terms and will sometimes not work at all. It involves the central value, unprovable like all values, of respecting the freedom of the human will that respects the freedom of other wills. It leads to a commonsensical position that the only thing that cannot be tolerated is intolerance, with the proviso that Voltaire's *bon sens* is a better guide to applying it than Isaiah Berlin's account of the Enlightenment would seem to imply (Berlin 1997, 334; compare 362–63). Tolerance is also more than a refusal to persecute. It is an abstaining from the techniques of silencing, marginalization, and misrepresentation, and it has a strong economic and ecological constituent (it would seem to imply a kind of bio-economics).

Even a theoretical knowledge of the Plotinian approach has value in modern society, both because the consciousness aspect of life is largely ignored, with potentially disastrous consequences, and because the Plotinian approach allows for whole realms of human experience that are beyond the ken of the materialistic sciences and opens up potential techniques of investigation that science does not have. Consciousness is never an object and cannot be studied as such. Our own consciousness is directly experienced, and reflection on its functioning is reflection upon ideas and memories of previous states of consciousness: in other words, engagement with objects of consciousness by directly experienced consciousness itself. The consciousness of others is not, or not usually, available to us, and its existence is usually not directly experienceable. Moreover, there are numerous states of consciousness and types of experience, recorded and in principle repeatable, that are totally unknown to modern Western mainstream thought (Forman 1990, 1998). There are states where consciousness is, but ordinary personal identity is not, such as the experience of almost infinite pure I-ness together with absolute infinitude, the whole itself consciousness so that there is no subject-object relationship. There is undifferentiated pure consciousness, without space or time. There is instantaneous holistic cognition beyond discursive temporality. There is the perception of the world in what might be called geological time. There is the intelligible light of the Platonists, and so on and on. And Plotinus is right that such states are not isolated incidents. They temper the everyday functioning of consciousness and can open up other practical possibilities, for instance that of accompanying the dying through and beyond physical death, and helping them. If such experience is repeated, corroborated by others, and effective, then it has just as much right to regard as experiences of the sense realm.

Science, materialist in bias and deprived of access to consciousness beyond the most commonplace, can only study brain functioning and the effects on everyday life of interference with and stimulation of the gross physical nervous system (I say the gross, since kundalini manifestations, for instance, use a subtler but still material level). The resulting speculations, such as the systems model of consciousness in Hofstadter's "Prelude . . . Ant Fugue" (Hofstadter and Dennett 1982, 149–91) certainly have interest for the personality ("actor's mask") level of consciousness, but equally do not explain consciousness away as Hofstadter seems to imply. Scientific knowledge relating to consciousness may be valuable, but is certainly partial. It is part of the relativity of all knowledge, and not an exclusively valid knowledge of experts, consigning other knowledges to oblivion.

The relativity of knowledge affects both the nature of language and the status of theism. Noetic thought is prelinguistic and nondiscursive. In the Vedic tradition of linguistics, discursive verbalization is preceded by *pashyanti*, total wordless concept uniting subject and object, devoid of discursivity or the sense of time, and this level is recognized also by Plotinus, though he does not speak of it in the context of language 4.3.30.284. The root of language lies even beyond this, in the first stirrings of thought, which for Vedic philosophers (Dasgupta 1988, 1991) and Plotinus reenact the emergence of the manifest from that which is beyond manifestation. There is thus a division between sign and referent in verbalization, but it is a division rooted in unity, and language as a signifying system is not totally arbitrary and from its root carries within itself its own transcendence. In this sense language is the birth of manifest or relative consciousness, it functions through consciousness, and liveliness of consciousness in its use will give it a tendency to draw listener or reader toward unity with the source that lies within them. Enactment rather than information becomes the highest function of language.

What then of theism, monotheism, androtheism? The ultimate

test of monotheism is experience, one experience among many. Recourse to supposed authority vested in some text merely pushes the need for experiential validation one stage back, as does reliance on a supposedly authoritative tradition of textual interpretation. The only alternative to reliance on our own experience is brainwashing, which most cultures are extremely good at. Given, however, an experientially based inclination to adopt monotheism in one of its forms, there remains a demand in our culture for at least some approximate linguistic definition. Once this was a relatively straightforward, if not easy, matter. Now it isn't, since language has itself become problematic, as modern linguistic sophisticates are well aware, since the study of rhetoric has become politicized, and since gender role and hierarchic authority are being subjected to savage questioning and frequent rejection (Ellis 1997). However, the discussion of these issues is often on a very crude level, as are many of the traditional descriptions of God and the operation of the divine in this world, as well as many of the references to God and consciousness in current books popularizing science, including works by Dawkins (Hofstadter and Dennett 1982, 141–44), Kosko (1993, 267–85), and Hawking (1988, 174–75).

If you describe what God is, you also describe what you are. As in the case of perception, subject and object are not divorced, object is perceived and described in terms of subject. In *Paradise Lost* the falling Adam exclaims, "But past who can recall, or done undo? / Not God Omnipotent" (9.926–27), thus placing God in time, not time in God, and making God an operator all-powerful only within a time sequence that is serially extended but otherwise similar to the time of the everyday world. Time thus becomes the ultimate reality. A similar way of thinking turned God into the divine watchmaker in the eighteenth century, and in the seventeenth had produced a divine watchmaker of less than perfect watches, for, according to Feyerabend, Newton held that God periodically intervened to adjust the motions of the planets in order to forestall the disintegration of the solar system that seemed to follow from Newton's (and God's) system of celestial mechanics. Such descriptions could only come from minds chained to the discursive levels of consciousness.

Enpantheism offers an alternative version or versions of monotheism that can more easily account for subtler consciousness. It was for this reason that it tended to be stated or implied by the En-

glish romantic poets. It also moves beyond the finality of a subject-
object divide, so that in theological terms an I-thou relationship
with the divine can be complemented by an I + divine-not-I-
within-me relationship. It is also implied in the Good of Plato and
the One of Plotinus, from which the universe radiates like light
from the sun. The idea has immense ethical implications, embodied
in the wisdom-and-compassion ideal of Buddhism, and implications for the role of consciousness in right action that are most inci-
sively analyzed in the *Gita*. In the Judaeo-Christian tradition
generally there has, however, been a tendency to place a great
chasm between God and creature, God and man, God and world,
and in the Christian imagination, especially in Western Christendom, God has often been transformed into a feudal lord.

Now, however, this will no longer do, and the *idea of* God, for
that is what it is, is being rethought. One of the most interesting
rethinkings that I have come across is in David Jasper's paper, "The
Death of God: A Live Issue?" in this collection. Take, for instance,
the following comment: "The critical notion of the 'death of the
author' is revisited as the 'death of God,' but carried further as this
death becomes an embodiment in the movement from speech into
silence, and silence as a total emptiness from which the genesis of
speech occurs. Only pure silence can be heard as silence, and only
in such silence is speech totally present because totally absent."
This is precisely the system of statement that is always and forever
misstatement transcending itself, and the reader/hearer transcending him/herself and time becoming timeless within the here and
now. Continuity as continuity is meaningless—always was—the
plottings, "plan," and patternings of a time-bounded God. Meaning
is the unspoken and forever speaking silence. Again, as David Jasper adds, "What this poetics, which is far beyond the hermeneutical, allows us is the impossible possibility of *thinking* about God."
This thinking lies through the process of mind and beyond mind,
not in a defined object of mind. Thus Blake is, in David Jasper's
phrase, "writing scripture" in *The Marriage of Heaven and Hell.*
The positivistic God of Western tradition is superseded. So is the
positivistic God of Western scientism (in the senses of both the scientific version of the God of modern Western religion and the arrogant hubris of science itself).

This stance has tremendous implications within Christian tradition, not least for the idea of faith. Kierkegaard would have under-

stood the implied transformation of faith; a positivist theologian would look for a stake, faggots, and a box of matches. The death of God, thus interpreted, could restrain even the murderous tendencies of positivistic theism and positivistic science. For such a practice of timelessness there is not much time left.

The death of God is God as *via negativa*, enacted in the history or myth of Christianity as narrative, and including the cruelty and suffering of life, as they are included for the Hindu in the figure of Kali. It has indeed similarities with the Hindu idea of Brahma withdrawing into himself in order to create and, in other versions of the myth, falling in consequence, but it does not necessarily reduce God to process, as Smullyan does in "Is God a Taoist?" (Smullyan's version of Taoism, like some modern Western philosophers' versions of Buddhism, is time-bounded: the Tao is the wisdom of the process of things, but it is also beyond process.) God as *via negativa* links, even unites Plato and Neoplatonism, Christendom and its persecuted mystics, Sufis, Hindus, and Buddhists, plus those like myself who are in and outside all these traditions (compare Coward and Fosbay 1992). What a gift for a multicultural multireligious world! The way forward is the way inward. As an Indian teacher said after an exhaustive discussion of the spiritual path, "The truth is there is no path and no one to tread it."

The *Tao Te Ching*, which never ventures far into words, puts it very succinctly, making play with the literal everyday sense of *tao* as "way."

> The Tao that can be told is not the eternal Tao.
> The name that can be named is not the eternal name.
> The nameless is the beginning of heaven and earth.
> The named is the mother of ten thousand things. (1)

TECHNO-ECONOMICS

All this, of course, is mysticism and not worth rational consideration, even though Plotinus did not belong to the theistic religions and scholarship that for their own purposes invented the category of mysticism, and even though he is as rational and ratiocinative as the next man. All experience is equal, but some kinds of experience are so much more equal than others that the others can be left out of account in this practical world of ours. The original English word for scientific experiment was experience.

If Feyerabend's free and open society is to be achieved, if tolerance is to become reality, then human beings, human society, and human interaction with the ecosystem require radical change. Awareness of new possibilities is not enough. We need also to grapple with the inertia in the systems we allow to form us, and therefore with the inertia in ourselves. The most powerful system at the moment, more powerful than politics, is economics.

Economics, it has been said, would be a science if it weren't for the human factor. Unfortunately, economics cannot be divorced from the human beings who form economic systems. The human factor is all-pervasive. On materialist assumptions economics is a specialization of the ecosystem. In our alternative psychology it is also a way of projecting into external symbol the mind's drive toward infinitude, and thus moves well beyond basic material need. Both aspects of economics, concern with material need and with something beyond it, are also there in rudimentary form in other animals. Through territoriality they attempt to control supplies of food and water. They also acquire wealth, and not merely by hoarding food. Magpies collect jewels and glittering objects; homo economicus collects art, curios, and of course money: gold or notes or notional figures in computer storage; the concept grows increasingly abstract and the materials concerned grow less beautiful.

Money does not measure any inherent value in objects purchased or any human worth in the moneyed; it does measure desirability, but since desires directed outwards toward flux perpetually fluctuate, money value fluctuates perpetually. It also confers status and influence in the social pack, though this conferring varies in kind and degree according to the type of society concerned. Utopians have tried to limit its influence, from Sir Thomas More's advocacy of gold pisspots in *Utopia* to the ruling philosophers' fastidious avoidance of money in Plato's *Republic*. The clever mathematical formulae used by economists to predict market behavior, based on economics conceived as a system, operate up to a point for a while, and then break down. Nonmathematical predictions are equally problematic. The present discussions concerning the boom and bust cycle, and whether it has now disappeared or has been flattened in its peaks and troughs or has had its periodicity extended, are an instance in point. Operative devices, notably monopoly, can stabilize a market but not indefinitely. Monopoly, however, is now out, in theory at least. We are after all in a free market economy based on open competition.

Free market economy and open competition are heartwarming slogans with as much relevance to what is going on as *liberté, égalité, fraternité* had to what was going on in the French Revolution. Joe Rogaly, the oracle of the *Financial Times,* commented on one instance of what is in fact happening:

> In the US, 14 states have adopted "food disparagement" acts, which bar negative comments about perishable comestibles. These bans amount to a protection racket for farmers and commodity merchants, following the powerful anti-green alliance between loggers and right-wing congressmen.
>
> It is curious that such a curtailment of free speech is acceptable to so many Americans. We may regard this as yet another indication of the change in the balance of power between elected representative institutions and free-ranging capitalist organizations. (*Rogaly* 1997)

To a foreigner the U.S. can seem over-regulated and litigious where its ordinary citizens are concerned, but the larger corporations influence much of the legislation, fund politics, or contribute greatly to funding politicians, and can afford litigation. Whole industries have likewise organized into powerful political lobbies. In our own country (the U.K.) the situation is little better, and the previous government was linked to business through a network of sleaze that had the look of comfortably established practice.

The regulation of markets is a matter of ethics, and ethics are of course mysticism; systems of ethics cannot be "proven," only supported by arguments based on differing assumptions. (There are some similarities with the epistemology of the sciences, where truths can be established within overall sets of assumptions.) The official ethic of a particular society tends to be one that suits the interests of dominant power groups. Ethical regulation raises the questions of whose ethics, operating in whose interests, and based on what assumptions.

The dominant market ethic tends to favor corporate interests and foster the symbiotic relationship between science and commerce. An instance is the contemporary rush into genetic engineering. Gigantic cattle are now being produced, as Colin Tudge pointed out

(1997), muscular mutants on feeble frames of bone, born with double muscle systems to satisfy our need for flesh. Pigs, chickens, cows, turkeys have been subjected to "engineering" or bred for the survival of the fittest—for the market. Some are unable to stand unsupported without their skeletons shattering under their own weight. Monsanto has spearheaded the introduction of genetically engineered soy beans with unforeseeable consequences for human health and the ecosystem and has mixed them unlabeled with virtually all U.S. supplies of soy bean. They have even penetrated into baby food in the States. Attempts to enforce labeling have been resisted with great vigor, not only in the U.S. but abroad. Genetically engineered organisms once released cannot be recalled, but the extensive field tests undergone for drugs have not been completed for these foods. Moreover, agricultural field tests themselves constitute an unacceptable risk in the case of genetic engineering, given the irreversibility of cross-pollination, dissemination, etc.: what is required is preliminary very thorough testing in environments within sealed laboratories. However, there is a majority scientific consensus that the risks involved are none or few, and a scientific consensus is as infallible as the Pope. Naturally the scientists involved, being genetic engineers, tend to have an enthusiasm for the industry and an interest, direct or indirect, in its commercial success. Nonetheless, it is in our own best interests in this free market economy that we should not have clear labeling of genetically engineered products, for we should not be permitted to diverge from authoritative scientific judgment. Living in democracy, we need to have our minds made up for us by experts, the only people qualified to do it. To adapt one of Hitler's slogans, "Our leaders think for us."

The principle that science decides, not politicians, let alone the people, is written into the sanitary and phyto-sanitary agreement of the WTO. Food imports can only be rejected for reasons of safety on the basis of positive scientific evidence, a market regulation that in combination with a lack of clear labeling precludes consumer choice. If corporations are able to demand positive scientific evidence of harm from their products before they can be refused admission to another country, and if they will not label them, then corporations are, to use one of the sports metaphors so beloved of economic commentators, on a safe wicket. "Establishing a link" between products and human disability can take decades, as the struggle over tobacco in the U.S. has shown, and often requires the kind of funding available only to corporations. Science and some scientists are being used as tools to protect markets. The link between science and finance is decisive.

We do, however, still have ultimate power. Boycotts and rejections can cripple corporations, but their effectiveness depends on concerted action and the availability of information and alternative ways of thinking. Hence the attempts to prevent labeling and the massive advertising campaigns launched worldwide by Monsanto and others (advertising appeals, of course, primarily to feeling, reasoning does not get much of a look-in; advertising, you might say, is mysticism, though it must be granted that it is rationally used). Thus responsibility devolves upon us, cannot be shouldered off on to political "leaders." As Charles Handy notes, corporations "are getting bigger than nation states . . . [which] means that they are effectively responsible or answerable to no one except themselves" (1997, 8–9). In consequence, "capitalism is too strong for governments. If we want to control it we must do so ourselves" (60) There are matters that are far too important to be left to the decision of scientists. Scientists have a legitimate voice, but should not be sole arbiters. One factor that involved science in international trade disputes is the unquestioned status it holds in U.S. culture as opposed to the much greater cynicism that it evokes in Europe.

THE QUESTION OF CULTURES

Most supranational corporations are currently based in the U.S. American culture and society helped to form them, and they have in turn shaped America. They now exert worldwide cultural pressure. Working practices are changing drastically. The family takes second place to the job. As Galbraith pointed out long ago, green spaces and other public amenities do not figure on balance sheets; they are only now beginning to be considered economic assets. The work ethic is destroying the anciently cherished institutions, even that of the Frenchman's leisurely lunch, no longer affordable in a wealthily efficient society. Handy remarks, "I remember my first economics teacher, a central European now working in America, and a winner of a Nobel prize, saying, rather wistfully, that he always preferred living in a country where the economy was in decline, because there was so much more time for lunch!" (1997, 27).

Working hours and habits do not change in isolation. Whole cultural narratives are also being altered fundamentally by "market forces" through the influence of the media. Such change has not always been for the worse, but it merits attention. A current instance has arisen in cinema. Disney has produced a cartoon of Hercules, which has been greeted with indignation in Greece and attacked in the *European* under the headline "Lock Up Your Legends": "You don't need to be a classical scholar to spot the howlers. The Medusa was killed by Perseus, the Minotaur by Theseus. Hades was not evil. The ancient Greek Heracles was . . . only a demi-god, and jealous Hera was his sworn enemy, not his doting mother" (1997, 9). Disney's changes polarize the film. There is a goody (Hercules) and baddies (Hades and the Minotaur), with no complicating jealousy from the queen of heaven caused by the sexual goings-on of her husband. The gods are united, all on one side, and they are either gods or not gods, not demigods born of copulation between god and human. Hades is evil, instead of being ruler over the varied postmortem worlds of mortals composed of starkly different regions allotted to the souls of the departed according to the merit of their lives on earth. Hades induces the mortalization of Hercules, who was born a god. In other words, the story is being forced into the mold of the old dualism of Christianity, good versus evil, each unambiguously identified, plus an incarnation to conquer or undo evil. It will leave the fundamentalists of the Midwest undisturbed by any alternative vision. Yet children in Europe will eagerly lap up the film, too, and their parents will take them to see it. The same is probably true in Japan and elsewhere. And Hollywood is indeed partly in Japanese ownership. This is making us a monoculture, which is why the world has grown increasingly boring.

One source of new and multicultural thought is or should be the humanities. In the realm of the sciences, Feyerabend has pointed out that ideas held in contempt and discarded for centuries have often made a comeback: atomism is a case in point. Science is one way of looking at things. Business economics is another. One of the tasks of the humanities should be to break out of such accepted mind-sets, and take a good look at *them* from outside. One of the resources, but only one of them, is the ideas of the past.

Ideas, however, are not enough, nor is structural change. Handy has stressed the need to humanize business so that it provides all of us with opportunity "to make the best of ourselves" by overcoming "tests" and "challenges," by developing ourselves in relationship and conflict with others while we move toward a finding of ourselves; our self-images, reflecting back from the selves (self-images?) of others, "come together as we get older, until we become one person, not several" (1997, 94). In this actualization of potential, interaction with others provides a "reality check" (98). Yet as death approaches, that identity as doer also slips away, together with the society and family that supported it. We move beyond habitual images, and indeed we can do so in life. Opportunity for self-realization is welcome, but identity based on self-image generated in flux is fragile, not an ultimate answer, if indeed there is an ultimate answer. In a world of images, the reality check is an unreality check. If obtainable, we need also what Shelley pointed to when he said, "the deep truth is imageless."

Plotinus is important because he points to the possibility of change in consciousness itself, as does Plato read in the light of Plotinus. Whether Plato's means to that change are the best or only ones is another matter. But the change is certainly needed. As Havel, quoted by Handy, puts it: "without a global resolution in human consciousness nothing will change for the better and the catastrophe towards which this world is headed will be unavoidable" (1997, 61).

THE HUMANITIES

It is in this current world, increasingly dominated by techno-economics and increasingly monocultural, that the humanities will have to survive, if they are to survive at all. The situation is modern, but not entirely unlike that of the traditional humanities. The study of Greek and Latin in earlier European centuries included the study of literature, and the literature was written not by Christians, but by pagans. They at least took their gods seriously, or if they had reservations about them they turned to skepticism, not a Christian orthodoxy. Their own religious myths were not as neatly polarized as the Christian; it was not always clear good against clear evil, the gods and the opposing Titans and other enemies had much in common, as they did in Norse myth. As Strindberg pointed out in connection with the Indian branch of Indo-European myth, the division between gods and *asuras* (gods and Titans) was not moral. Often

there was a confused power struggle, as in human life. The gods
were not noticeably more moral than the world they ruled over.

Both Greeks and Indians eventually attempted to square their
myths with morality, never an easy task. They resorted to hermeneutics and allegory to circumvent difficulties. Under Christendom
the effort often had to go the other way, for the officially just myth
was far more dubious in its morality than was claimed. Ayer's comment (in a public debate at Oxford in 1953) that he saw no reason
why God should be love, He could just as well be hate, is a modern
continuation from this.

Graeco-Roman culture in western Europe after the fall of the Empire survived in creative tension with the dominant Christian culture. In the Middle Ages the gods were primarily astrological
figures, yet the goddess Fortuna and her wheel symbolized an aspect of existence not projected by an absolute all-embracing and
infallible divine providence (as Napoleon remarked, a man must
have luck). Venus also focused the natural drives of sexuality and
sexual love, never well accommodated in Christianity. In less liter-
ate strata of society, folk figures such as the Green Man focused
other aspects of the natural environment. After the Renaissance the
tension became more marked, as the classical gods were either allegorized or rejected in an attempt to produce intellectual consistency
by harmonizing them with radical developments in Christian doctrine. At the same time a revived Platonism enriched Christian theology, while again existing in tension with it. By the earlier
eighteenth century, with its undertow of philosophical skepticism,
many of the British merchants, soldiers, and administrators in the
East India Company, brought up on Homer and the classics, found
the pagan society of India not totally alien (later the growing dominance of middle-class Christianity and the arrival of the memsahibs
tended to change this). Even the Hindu idea of reincarnation was
familiar from the myth of Er in Plato, the vision of the future
Roman heroes awaiting incarnation in the *Aeneid*, and its recurrence
in a good deal of Greek thought.

Such a role for the classical humanities may now be played out,
though (like the ecosystem) the myths of Greece have proved remarkably resilient. They have enabled us to express a great deal
that is otherwise difficult to formulate. They were useful to nineteenth-century psychology and postwar existentialism, as they had
been useful in earlier centuries (Linnaeus, for instance, textured his

work with classical references), and the Greeks themselves had used their own myths in literature and philosophy to probe the nature of human life and its place in the universe.

Whatever the future of Graeco-Roman myth and literature, the open spirit of inquiry that was the distinguishing characteristic of Greek civilization at its best is most certainly needed today. The modern monoculture is imposing a gray conformity more deadly than the top-hatted conformity of the old bourgeoisie. Even in mourning we call upon experts and counselors to take us through the official steps in due order—and for a small fee. When the spontaneous mourning in communist North Korea for Kim Il-song is virtually indistinguishable from the spontaneous mourning in Britain for Princess Diana, then something is badly wrong.

Justinian shut down the old Platonic Academy as a political and religious inconvenience. We need to open it anew, with a freedom greater than that of the original. Nothing is too sacred to be questioned openly and all questions have to be answered, even if the answer is an explanation of why the question cannot be answered. It is the job of the humanities to ask and keep asking the old and probably unanswerable questions. What is the or a good life? What is the basis of authority? What is the basis of religion? What are politics for? What are economies for? What is the state for (good citizenship is a secondary matter, there is no point in being a good citizen of a bad state)? What is democracy and why should it be considered a good thing? What is science and what kind of heed should we pay to it? Why do we think in the categories we do, and what might be the basis for what duties to the ecosystem?

Since these are life questions, not theory, we need life answers and life investigations. Literature, drama, philosophy all have a role, as does our own experience of the potential of human consciousness. But to arrive at answers we need time and some peace of mind, and since such activity is not money-spinning, we need to go back and examine our economic priorities.

Modern economies are producing prosperity, not well-being. Well-being implies physical well-being, which implies at the very least pure air, pure water, pure and nutritious food, adequate clothing, and shelter. The water drunk by the Romans was meticulously selected for purity and often ducted over long distances; we draw water from polluted sources and need filters on our taps. Air in nearly all modern towns is chemically polluted, as it was not in a

Roman city. Our food no longer has the quality or savor of organic food, and while gross starvation in Western towns is not what it was in the thirties, it has not disappeared. And we are the world's wealthy.

Well-being also implies mental and emotional well-being. Part of the "product" of an economy is the happiness of the work force and management, and of those who receive services and goods, and happiness is at least long-term contentment. Since we are not alone on the planet—yet—well-being also extends to a symbiotic relationship with the ecosystem, living and conscious. Cruelty to our fellow animals diminishes us by limiting our range of awareness. We cramp our own potentialities in consciousness and our own ability to develop them. Morality is the highest form of selfishness.

Meanwhile, our techno-economic juggernaut rolls on. Devotees of the original juggernaut throw themselves beneath its wheels to achieve salvation. Our juggernaut promises material salvation at a price and crushes us whether we wish to throw ourselves beneath it or not. Or can we have the wit, the *nous* in Plotinus's sense, to escape? The humanities are dead. Long live the humanities.

NOTES

I would like to thank Theo Malekin for editorial assistance in this chapter.

1. There are indeed grounds for optimism that the rate of progress may increase exponentially. In a very recent special issue of *Time* devoted to the future of humanity in this world, Niles Eldredge of the American Museum of Natural History estimates that thirty thousand species are becoming extinct every year (Eldredge 1999, 79). This is a rate of one every seventeen and a half minutes, a considerable advance on one every half hour. It is indeed a rate of over eighty-two species extinct every day. If that rate could be maintained steadily, it would be possible to extinguish ten million species in only 333.33 years, not even allowing for leap years. This of course would include our own extinction.

2. In the same issue of *Time* noted above, Michael D. Lemonick mentions the possible demise of the Gulf Stream, and Richard Preston points out that since 1994 at least thirty new viruses have appeared as well as mutant bacteria untreatable with antibiotics, while the concentration of populations means that by 2030 nearly 60 percent of the world's population will be urbanized (Lemonick 1999, 89; Preston 1999, 59). Preston also alludes to the awe-inspiring possibilities inherent in biological weaponry.

While other articles in the same issue evince a childlike faith in the power of technological medicines to cure all or most physical human ills (and this faith could bear some fruit through the placebo effect alone), this too could be a positive factor. While the public is dazzled by the glorious future of medicine it will be distracted from attending to other measures that might slow the overall rate of progress.

3. Dean Radin's *The Conscious Universe: The Scientific Truth of Psychic Phenomena* (1997) gives a survey of the factors, mostly subjective factors, influencing scientific replication, experimental design, the psychology of the interpretation of results and the number of experiments required for orthodox science to accept a particular finding as valid or even conceivable. It also points out the consequent advantages of meta-analysis (33–58). Since Radin's own area of research often deals with phenomena inexplicable within the paradigms of current conventional science, since fraud, sloppy methodology, and other possible explain-away factors have been virtually ruled out by experimental procedures and statistical checks, and since the meta-analytically established odds against chance are very high, in some cases a billion or more to one, there is very good evidence that Radin is right in foreseeing an imminent upheaval in the scientific paradigms with regard to attitudes, underlying metaphysical assumptions, and methodologies.

Both Sheldrake and Benveniste appear to have survived hereticization. Information about Benveniste's current researches can be found on <http://www.digibio.com> and about Sheldrake's on <http://www.sheldrake.org>. Jacques Benveniste, a highly respected specialist on the mechanisms of allergy and inflammation, was a Research Director at the French National Institute for Medical Research. He stumbled on "dilution phenomena," occurring when a substance was diluted in water to such a degree that none of the original molecules remained in the solution, yet it provoked reactions as if they were still present. Sir John Maddox, editor of *Nature,* impartially "investigated" Benveniste's experiments accompanied by an undercover conjuror and an undercover investigator of the paranormal. Benveniste's funding was withdrawn by INSERM, but his laboratory and work has continued and flourished supported by private funding. Rupert Sheldrake had a very brilliant career at Cambridge and Harvard, became a Research Fellow at Clare and at the Royal Society, and developed ideas of the telepathic transfer of learned ideas between animals of the same species and the existence of a kind of species memory, probably based on consciousness as a field. It was again Sir John Maddox who laid into these ideas. Meanwhile Sheldrake has gone on to the conception of holistic science and experiments that can potentially be performed by independent individuals rather than massively funded institutions. Radin treats Sheldrake's concept of morphogenetic fields with respect, though in passing, in his discussion of "downward causation" (Radin 1997, 261). Sheldrake has, of course, hit the usual problem of lack of funding for experiments to support or falsify hypotheses in conflict with current paradigms.

4. References to Patanjali's *Yoga Sutras* are by chapter and *sutra* only.

Works Cited

Ayer, A. J. 1973. *The Central Questions of Philosophy*. London: Penguin.

Berlin, Isaiah. 1997. *The Proper Study of Mankind: An Anthology of Essays*. Ed. Henry Hardy and Roger Hausheer. London: Chatto.

Chidbhavananda, Swami. 1971. *Facets of Brahman; or, The Hindu Gods*. Tiruchchirappalli, India: Sri Ramakrishna Tapovanam.

Coward, Harold, and Toby Foshay, eds. 1992. *Derrida and Negative Theology*. Albany: State University of New York Press.

Dasgupta, Surendranath. 1988. *A History of Indian Philosophy*. Vol. 1. Delhi: Motilal Banarsidass.

———. 1991. *A History of Indian Philosophy*. Vol. 2. Delhi: Motilal Banarsidass.

Davies, Paul. 1983. *God and the New Physics*. New York: Simon and Schuster.

Eldredge, Niles. 1999. "Will Malthus Be Right?" *Time*, 8 November, 78–79.

Ellis, John M. 1997. *Literature Lost: Social Agendas and the Corruption of the Humanities*. New Haven: Yale University Press.

European. 1997. 28 August—3 September. [9]

Feyerabend, Paul. 1987. *Farewell to Reason*. London: Verso.

———. 1993. *Against Method*. 3d ed. London: Verso.

Forman, Robert K. C., ed. 1990. *The Problem of Pure Consciousness: Mysticism and Philosophy*. New York: Oxford University Press.

———, ed. 1998. *The Innate Capacity: Mysticism, Psychology, and Philosophy*. New York: Oxford University Press.

Handy, Charles. 1997. *The Hungry Spirit: Beyond Capitalism—A Quest for Purpose in the Modern World*. London: Hutchinson.

Hawking, Stephen W. 1988. *A Brief History of Time: From the Big Bang to Black Holes*. London: Bantam.

Hayles, N. Katherine, ed. 1991. *Chaos and Order: Complex Dynamics in Literature and Science*. Chicago: University of Chicago Press.

Hofstadter, Douglas R., and Daniel C. Dennett, eds. 1982. *The Mind's I: Fantasies and Reflections on Self and Soul*. London: Penguin.

James, William. 1961. *The Varieties of Religious Experience*. New York: Macmillan.

Jones, Prudence, and Nigel Pennick. 1997. *A History of Pagan Europe*. London: Routledge.

Kosko, Bart. 1993. *Fuzzy Thinking: The New Science of Fuzzy Logic*. London: Flamingo.

Kuhn, Thomas. 1970. *The Structure of Scientific Revolutions*. Chicago: University of Chicago Press.

Lemonick, Michael D. 1999. "And Then How Cold?" *Time*, 8 November, 89.

Lessing, Doris. 1972. *Briefing for a Descent into Hell*. London: Grafton.

Maddox, John. 1981. "A Book for Burning?" *Nature* 293: 245.

Plotinus. 1991. *The Enneads*. Trans. Stephen MacKenna, ed. John Dillon. London: Penguin.

Popper, Karl. 1963. *Conjectures and Refutations: The Growth of Scientific Knowledge*. London: Routledge.

———. 1979. *Objective Knowledge: An Evolutionary Approach*. 2d ed. Oxford: Clarendon.

———. [1959] 1980. *The Logic of Scientific Discovery*. London: Routledge.

Preston, Richard. 1999. "What New Things Are Going to Kill Me?" *Time*, 8 November, 58–59.

Radhakrishnan, S, ed. 1992. *The Principal Upanishads*. Delhi: Oxford University Press.

Radin, Dean I. 1997. *The Conscious Universe: The Scientific Truth of Psychic Phenomena*. San Francisco: Harper Edge.

Rogaly, Joe. 1997. *Financial Times* 3, 23–24 August.

Sheldrake, R. 1981. *A New Science of Life: The Hypothesis of Formative Causation*. Los Angeles: Tarcher.

———. 1995. *Seven Experiments That Could Change the World*. New York: Riverhead Books.

Smullyan, Raymond M. 1982. "Is God a Taoist?" In *The Mind's I: Fantasies and Reflections on Self and Soul*, ed. Douglas R. Hofstadter and Daniel C. Dennett. London: Penguin.

Tao Te Ching. 1974. Trans. Gia-Fu Feng and Jane English. London: Wildwood House.

Tudge, Colin. 1997. *The Times* (London), 3 September.

The Death of God: A Live Issue?

DAVID JASPER

IN HIS 1960 ESSAY "WILLIAM BLAKE AND THE ROLE OF MYTH," THE American theologian Thomas Altizer wrote:

> Blake belongs to a large company of radical or spiritual Christians, Christians who believe that the Church and Christendom have sealed Jesus in his tomb and resurrected the very evil and darkness that Jesus conquered by their exaltation of a solitary and transcendent God, a heteronomous and compulsive law, and a salvation history that is irrevocably past. Despite its great relevance to our situation, the faith of the radical Christian continues to remain largely unknown, and this is so both because that faith has never been able to speak in the established categories of Western thought and theology and because it has so seldom been given a visionary expression. (reprinted Altizer and Hamilton 1968, 182)

Altizer's "death of God" theology caused an almighty furor in the conservative Deep South of America where he was then teaching. *Time* magazine announced:

> ATLANTA, Ga., Nov. 9, 1965—God, Creator of the Universe, principle deity of the world's Jews, Ultimate reality of Christians, and most eminent of all divinities, died late yesterday during major surgery undertaken to correct a massive diminishing influence.
>
> Reaction from the world's great and from the man in the street was uniformly incredulous—From Independence, Mo., former President Harry S. Truman, who received the news in his Kansas City barbershop, said, "I'm always sorry to hear someone is dead. It's a damn shame." (1966, 82)

In fact, I would suggest, Altizer's theology was and remains deeply Christian and has uniquely survived into the era of postmodernity in Altizer's own continuing work, such as his most recent book, *The*

Genesis of God (1993) and, in different ways, in the writings of younger radical "a-theologians" like Mark C. Taylor and Charles Winquist, at least in the United States. The story in Europe, as I will suggest, is somewhat different. Here the themes of Altizer's work have continued to be heard not through theologians, but in the writings of novelists and the literary world.

Altizer himself began his career as a professor of English, and his fundamental *critical* moves are literary rather than theological. That is, his profound sense of divine *kenosis*—the self-emptying of God as the ground of the self-embodiment of God (the title of a book published in 1977)—begins in a radical and dramatic move from author to reader. In this move the author and reader literally *enact* the divine dramatic move of death/genesis in an apocalypse of reading, though in this enactment the two cannot finally be distinguished. Thus, Altizer writes in *The Self-Embodiment of God*: "The intention of the book is to break through to a new theological language, a language biblical and contemporary at once and altogether. The language sought here can have no meaning or reality apart from the response of the reader for here the reader is simultaneously listener and speaker, and is fully reader only by being the author of what is read. . . . Only when God disappears as object, or as 'God,' does God fully speak" (1977, 19). The critical notion of the "death of the author" is revisited as the "death of God," but carried further as this death becomes an embodiment in the movement from speech into silence, and silence as a total emptiness from which the genesis of speech occurs. Only pure silence can be heard as silence, and only in such silence is speech totally present because totally absent.

This pure apocalypse is beyond the capacity of traditional theology or so-called "Christian" language to endure, which therefore becomes deadly and deeply heretical in its failure to countenance radical *kenosis* and in its irresistible urge toward Docetism. That is, Christian theology has always tended to avoid the utterly radical consequences of a Christology that can sustain pure *kenosis*—the self-emptying of God as his self-embodiment. And since the literature of the New Testament itself, Christian apocalyptic has repeatedly diluted apocalyptic vision by involving it with a view of history that might explain present miseries and crises. What was born from such visions of the end of the world was not a truly radical and apocalyptic Christianity, but rather the Church and Christendom (see McGinn 1995, 58–89), agencies that, as we have seen, "have sealed Jesus in his tomb" (Altizer and Hamilton 1968, 182). Only a poet as profoundly radical as Blake has issued a genuinely apocalyptic protest against the "Christian God" in a radical immediacy: a reading that he shares, Altizer believes, with Dante, with James Joyce in *Finnegans Wake*, and with few others. In these poets, Altizer suggests: "The very enactment of the Christian imagination is an assault upon Christian orthodoxy, but an assault which is itself a renewal of the Bible, and a renewal of the Biblical ground which itself had been subverted by Christian orthodoxy, and nothing was more profoundly subverted by that orthodoxy than the original apocalyptic ground of Christianity" (1993, 167).

In this assault, as is immediately apparent in a work like *Paradise Lost*, even more than in Milton's earlier treatise *De Doctrina Christiana*, is contained an understanding of God and Christ that orthodoxy has never dared or had the energy (spiritual, poetic, or intellectual) to sustain—an understanding that is a deep imaginative engagement with utter scandal. Blake saw this most readily in Milton in the memorable note in *The Marriage of Heaven and Hell*, usually totally misunderstood because quoted only in part: "Note: The reason why Milton wrote in fetters when he wrote of Angels & God, and at liberty when of Devils & Hell, is because he was a true Poet and of the Devil's party without knowing it" (Blake 1972, 150). The true poet is, indeed, a maker, engaging in an activity as close as anything human to the divine act of creation. So Coleridge describes the "primary Imagination," which is "the living Power and prime agent of all human Perception, and . . . a repetition in the finite mind of the eternal act of creation in the infinite I AM" (1817, Ch. 13).

Thus the true poet is scandalously close to the apocalyptic moment that is both the genesis and death of God, the infinite I AM. The speech of the true poet, in its imaginative enactment, is utter *kenosis*—a self-emptying into silence that is at the same time a realization of all speech.[1] And this imaginative enactment is nothing less than scriptural—that is, not Torah and not a derivation from or commentary upon the canonical books of the Bible, but "a scripture which is scripture and only scripture, or scripture which is wholly and only the consequence of inspiration (Altizer 1990, 46). For Altizer this is uniquely realized in Nietzsche's "gospel" *Thus Spake Zarathustra*, and only Blake in his apocalyptic writings is Nietzsche's true precursor, for both share a common image of Jesus and a belief, expressed by Nietzsche in *The Antichrist* (1990), that what has been called the gospel in Christianity is the exact opposite of the gospel that Jesus lived.

Blake was doing nothing less than writing scripture, and thus dares to be wholly apocalyptic. In Harold Bloom's words, "Milton and the Bible have enclosed Blake" (1989, 129) so that he inhabits Scripture in a pure condition of complete absorption beyond the discursions of commentary. As he expresses that condition in *Jerusalem*: "I know of no other Christianity and no other Gospel than the liberty both of body & mind to exercise the Divine Arts of Imagination. . . . The Apostles knew of no other Gospel" (1972, 716–17). In Blake we move beyond a mere crisis in language or the supposed critical options of postmodernity to an *absolute* poetics, that is, a poetics created purely out of nothing except pure imagination, in which the absolute and absolutely necessary death of God *is* the genesis of god, and pure presence is realized only as pure absence.

What this poetics, which is far beyond the hermeneutical, allows us is the impossible possibility of *thinking* about God (that is quite different from thinking about theology, which is generally a huge waste of time) in a tireless conversation, a radical dialectics, which has no terms or planes of argument of its own, but acknowledges the place that denies the place that theology insistently and profanely occupies through its philosophical and systematic claims. A few, a very few, modern theologians have dared to propose such a thoroughly dialectical theology; perhaps supremely Karl Barth in his *Romerbrief* (1968) who, like Altizer, focuses upon *kenosis* and crisis and returns insistently to Kierkegaard. For Barth in his early work, written in the aftermath of the trauma of the First World War (and typically theologians have concentrated on the later, and far less radical, *Church Dogmatics*), the life of Christ *is* his death on the cross. So the true death of God is also his genesis in the one truly apocalyptic act that is wholly other, a truly absent presence both end and beginning, beginning and end. In Jesus this apocalyptic act is pure negation, a "negative achievement." As Barth expresses it:

> Jesus stands among sinners as a sinner; He sets Himself wholly under the judgment under which the world is set; he takes His place where

God can be present only in questioning about Him; He takes the form of a slave; He moves to the cross and to death; His greatest achievement is a negative achievement. . . . Nevertheless, precisely in this negation, he is the fulfillment of every possibility of human progress . . . , because there is no conceivable human possibility of which He did not rid Himself. The Messiah is the end of mankind, and here also is God found faithful. (1968, 97)

The Christian tradition has never dared to take with utter seriousness, in the primary language of the poet, its own original insight into the death (which is the true life) of the Messiah, being continually sidetracked into false narratives, stories, and philosophies. Notoriously, the young Karl Barth made a radical distinction between revelation and culture, between God's word and the human production of art (though he later granted theological significance to the music of Mozart, it was only in a parabolic way), and did not translate his reflections in the *Romerbrief* into the radical vision, which only a poet like Blake has done. Nietzsche, in his own explosive scriptures, also dared to celebrate the abolition of "the Christian conception of God—God as God of the sick, God as spider, God as spirit—[which] is one of the most corrupt conceptions of god arrived at on earth." This is God in whom "nothingness is deified, the will to nothingness sanctified" (1990, 138), and it is this God whom Blake knew as Satan.

This is utterly other than the voice that, in Barth's terms, utters the No to our Yes (and the Yes within that No). Taken to its absolute apocalyptic end (which is also its beginning, and therefore truly poetic), this voice has barely been heard in the Christian Church, which has never dared to take the ultimate step (today forced upon us in our so-called "postmodern condition" of nuclear, ecological, and economic collapse, it might be argued) of thinking the unthinkable—never, that is, except in the case of one or two mystics like Meister Eckhart, and a few madmen and madwomen through the centuries. Michel de Certeau in *The Mystic Fable*, a "postmodern" work that "emerges from a mourning, an unaccepted mourning that has become the malady of bereavement, perhaps akin to the ailment melancholia," suffering the pangs of absence, argues that in Western traditions of mysticism are found marginalized groups reflecting an apprehension of selfhood, society, and culture and experiencing relationship with God as "absence" (1992, 1–2). In

this savage and humiliated tradition are to be found idiots and luna-
tics who celebrate this supreme absence, which is the absence of
meaning or sense—a nothingness that cannot be borne and a realization of *kenosis* that the world will always reject. In Palladius's
Lausiac History (c. 419 C.E.), there is the Idiot Woman whose madness may (or may not) be evidence of a profound sanity—the question is unresolvable. Palladius writes:

> In this monastery there was a virgin who pretended to be mad, pos-
> sessed by a demon. The others became so disgusted with her that no one
> ate with her, which she preferred. Wandering through the kitchen, she
> would render any service. She was, as they say, the sponge of the mon-
> astery. In reality, she was accomplishing what is written: "If someone
> intends to be wise among us in this life, let him become a fool to be-
> come wise." She had tied a rag around her head—all the others are
> shaven and wear hoods—and it is in this attire that she performed her
> duties. Of the four hundred [sisters], not one ever saw her chew any-
> thing during the years of her life; she never sat at table; she never broke
> bread with the others. She was happy with the crumbs she wiped up and
> the water from the pots and pans she scoured, without offending anyone,
> without murmuring, without speaking little or much, though she was
> beaten with blows, insulted, laden with curses, and treated with disgust.
> (quoted in Certeau 1992, 32)

The woman is a sponge that, in Derrida's words, "finds its irresistible force in a passivity without limit, absorbing everything"
(1984b, 66), absorbing all our readings, all our filth; the opposite of
Franciscus Pontius—the name once used in a signature by the poet
Francis Ponge himself, thereby becoming Ponge Pilate, who
(claims the poet in *Le Savon*) "washed his hands clean of the death
of the Just Man (or the fanatic)[*ou de l'exalté*], and thus [became]
the only person in the story to have gone into history with pure
hands" (quoted in Derrida 1984b, 110; see also Moore 1992, 48–49).
  Like the Christ-sponge who shed his blood for many and absorbed their sins (Mark 14:24), or the disciple finding itself at the
end of *Finnegans Wake*, "I sink, I'd die down over his feet, humbly
dumbly, only to washup" (1966, 278), she is the leftovers, infinitely
nothing. The opposite of the imagery that comes to characterize the
Blessed Virgin Mary (though herself a virgin), the woman utterly
resists meaning. Absolutely nothing herself, she nevertheless
makes the identity of the whole community possible. She is the ab-

sence that is utterly and unbearably present. According to Palladius, finally gaining the esteem of the community, she leaves the convent, and "where she went, where she hid herself, how she ended her days, no one has found out." She is why what has been called the gospel in Christianity is the exact opposite of the gospel that Jesus lived (see Altizer 1990, 146). "In fact there have been no Christians at all"—as Nietzsche, another madman, proclaimed (1990, 161). Devastatingly, and at the impasse that lies at the heart of all true theology, we continually hunt for a way out and seal ourselves into the impasse the more inextricably, and only here are we rendered similar to God—that is, similar to nothing. As Georges Bataille expresses it in his preface to *Madame Edwarda*: "God is nothing if He is not, in every sense, the surpassing of God. . . . Hell is the paltry notion God involuntarily gives us of Himself. But it requires the scale of limitless doom for us to discover the triumph of *being*—whence there has never lacked anything save consent to the impulse which would have been perishable" (1989, 2–3). In nothing, or pure emptiness, is the apocalyptic presence of the God who is wholly other, wholly absent. This conjunction of apocalypse and genesis is utterly scriptural: that is, a scripture that is realized only, and without excess or deficit, in the act of reading wherein the reader is also fully the author of what is read. Such is the scripture that constantly invites and constantly confounds interpretation, realized most profoundly in the apocalypses of Daniel and Revelation and in the epic poetic tradition of Dante and Blake, and preeminently in our own century in James Joyce's *Finnegans Wake*.

To read the opening of *Finnegans Wake* is to come close to this realization in the act of reading. Altizer has suggested that it would not be amiss to interpret these pages (though in a sense they utterly defy interpretation and hermeneutics, and can only be, precisely, *read*), as an enactment of the genesis of God that is also a fall of God (1993, 5). It might be said that this event in reading envelops, even *consumes* Scripture itself, from Eve and Adam, to "bland old Isaac," the fall, "the great fall of the offwall."

riverrun, past Eve and Adam's, from swerve of shore to bend of bay, brings us by a commodius vicus of recirculation back to Howth Castle and Environs. . . . The fall (bababadalgharaghtakamminarronnkonnbronnton nerronnkonnbronntonnerronntuonnthunntrovarrhounawnskawntoo- hoohoordenenthurnuk !) of a once wallstrait oldparr is retaled early in

bed and later on life down through all christian minstrelsy. The great
fall of the offwall entailed at such short notice the pftjschute of Fin-
negan, erse solid man, that the humptyhillhead of humself prumptly
sends an unquiring one well to the west in quest of his tumptytumtoes:
and their upturnpikepointand place is at the knock out in the park where
oranges have been laid to rust upon the green since devlinsfirst loved
livvy. (Joyce 1966, 27)

Not only does this look back to the childhood scenes in the opening pages of Joyce's *A Portrait of the Artist as a Young Man* (1916),
but also to *Ulysses* (1922), which initiates us into that Christ who
is Satan (Altizer 1990, 170–73), and forward to Book II of the *Wake*
(the earliest part to be written), which is a divine acceptance of
death and an actualization of the "original sun" that emerges from
the God in the "*felix culpa*" poetically (though not theologically—
theology had failed in his earlier work *De Doctrina Christiana*) realized by Milton in *Paradise Lost*. In Joyce's epic is actualized an
utter *coincidentia oppositorum* in a Eucharist ("EUCHRE RISK")
in which Christ and Satan are fully one, a darkness that is a celebra-
tion of light, a death that is a genesis in pure apocalypse. Thus, just
as *Ulysses* ends with Molly Bloom's great "Yes" (the Yes within
the No), so *Finnegans Wake* concludes with a great open-ended vision, like the Book of Revelation (and like *The Divine Comedy* and
even *The Pilgrim's Progress*), and in the ending is the beginning:

Yes. Carry me along, taddy, like you done through the toy fair! If I seen
him bearing down on me now under whitspread wings like he'd come
from Arkangels, I sink I'd die down over his feet, humbly dumbly, only
to washup. Yes, tid. There's where. First. We pass through grass behush
the bush to. Whish! A gull. Gulls. Far calls. Coming, far! End here. Us
then. Finn, again! Take. Bussoftlhee, mememoree! Till thousendsthee.
Lps. The key. Given! A way a lone a last a loved a long the (1966, 278)

Here one *is* reminded of William Blake and his reading of Milton, whose deep originality lies not in a quest for the recovery of
ancient mythical forms of Christianity, but a radically, absolutely
new poetic myth of redemption as yet beyond the arena of our totally fallen history. The gospel of Christian atheism, like the cruci-
fixion itself, is wholly unique, wholly new, and independent of
precedent, though, aporetically, always renewable. Blake's "true
poet" realizes that discontinuity (see Bloom 1973, introduction)

that radically breaks the tradition in an eternal return that totally absorbs what has been and reveals a deeper continuity in which the coincidence of Christ and Satan in the death of God is a *felix culpa*, utterly redemptive, as Satan *is*, finally, Christ. Blake indicates why in the end Andrew Marvell was right to suspect that Milton was guilty of the ruin of sacred truths, and wrong to conclude that in *Paradise Lost* there was no violation, and why Samuel Johnson was justified in his profoundly guilty unease at the poem in his *Life of Milton*. For in the true epic, and in Blake himself, there is a poetic reversal of our Christian religious tradition and its mythical expressions, an absorption of the sacred into the profane that is a kenotic and a redemptive move. In Altizer's words in "Blake and the Role of Myth": "The Blake who proclaimed that God must eternally die for man, that a primordial Totality must pass through 'Self-Annihilation,' was the Blake who envisioned a uniquely contemporary Christ, a Christ who becomes Antichrist before he is resurrected as Jerusalem" (Altizer and Hamilton 1968, 188). In fact this apocalyptic *coincidentia oppositorum* lurks, usually unacknowledged, within much contemporary discourse and literature. As always, theologians have almost universally avoided its full radicalism and risk, and writers most deeply enmeshed in the dire consequences of a "Christian" upbringing, most notably D. H. Lawrence, have been too damaged by it to escape its malign influence on their thinking and imagination. Haunted by memories of the Book of Revelation propagated through the grim chapels of his childhood, Lawrence wrote in *Apocalypse* (1931) that "Revelation had to be included in the New Testament, to give the death kiss to the Gospels" (1974, 18). Ironically he was right, but for exactly the opposite reason from that which he intended.

Other novelists have responded to the urgencies of our time in apocalyptic "fictions" revealing the unthinkable and unutterable, and not only writers like J. G. Ballard in *The Atrocity Exhibition* (1970) or Margaret Atwood in *The Handmaid's Tale* (1986),[2] but others who have engaged more profoundly with the issue of the death of God, such as Iris Murdoch in *The Time of the Angels* (1966) and A. S. Byatt in *Possession* (1990). Murdoch's early novel explores the power of a priest who believes that "the death of God has set the angels free. And they are terrible." Since that deeply pessimistic and even nihilistic book, postmodern critical thought also has repeatedly returned to the theme of apocalypse, not least in the work of the Jewish thinkers Edmond Jabès and Jacques Derrida.

In Derrida's writings, increasingly absorbed in religious thinking up to his recent book *The Gift of Death* (1995), with their "series of detours, relays and extravagant swerves from destination" (Norris 1995, 235), we experience a rhetorical incorporation of apocalyptic poetics into our traditions of thinking and philosophic reason. After the collapse of the ancient literary tradition of mimesis, the Derridean suspicion of logocentricity, the desert silence of Edmond Jabès, the specter of total annihilation and demise of the subject, present us with the possibility of an actuality that cannot be avoided or diluted by interpretation or any historicisms and yet is wholly contemporary. Derrida acknowledges this demise above all in the "gift" of that one great humanizing experience that none of us will ever experience "as ourselves," though it is common to all of us— our death. It is only in the apocalyptic context of nuclear catastrophe, Derrida argues, that this common event of our deaths is again made "real" and absolute:

> Culture and memory limit the "reality" of individual death to this extent, they soften or deaden it in the realm of the "symbolic." The only referent that is absolutely real is thus of the scope or dimension of an absolute nuclear catastrophe that would irreversibly destroy the entire archive ["the juridico-literary . . . basis of literature and criticism"] and all symbolic capacity, would destroy the "movement of survival," what I call "survivance," at the very heart of life. This absolute referent of all possible literature is on a par with the absolute effacement of any possible trace; it is thus the only ineffaceable trace, it is so as the trace of what is entirely other, "trace du tout autre." (1984a, 28)

My argument here would retrace some of the steps taken by Derrida in this essay in *Diacritics*, "No Apocalypse Not Now (Full Speed Ahead, Seven Missiles, Seven Missives)" (1984a) from the immediacy of nuclear disaster and suggest that in spite of all that religious tradition has done to efface it, there has *always* been a poetic voice that has revealed the apocalyptic and necessary vision of absolute absence and absolute presence, of the coincidence of opposites in the dissolution of God and the inauguration of His will. Because this self-embodiment of God in His own death involves a *kenosis* that is also a self-emptying of speech itself, it involves also a silence that is actually unhearable, though only then is it heard everywhere (Altizer 1977, 85). It is this silence that we encounter in the poetics of Blake, undiluted by the possibility of interpretation or any temporary historicisms. It is a silence heard in language, which has no meaning or reality apart from the response of the reader (who has thus become wholly author). Only thus can we finally read the Book of Revelation or the poetry of Blake, and it may be for this reason that Blake is in the end impossible to "teach." This presencing of the wholly other, a literal experience of the gift of death, which is life itself, is, I suggest, finally and uniquely achieved in the apocalypse of the death of God.

NOTES

1. See further Altizer 1977, "Apocalypse," 92–93. " 'I am' only wholly enacts its own silence by finally bringing an end to the speech of 'I AM.' The voice of silence is the voice of speech only insofar as the self-identity of speech has come to an end. Or, rather, the voice of silence is the voice of speech when the voice of speech has passed into silence. This can occur only by way of an actual end of the voice of speech. An actual end is an actual ending, a real ending of the voice of 'I AM.' " This, it seems to me, is another way of expressing Blake's apocalyptic insight into Milton as "the old Devil's party," and a true poet.

2. For discussion of the novels as apocalyptic fictions, see Detweiler 1990.

WORKS CITED

Altizer, Thomas J. J. 1977. *The Self-Embodiment of God*. New York: Harper and Row.

————. 1990. *Genesis and Apocalypse*. Louisville: Westminster/John Knox Press.

————. 1993. *The Genesis of God: A Theological Genealogy*. Louisville: Westminster/John Knox Press.

Altizer, Thomas J. J., and William Hamilton, eds. 1968. *Radical Theology and the Death of God*. Harmondsworth: Penguin.

Barth, Karl. 1968. *The Epistle to the Romans*. Trans. Edwyn C. Hoskyns. Oxford: Oxford University Press.

Bataille, Georges. 1989. *Madame Edwarda*. Trans. Austryn Wainhouse. London: Marion Boyars.

Blake, William. 1972. *Complete Writings*. Ed. Geoffrey Keynes. Oxford: Oxford University Press.

Bloom, Harold. 1973. *The Anxiety of Influence*. Oxford: Oxford University Press.

————. 1989. *Ruin the Sacred Truths*. Cambridge: Harvard University Press.

Certeau, Michel de. 1992. *The Mystic Fable*. Vol. 1. Trans. Michael B. Smith. Chicago: Chicago University Press.

Coleridge, S. T. 1817. *Biographia Literaria*. Boston: Charles E. Tuttle.

Derrida, Jacques. 1984a. "No Apocalypse Not Now (Full Speed Ahead, Seven Missiles, Seven Missives)." *Diacritics* 14(2):28.

———. 1984b. *Signsponge*. Trans. Richard Rand. New York: Columbia University Press.

Detweiler, Robert. 1990. "Apocalyptic Fiction and the End(s) of Realism." In *European Literature and Theology in the Twentieth Century*, ed. David Jasper and Colin Crowder. London: Macmillan.

Joyce, James. 1966. *A Shorter Finnegans Wake*. Ed. Anthony Burgess. London: Faber.

Lawrence, D. H. 1974. *Apocalypse*. Harmondsworth: Penguin.

McGinn, Benard. 1995. "The End of the World and the Beginning of Christendom." In *Apocalypse Theory and the Ends of the World*, ed. Malcolm Bull. Oxford: Oxford University Press.

Moore, Stephen D. 1992. *Mark and Luke in Poststructuralist Perspective*. Newhaven: Yale University Press.

Nietzsche, Friedrich. [1895] 1990. *The Antichrist*. Trans. R. J. Hollingdale. Harmondsworth: Penguin.

———. 1993. *Thus Spake Zarathustra*. Trans. Thomas Common. New York: Prometheus Books.

Norris, Christopher. 1995. "Versions of Apocalypse: Kant, Derrida, Foucault." In *Apocalypse Theory and the Ends of the World*, ed. Malcolm Bull. Oxford: Oxford University Press.

Time. 1966. "Toward a Hidden God." 8 April.

Part II
The Arts and the Transformation of Consciousness

Consciousness and the Future of Theater

DANIEL MEYER-DINKGRÄFE

AFTER ABOUT A YEAR OF STUDYING DRAMA, STUDENTS WILL GENER-
ally indicate that they now find it much easier to analyze a theatrical
production in terms of elements they had discussed in class, ranging
from literary aspects like genre to technical details like the kind of
equipment used by the lighting designer to achieve specific effects.
In most cases this analysis takes place while the students are watching the performance, and usually is used to describe, or find reasons
for, all kinds of things that "do not quite work" in such productions. Analytic activity that starts and continues during the performance tends to be highly critical.

On the other hand, many students indicate that they have experienced performances during which their analytical activity took second place to just "being with the experience," or was not present at
all. There was no awareness of time passing, and students found it
difficult to say more than "I enjoyed that performance" immediately after the show was over. They found that embarrassing because they felt that as drama students they should be able (and
would be expected) to provide a sound and thorough analysis of a
production immediately after having watched it. The extraordinary
performance, the performance that makes the spectators forget they
are in the theater, that makes them forget the passing of time, that
engages them fully in the here and now, the present moment, somehow seems to escape the immediate analytical abilities of the intellect. Only in retrospect will it be possible to talk about such a
production. When such extraordinary, quite infrequent experiences
in the theater are discussed, the discourse mirrors the different nature of such encounters: terminology tends to be vague, concepts
fuzzy, and the students seem reluctant to employ the critical analytical terms they easily employ when they condemn a "bad" production because they feel their inadequacy for the experience they have

had. It is easy and convenient to use critical discourse taught in theater studies to find and give reasons for faults and errors in a production. When it comes to praise, however, critical vocabulary appears inadequate; terminology that appears more appropriate is not fashionable in the university context: the world of emotions, feelings, hunches, intuition, even experiences that go beyond ordinary sensory experience and therefore beyond the grasp of language. I overheard a conversation among students after one production: "It was funny, first I tried to understand what was going on, I tried to analyze why they had used this kind of set, and all those things we are supposed to do, but I just didn't get anywhere, I got rather frustrated. Then I just let go, switched off my mind, and just watched, and, actually, it was quite curious, really, I enjoyed myself tremendously, it was all so different." Please note that this student, and other students with similar experiences, agreed unanimously and independently that such experiences in the theater were far more desirable than the ones open to immediate critical analysis. The absence of critical assessment was not regarded as alarming or unwanted, but as more rewarding. How to explain and interpret such differences of discourse? How can they affect the future of the theater and theater studies? The majority of theater today may be interesting, but there are only a few isolated experiences in the theater that are *extraordinary*. Attempts to create conditions that will allow such experiences to recur have not led to techniques or combinations of methods that allow a systematic re-creation of those extraordinary experiences. The terminology used to describe and conceptualize extraordinary experiences in the theater has tended to be vague, if poetic. I locate the problems of an appropriate discourse in a lack of proper understanding of human consciousness. How can he explain extraordinary experiences in theater?

In drama and theater, it has been traditional ever since Aristotle to show some sort of conflict within or among humans, or between humans and gods or God, or between humans and forces of nature. In various forms, the nature of evil has always fascinated humans, and the formula of conflict for drama is closely related to that fascination. Is it surprising that the function of theater for Aristotle was not only entertainment, but the catharsis of negative qualities, especially pity and fear? According to the *Natyashastra*, the ancient Indian treatise on dramaturgy, theater had its origin in its purpose to restore the state of perfection that humans enjoyed in the golden age (Ghosh 1950). Perfection has only recently become a focus of modern psychology, which started as an investigation of abnormal behavior, behavior in need of improvement through treatment. Later, branches of psychology interested in well-being, in peak experiences and desirable altered states of consciousness, were at least initially regarded with suspicion and ridicule from the hard core of the discipline.

If we look at imperfection or conflict as a condition for drama, the questions must be what form this "conflict" takes, and what is shown through conflict. The advent of realism and naturalism as modes of writing and performance in the late nineteenth century strongly enhanced the importance of conflict, because it provided an opportunity, in drama as text and in theater as performance, to present reality in all its details. For the sake of conflict in its massappeal, sensational aspect, those details were often rather gross, showing the dark side of human nature and daily life. As modern psychology developed, drama and performance delved deeper into the hidden crimes of individual minds.

Conflict in the theater can mean the presentation, in a socially acceptable frame, of human problems, human degradation. However, does conflict, as a basis for interesting theater, have to be rooted in the dark side of human nature so exhaustively studied and described by psychology, psychiatry, and criminology? Some recent developments in theater, both traditional and experimental or innovative, suggest that fascinating, deeply moving theater can be achieved without recourse to psychopathology. The experiences of the students in some rare productions in which they forgot the time and their critical functions were suspended confirm this development. There are specific productions of classic works, Shakespeare's plays for example, that allow this extraordinary experience: an enchanting production of *Twelfth Night* or *As You Like It*. There are contemporary mainstream plays that have a similar effect: for me it was the opening night of Peter Shaffer's *Amadeus* in November 1979 at the National Theater in London, directed by Peter Hall, with Paul Scofield, Simon Callow, and Felicity Kendal. After the show, I knew that this was great theater, but found it difficult to analyze the precise reasons why. In *Amadeus*, genius Mozart is beset by the machinations of mediocre rival Salieri. To give only three further examples: mental health problems in Edna O'Brien's *Virginia* about Virginia Woolf; the First World War and its impact on the friendship on poets Wilfred Owen and Siegfried Sassoon in Stephen MacDonald's *Not about Heroes*; political power and tyranny in the person of Stalin against the composers Prokofiev and Shostakovich in David Pownall's *Master Class.* In these and many similar plays, the human frailty of the artist characters brings them closer to the spectators, and idolization is demolished. At the same time, in the face of adversity, the artistic qualities of the characters are shown to be strong, not subject to any compromise. In the spectator's mind, this raises the status of the artist to a level of genuine appreciation (to call it admiration would be too close to less desirable idolization), much more so than may have existed before watching the play. In such plays, then, we have conflict indeed, but desirable ways of coping with adverse situations. In the case of *Amadeus*, the person/character Mozart is dead in the end, but his music, which was the dominant content of his entire life, survives.

But not only mainstream drama and performance have the potential of thus leading to fascinating experiences in the theater. When I asked current final-year students about their most impressive experience while studying drama at the University of Wales, Aberystwyth, the almost unanimous response was: *The Labyrinth.* This was a nontraditional, nonmainstream event, presented by a group of Colombian performers. They created a labyrinth of pathways within the theater space, leading to individual defined spaces, such as a children's nursery, a schoolroom, a space covered with sand where a performer dressed as a gypsy sat by a real fire, performing magic spells and manipulating the fire. Spectators went through the labyrinth on their own, groping their way along the black cloths in total darkness, sometimes guided by the performers' touch or sound, encountering various "characters" in the defined spaces, and experiencing a wide range of smells, sounds, and touches without being able, in many cases, to *see* the origin of the sensory impression. In one installation, spectators had to crawl though a well-lit, comfortably padded "umbilical cord," leading to a pitch-dark end where they had to slide downward into the unknown. Some were initially too afraid to take the risk, but returning was impossible. At the end of the slope, they ended up in a large mass of unroasted coffee beans, stroked and comforted by a performer. The reaction of individual spectators was different to each of the defined spaces, the installations, and whatever went on in them, but all agreed that the experience had remained vividly in their minds, unlikely to be forgotten ever, and the nonvisual impressions, especially the unfamiliar but generally pleasant smells, had stayed with them for days. It was difficult to stop the students discussing *The Labyrinth* encounters on an experiential level. They found it difficult, if not impossible, to analyze their experience in traditional critical terminology. Is analysis helpful beyond being a reasonable tool for examination? You can assess if a student has grasped the meaning and implications of a specific concept, but it is much more difficult to assess a personal appreciation of a theater impression. Are we less capable of enjoying if we are unable to analyze?

Both current mainstream theater and experimental theater have been able to trigger experiences in the spectators (and in the performers as well!) that go beyond critical analysis. Peter Brook has argued for a "total theater" (1987), and Grotowski's "poor theater" aimed at a state of "translumination" in the performer and through the performer in the spectator (1969). Eugenio Barba has written about the "transcendent" in the theater, the performer's presence, based on the initial question: "when two performers are doing apparently the same thing, why does one performer fascinate me, and the other one not?" (1985, 12). Brook's, Grotowski's and Barba's theater are only some of the more well-known examples of attempts in the theater to reach levels of the mind that go beyond the analytical intellect, even beyond the emotions. "Translumination," for example, has been described as a state in which the split between subject and object no longer exists, a state in which there is no time lapse between an impulse and carrying out the impulse (Grotowski 1969, 12). A close look at the work of these theater artists suggests that they have themselves experienced such altered states of consciousness, which they conceptualize in terms such as total "theater," "translumination," or "presence" (or they have at least closely observed their colleagues who have reported such experiences). Their theater work represents the attempt of re-creating or stabilizing such experiences. The terminology they use is poetic, metaphorical, and, therefore, vague. Their discourse essentially resembles that of the students I wrote about earlier (albeit, of course, on a different level of complexity, in line with their professional expertise).

Given the insight that theater has the potential of creating desirable experiences in performers and spectators that go beyond the analytical abilities of the mind and at best even beyond emotions and intuition, the question arises why all theater today does not make use of that potential. The answer is related to the vagueness of the discourse, and the related unease with the experiences, which can only be related in such poetic, often beautiful, but still vague terminology. What is needed is a cogent model of consciousness that enables us not only to explain the experiences on which much current theater work is based, but also to systematically develop such desirable experiences. I propose that Indian philosophy offers just such a model of consciousness. Elements of it are found in the systems of Indian philosophy, especially samkhya and yoga. Malekin and Yarrow have described the fourfold classification of consciousness by Gaudapada in his verse commentary (*Karika*) on the *Mandukya Upanishad*: in addition to waking, dreaming, and deep sleep, Gaudapada conceptualizes *turiya*, "an underlying unconditioned consciousness which appears limited when reflected through the three contingent states of the individual mind" (1997, 38). Alternation of pure consciousness with the three ordinary states of consciousness will gradually lead to glimpses of a simultaneity of *turiya* with any one of waking, dreaming, or deep sleep (Forman 1990). Such glimpses can be dualistic in nature, with a clear separation between the individual Self in *turiya* and the characteristics of ordinary waking, dreaming, or deep sleep states of consciousness. Refined perception may accompany the development of *turiya*, and ultimately a unity of Self and objective world is characteristic of full development of *turiya*. "Various stages thus intervene between ordinary consciousness and the full establishment of or in *turiya* (Malekin and Yarrow 1997, 39).

The model of the mind proposed by Indian philosophy allows us to explain seemingly extraordinary experiences described in the theater. The model also helps us understand that theater is, at least potentially, very powerful indeed, more so that many people would currently concede. It can function to obstruct the experience of pure consciousness in production team and audience alike, can lead to maladaptive states of consciousness that can be experienced as undesirable and even in need of treatment. Or it can be a means of developing higher states of consciousness in all people involved in it.

ACTING

Should the actor feel the emotions the character is supposed to be feeling? This question has been at the forefront of theater theory not least since Diderot formulated his famous paradox: actors should not be involved emotionally; rather, they should closely observe reality and reproduce in performance the outward signs of emotions. Only in rehearsal are they allowed to feel with the character's emotions. The actor, Diderot said, "must have within himself an unmoved and disinterested onlooker (1955, 14). The paradox is that an emotionally uninvolved actor is able to emotionally move and involve the spectator. With Stanislavsky, this paradox takes a decisive shift: it no longer exists in the relationship between actor (uninvolved) and spectator (involved), but within the actors themselves: Stanislavsky expects them to be simultaneously deeply emotionally involved (by help of his psycho-technique, they will ideally reach the level of the subconscious) and yet still in conscious control of the acting through their ability to watch their involved acting. A kind of dual consciousness is what Stanislavsky has in mind here.

Diderot's theory of the emotional stimulation of the spectators through an emotionally uninvolved actor is paradoxical on the level of an ordinary waking state of consciousness as described by Indian philosophy. On this level of consciousness, the Self as the basis of the mind is not open to direct experience. It is overshadowed by the (sensory) objects of experience. The Self identifies with the objects of sensory perception, or with the emotions and feelings. In such a state, detachment from one's own experiences and actions is difficult, and ordinarily considered undesirable. According to Indian philosophy, the development toward established *turiya* is characterized by a phase when the Self is by definition experienced as separate from the manifest levels of the mind (ego, feelings, mind, intellect, senses). This liberated Self could be associated with Diderot's "disinterested onlooker" whom the actor must have in him/herself. The actor's development toward that stage is characterized by his/her increasing ability to perform with growing realization of the Self. This growth will be experienced both in time quantity, and in quality—that is, depth. Initially, the experience of "witnessing," characteristic of the dualistic phase on the way toward established *turiya*, will be experienced for short periods during a performance, the length of experience will increase, and ultimately the experience of the Self will be maintained throughout activity, no longer limited to acting on stage. Simultaneously, the functioning of the expressed levels of the mind will be improved, so that the actor can meet Diderot's demand for penetration, an intellectual quality. Moreover, the actor's ability to observe nature as a source for imitation will be enhanced by heightened sensory functioning.

The proposed solution to Diderot's paradox from the perspective of Indian philosophy also applies to Stanislavsky: Indian philosophy would argue that the actor's deep emotional involvement is facilitated through the actor's development of consciousness. This development goes along with the growing ability to experience the Self as a witnessing agency of consciousness together with the witnessed objects of (sensory) perception, together, that is, with any activity.

Grotowski has taken claims for extra-ordinary states of consciousness further: he aims for a state of consciousness and body where the actor transcends incompleteness and the mind-body split, where he achieves totality, full presence, where he becomes a "holy actor" (1969). Such "translumination" is clearly an experience of not only the dualistic phase of development, characterized by a separation of Self and activity, but a developed experience of *turiya* as defined by Indian philosophy: knower and known are experienced as a unity, the striking duality of Self and expressed levels of consciousness, characteristic of the dualistic stage, disappears. For the duration of the experience of such higher states of consciousness, all action, performative or other, is fully spontaneous: there is no longer a time lapse between inner impulse and outer action.

The aim of theater that follows the principles of Indian aesthetics—and encompasses Indian architecture, Indian medicine, and Indian astrology, to mention only a few disciplines—is to develop the level of consciousness toward enlightenment. What does enlightenment mean for the theater? I will elaborate with reference to the actor.

The enlightened actor will not be emotionally involved while acting. In the initial stages of developing *turiya*, his/her self will be separate from the activities of the waking state of consciousness; the actor will witness his activity of acting. Once *turiya* has been fully developed, the Self and its expressions are experienced as one.

A fully concentrated mind, a mind established in *turiya*, is demanded of the actor in the *Natyashastra* (Ghosh 1950, 143). This is a mind in which the Self is in a noninvolved state, while the expressed aspects of the mind are fully developed and thus capable of full concentration. This concentration pertains to the senses, the mind, the intellect, the emotions, and the ego. The actor's concentration extends even to the autonomous nervous system commonly assumed to be beyond intentional control by the will. From the dualistic experience of *turiya* onward, the actor can voluntarily induce any means of historic representation required to create specific aesthetic experience in his audience (Ghosh 1950). Such full concentration will enable the actor to fully understand and feel the emotions the character is supposed to be feeling. He or she may fully appreciate the dramatist's intentions, but may also go beyond those conscious intentions. This implies that the work and its meaning are not established and fixed *sub specie aeternitatis*.

Indian philosophy holds that knowledge is different in different states of consciousness. Different spectators will react differently to the same play, depending on their state of consciousness. This concept is not even highly philosophical: if the spectator is tired after a long day in the office, he/she will appreciate the play differently from a relaxed spectator, determined by the difference of alertness in his/her mind, in turn interdependent with the state of the nervous system—tired or fresh. All possible reactions of all possible spectators latently exist in the field of *turiya*, a field that connects all individuals. Thus if the actors gain access to that level in their own minds, they will be able to use a large variety of ways of rendering the different dimensions of meaning associated with a particular role in a particular play. They can choose from that reservoir to suit the historically specific needs of specific spectators at a specific performance, and to vary the chosen elements of rendering in the next performance.

Two aspects of the concept of enlightenment need further explanation. First, what makes an actor an actor: from among a shoemaker and an actor who have both reached full development of *turiya*, the actor would be the better actor. The concept of dharma, central to Brook's interpretation of the *Mahabharata* (Brook 1987, 164), is essential to this issue. On a general level, dharma is "that invincible power of nature which upholds existence. It maintains evolution and forms the very basis of cosmic life. *Dharma* can be

associated with law, justice, customary morality, reflective morality, duty and conscience (Kuppuswami 1977, 24). According to
Kakar, dharma refers to the "ground-plan" of any person's life, as
the individual's "life-cycle," *ashramadharma*, and most important
the individual's "own life-task, his *svadharma*" (1981, 37). According to *The Bhagavad-Gita*, each individual has "his own in-
born nature, *svadhava*, and to make it effective in his life is his
duty, *svadharma*" (Kuppuswami 1977, 129). This individual life-
task is not absolute, but embedded in the individual's historical
condition: "Hindu philosophy and ethics teach that 'right action'
for an individual depends on *desa*, the culture in which he is born;
and *kala*, the period of historical time in which he lives; on *srama*,
the efforts required of him at different stages of life; and on *gunas*,
the innate psycho-biological traits which are the heritage of an individual's previous lives" (Kakar 1981, 37). In the course of time,
Kakar argues, *svadharma* came to mean "traditional action . . . in
the sense that an individual's occupational activity and social acts
are right or 'good' if they conform to the traditional pattern prevalent in his kinship and caste group."

It is important to note that the concept of dharma functions on
two levels: relative and cosmic. Dharma originally describes how
nature functions. This applies to the level of enlightenment, where
functioning in accordance with the laws of nature, of the cosmos, is
automatic, spontaneous, fully life-supporting for all concerned, and
not subject to manipulation or misuse. The descriptive function of
dharma consists in laying down rules intended to serve as guidance
for nonenlightened people on their path to enlightenment. Such
rules originate from enlightenment itself. However, applied rules of
dharma vary according to the historical and cultural circumstances
of the times in which they were written down. For example, in
Vedic times (2500 B.C. to 500 B.C.), women enjoyed equal status
with men, participating fully in religious and social activities (Kuppuswami 1977, 183). At a later stage, documented in the *Manusm-
ritis*, a major text in the canon of *dharmashasta*, holy texts on
dharma, the role of women in society had changed considerably
(Doninger 1991). Thus, as soon as dharma becomes open to individual, culture-bound interpretation, it becomes open to manipulation and misuse. Someone might, for example, wish to maintain his/
her status of power by convincingly suggesting to others that their

dharma is in a position of comparatively less power. Once open to ignorance, dharma as a concept may be misused. As a cosmic, universally applicable force or pattern of nature's functioning, however, dharma is not changed by such misuse. On a relative level, open to misuse, there may well be clashes between what someone is told to be his or her duty, and that same person's "real" dharma or vocation in life. If dharma has its own way in an enlightened society, duty and vocation will be the same. As this section of my chapter deals with the enlightened actor, for him/her, then, allotted duty and vocation are the same.

The precondition or characteristic of enlightenment is that the individual follows his or her dharma, allotted duty, because only then will evolution take place. Consequently, the person who has gained enlightenment will fully live his or her dharma. Thus by definition the enlightened actor is an individual whose dharma or purpose in life is to be an actor; he or she will thus be a better actor than the enlightened shoemaker, whose dharma is to be a shoemaker.

The second aspect of enlightenment that needs further explanation regards the question: will there be a difference in the acting of two actors who are enlightened? Yes, there will be. According to Kuppuswami, "the ruling idea in ancient Indian thought is unity in diversity, not uniformity" (1977, 183). Although the basis of creation, pure consciousness, is the same everywhere and links all individuals, and thus all actors, the infinite dynamism and the potential for infinite possibilities that characterize this field cause the infinite variety of manifest creation, including the variety among human beings. Thus people will not become more alike on their path to enlightenment. On the contrary, each person will develop the full potential of his/her individuality. This applies to every person in every profession. It follows that two actors who have gained enlightenment will have distinct fully developed personalities, characteristics, traits, and the like.

Now that the concept of a fully developed actor has been described, the question arises: what about the actor who is not enlightened? A person whose dharma it is to be an actor will find the learning and training process for the art and skills of acting easier and more enjoyable, no matter whether his training is based on the *Natyashastra* or on Western principles.

ACTOR TRAINING

A very important question that has to be addressed if one wants to reach an ideal of theater on the basis of Indian philosophy is: how to train actors in such a way that they reach higher levels of consciousness themselves and are able to raise the level of consciousness in the spectators. In their attempts to re-create desirable experiences variously described as "translumination," "presence," tradition of traditions," or "total theater," Western theater artists such as Grotowski, Barba, and Brook have developed nonsystematic approaches to actor training: they pick some ideas and techniques from assorted sources and mix them into their own training programs (a bit of *Kathakali,* a bit of Yoga, a bit of Noh, a bit of Tai-Chi, and a bit of Stanislavsky or the Method). I fear that the nonsystematic nature of this approach is not very helpful in systematically achieving desirable higher states of consciousness in the production team and audience. Indian (theater) aesthetics holds a possible solution to this dilemma, in that it claims to provide the techniques for developing higher states of consciousness. Empirical studies will have to be developed to test this claim. Philosophical debate is ongoing about the applicability of Eastern concepts and techniques for people in the West (Shear 1997; Varela and Shear 1999). At present, I would like to tease out the implications of taking this claim at face value. The *Natyashastra,* the classical Indian treatise on drama and theater, can be interpreted as having a twofold function: it serves as a detailed description of what an actor who has reached a higher level of consciousness spontaneously does on the stage to create a specific effect on the spectator, and it serves as a manual of how to develop to higher states of consciousness.

To understand how the techniques of histrionic representation described in the *Natyashastra* function to raise the level of the actor's and the spectator's consciousness, it is necessary to remember, first of all, that although the *Natyashastra* and later works on Sanskrit dramaturgy devote much space to the description of the physical techniques, they emphasize the representation of the temperamental states as being most important in the creation of an aesthetic experience for the spectator (Bhat 1981). The actor, through a specific mode of acting (*sattvika abhinaya*) portrays the temperamental states (*sattvika bhava*). The meaning of *sat* is "eternal, absolute." In Sanskrit, pure consciousness is referred to as *Sat-Chit-Ananda,* eternal or absolute (*sat*) bliss (*ananda*) consciousness (*chit*). This is the meaning of *sat* within the unmanifest, transcendental field of life, which is beyond the level of the senses, the mind, the intellect, the emotions, and the ego. It is a quality of the unmanifest Self, at the basis of all manifestations. On the level of manifestations, the term *sat* is found in the term *sattva*. This is one of the three *gunas*, elementary forces of nature, the others being *rajas* and *tamas*. Jhanji further explains that according to Indian philosophy: "*Sattva* which refers to the freedom from all willing is the state of detachment from the pragmatic world, and it is the state of pure knowledge. *Rajas* is understood in terms of all qualities of will and all the psycho-physical activities have their origin in terms of this quality. *Tamas* refers to the state of ignorance and lack of consciousness. The entire life of an individual represents the varied combinations of these three gunas. Beatitude and knowledge are associated with sattva; greed with *rajas*, and ignorance and illusion with *tamas*" (1985, 5). On the relative level, the proportion of the three *gunas*— *sattva*, *rajas*, and *tamas*—can vary. A predominance of *tamas* will lead to stagnation and suffering, and a predominance of *sattva* to increasing happiness that is eventually transformed into bliss-consciousness. Thus it is evident that on the relative level of life, among the three *gunas, sattva* is closest to the eternal quality, *sat*, of pure consciousness. By performing in a state of consciousness in which the level of *sattva* dominates the levels of *rajas* and *tamas*, the actor gradually, by continued practice, rises more and more in the *sattva* quality until he/she is able to maintain pure consciousness while acting, initially only for short periods of time, but eventually as a permanent phenomenon. Acting simultaneously stimulates the same processes in the spectator.

How does the actor manage to saturate his/her mind with the quality of *sattva*? Vedic literature describes three aspects of yoga, unity: the body has to be free of restricting impediments, the mind focused, and the spirit liberated. To achieve the state of yoga for body, mind, and spirit, three methods are prescribed: physical exercises, *asanas* (often the only association with Yoga), create yoga in the body; breathing exercises, *pranayama*, lead to a focused mind, and meditation produces a liberated spirit. All three methods are applied together, and together they lead to the state of yoga. The gestural means of histrionic representation, *angika abhinaya*, function in parallel to *yoga asanas*, conditioning the body to sustain the experience of *sattva*. Control of breath is also crucial in perform-ance, both in the West and in India. As Zarrilli points out in his studies of *Kathakali*, breath, associated with energy, is of vital im-portance in making "otherwise mechanical facial configurations," in which are "encoded the message pleasure/ erotic or fury," "live with presence" (1990, 142). Accurate control of breath, life force, is also at the center of the actor-spectator relationship:

> In all such precise psychophysical moments, the "character" is being created—not in the personality of the actor but as an embodied and pro-jected/energized living form between actor and audience. These Asian forms assume no "suspension of disbelief," rather the actor and specta-tor co-create the figure embodied in the actor as "other." The "power of presence" manifest in this stage other, while embodied in this partic-ular actor in this particular moment, is not limited to that ego. That dy-namic figure exists between audience and actor, transcending both, pointing beyond itself. (142)

Acting according to the guidelines of the *Natyashastra*, then, al-ways employs techniques parallel in effect to *asanas* and *pranay-ama*, conditioning the body and the mind to sustain experiences of higher states of consciousness. Further conclusive research is needed to establish ways of how to make use of the knowledge con-tained in the *Natyashastra* for the purposes of developing higher states of consciousness. It will not be advisable to try to go back to some mythical roots. A practical set of techniques for the contem-porary performer is needed. However, the probable mistake of ear-lier attempts at re-creating desirable extraordinary experiences in the theater, the rather careless and uninformed mixing of various bits and pieces from different, quite heterogeneous sources, must be avoided. To this end, theater artists should seek direct input from established experts in Indian philosophy.

In the emerging model of the theater, based on Indian philoso-phy, theater has a profound and specific function for the production team and the audience: it will appeal to all levels of the mind. Thus it will be entertaining, intellectually challenging, emotionally in-volving, and it will have an impact on the level of pure conscious-ness (*turiya*), the Self. Theater can serve the function of raising the level of consciousness of production team and spectators; it can lead their minds to experiences of pure consciousness together with the stimuli of the performance.

WORKS CITED

Barba, Eugenio. 1985. "Interview with Gautam Dasgupta." *Performing Arts Journal*, January.

Bhat, G. K. 1981. *Sanskrit Dramatic Theory*. Bhandarkar Oriental Institute Post-Graduate and Research Series, no. 13. Poona: Bhandarkar Oriental Research Institute.

Brook, Peter. 1987. *The Shifting Point: Forty Years of Theatrical Exploration: 1946–1987*. London: Methuen.

Diderot, Denis. 1955. *The Paradox of Acting*. New York: Hill and Wang.

Doninger, Wendy, with Brian K. Smith, trans. 1991. *The Laws of Manu*. Harmondsworth: Penguin Books.

Forman, Robert K. C. 1990. *The Problem of Pure Consciousness*. New York: Oxford University Press.

Ghosh, Manomohan, ed. and trans. 1950. *The Natyashastra: A Treatise on Hindu Dramaturgy and Histrionics*. Calcutta: Royal Asiatic Society of Bengal.

Gorak, Jan. 1991. *The Making of the Modern Canon: Genesis and Crisis of a Literary Idea*. London: Athlone.

Grotowski, Jerzy. 1969. *Towards a Poor Theater*. Ed. Eugenio Barba with a preface by Peter Brook. London: Methuen.

Jhanji, Rekha. 1985. *Aesthetic Communication: The Indian Perspective*. Delhi: Munshiram Mancharlal.

Kakar, Sudhir. 1981. *The Inner World: A Psychoanalytic Study of Childhood and Society in India*. Delhi: Oxford University Press.

Kuppuswami, B. 1977. *Dharma and Society: A Study in Social Values*. Columbia, Mo.: South Asia Books.

Malekin, Peter, and Ralph Yarrow. 1997. *Consciousness, Literature and Theater. Theory and Beyond, Studies in Literature and Religion*. Ed. David Jasper. Basingstoke: Macmillan/St. Martin's Press.

Meyer-Dinkgräfe, Daniel. 1996. *Consciousness and the Actor*. Frankfurt/Main: Peter Lang.

Orme-Johnson, Rhoda. 1987. "A Unified Field Theory of Literature." *Modern Science and Vedic Science* 1.(3). 323–73.

Shear, Jonathan, ed. 1997. *Explaining Consciousness—The Hard Problem*. Cambridge: MIT Press.

Varela, Francisco, and Jonathan Shear, eds. 1999. *The View from Within* (special issue). *Journal of Consciousness Studies* 6(2/3).

Zarrilli, Phillip B. 1990. "What Does It Mean to 'Become the Character': Power, Presence, and Transcendence in Asian In-Body Disciplines of Practice." In *By Means of Performance: Intercultural Studies of Theater and Ritual*, ed. Richard Schechner and Willa Appel. Cambridge: Cambridge University Press.

The Eloquence of Mercury and the Enchantments of Venus: *Humanitas* in Botticelli and Cervantes's *Don Quixote*

FREDERICK A. DE ARMAS

ALTHOUGH IN OUR CENTURY THE TERM "HUMANISM" HAS BEEN THE subject of so many broad definitions that it has lost much of its specificity and positivity, such was not the case in early modern Europe. In its inception, the term carried with it the excitement and fascination of discovering, editing, and coming to an understanding of recently rediscovered works from classical antiquity. The term *umanista* "was used, in fifteenth-century Italian academic jargon, to describe a teacher or student of classical literature and the arts associated with it" (Mann 1996, 1).[1] While Kristeller argues "against the repeated attempts to identify Renaissance humanism with the philosophy, science, or the learning of the period as a whole" (1979, 23), more recent studies strive to cautiously broaden the term in its original context, without losing specificity. Countering the view "that Renaissance humanism was a narrowly philological enterprise," Jill Kraye has assembled a collection of essays that shows that it was "a broad intellectual and cultural movement, which contributed to, or at any rate engaged with, disciplines such as biblical studies, political thought, art, science and all branches of philosophy" (1996, xv). As for the value of humanistic endeavors, Petrarch was quite clear in his pronouncement that *studia humanitatis*, "the study of literature, and in particular classical literature, makes a man good" (Mann 1996, 14).

Since the "goodness" and "humane values" of humanistic endeavors are being questioned and even rejected by many today, this study seeks to show how such questioning was already present in early modern Europe—and how a study of the problematics of humanism yielded a more modern yet at the same time a strikingly positive assessment in Cervantes's *Don Quixote*, where in the tenth chapter of part 2, the complexity of *humanitas* is brought to light through an *ekphrasis*[2] based on Botticelli's *Primavera*. Some may argue that the leap from humanism to art is too great. Others might add that a literary text that is said to imitate the chivalric rather than the classical may place us at too far a distance from humanism to be able to consider it as part of the textuality of *Don Quixote*. However, Charles Hope and Elizabeth McGrath have shown that although humanism "was principally concerned with texts which few if any artists would have read" (1996, 161), there are a number of ways in which humanists and artists came together, the most important being through their interaction in iconographic schemes and particularly "the devising of attributes for mythological figures and especially for personifications" (173). Indeed, Hope and McGrath point to Botticelli's *Primavera* as one of the most noted examples of humanist involvement: Botticelli must have sought advice from humanists for his depiction of the transformation of Chloris into Flora after she was ravished by the wind god Zephyr. His depiction of these figures "seems to correspond to a passage in Ovid's *Fasti*" (5.195–222).[3]

"Primavera" by Sandro Botticelli (1444–1510). Uffizi, Florence, Italy. Courtesy of Alinari/Art Resource, NY.

Although some have seen Cervantes's imitation of the novels of chivalry in *Don Quixote* as a barrier to understanding his humanistic pursuits, at least one modern critic has argued that "the parody of the novels of chivalry was in reality only a smoke screen intended to mask Cervantes' primary intention in *Don Quixote*, which was to imitate and improve upon Virgil's *Aeneid*" (McGaha 1980, 34). Indeed, Luis Murillo has asserted that *Don Quixote* must be studied within the tradition of the Renaissance epic. Showing how Cervantes was influenced by theoreticians of the epic and humanist scholars, Murillo argues that he was not bound by them since as a storyteller he "subordinates all elements and influences from either learned or popular traditions into one fabric of narrative" (1980, 68). Finally, the humanist concern with *imitatio* of classical literature (Mann 1996, 13) can be found in the Cervantine text not only in the uses of Virgil, the Renaissance epic, and Botticelli's own humanistic program, but also in his rather complex utilization of Plato, Herodotus, Apuleius, and many other classical authors (de Armas 1992).

At the beginning of the tenth chapter of *Don Quixote* part 2, the narrator confesses to the reader that he would almost prefer to "pass over them [the events that transpire in this chapter] in silence, as he fears that he will not be believed. For Don Quixote's madness here reaches a point beyond which the imagination cannot go, and even exceeds that point by a couple of bowshots" (1949, 565; 1978 2.102–3). Not only does the chapter include one of don Quixote's greatest *locuras*, it also represents the climactic point in the development of Sancho's imagination. This chapter also changes the nature of don Quixote's quest. The knight has traveled to El Toboso to visit Dulcinea. Sancho, who had mendaciously told don Quixote that he had delivered a letter to the fictional Dulcinea, is now in a very awkward position since don Quixote wants him to find the princess to whom he delivered the letter, warning him "not to appear in his master's presence again until he should first have spoken in person to the lady Dulcinea and begged her to be pleased to grant her captive knight a glimpse of her" (1949, 566; 1978, 2:104). Not knowing what to do, Sancho sits under a tree and tries to determine his future course. Reasoning that his master believes that windmills are giants, he figures it would not be too difficult to persuade him that any woman is in reality Dulcinea (1949, 568; 1978, 2:107).

Returning late in the afternoon to where don Quixote awaits, Sancho sees three peasant women riding on donkeys. He tells his master to emerge from the woods where he had been waiting so that he can see his beloved Dulcinea and two of her ladies. Erich Auerbach, who has devoted considerable attention to this chapter, explains the transformation that takes place at this point: "for the first time roles are exchanged. Until now it had been Don Quixote who, encountering everyday phenomena, spontaneously saw and transformed them in terms of the romances of chivalry, while Sancho was generally in doubt and often tried to contradict and prevent his master's absurdities. Now it is the other way around. Sancho improvises a scene after the fashion of the romances of chivalry, while Don Quixote's ability to transform events to harmonize with his illusion breaks down before the crude vulgarity of the sight of the peasant women" (1968, 339). Indeed, don Quixote responds to Sancho's imaginings by saying, "I see nothing . . . except three farm girls on three jackasses" (1949, 570; 1978, 2:109). He insists that is all they are. His vision is no longer one of giants and princesses. He does not see these women riding hackneys: "It is as true that those are jackasses, or she-asses, as it is that I am Don Quixote and you Sancho Panza" (1949, 570; 1978, 2:109). Don Quixote makes quite an effort to perceive "a village wench, and not a very pretty one at that" (1949, 570; 1978, 2:110) as the beautiful princess Dulcinea. Although he fails to transform his vision, the knight does kneel in her presence. Auerbach adds: "He finds a solution which prevents him both from falling into despair and from recovering sanity: Dulcinea is enchanted" (1968, 340). This ideal will carry through the second part of the novel, becoming its central motif, according to both Auerbach and El Saffar.[4]

Auerbach adds that on recovering from shock, don Quixote pronounces a perfect speech. It begins with an *invocatio* that has three parts, emphasizing "an absolute perfection, then a perfection in human terms and finally the special personal devotion of the speaker" (1968, 341). Before beginning the central section, the *supplicatio*, a complex sentence, also composed of three parts, creates rhythm and suspense.[5] Finally, the *supplicatio* is also divided into three parts. Thus we have a speech with three sections, each having three parts. For Auerbach, the important point here is its technical perfection. But the emphasis on the number three has further significance. It parallels the appearance of three peasant women rather than just one Dulcinea.

By foregrounding the number three throughout this chapter,[6] the narrator alerts the reader that there is a mystery here that needs to be deciphered. After all, the Renaissance Neoplatonists saw "vestiges of the Trinity" (Wind 1968, 41) in pagan triads and particularly in the three Graces. Cervantes seems to acknowledge this "pagan mystery" in the *prólogo* to the first part of *Don Quixote*. Here, a friend advises the author on how to adorn his narrative, parodying the ways in which some writers feign knowledge of humanism and classical learning. Among these adornments are two sets of three classical women, which can serve to parody the pagan trinities: one set is composed of wanton lovers (Lamia, Laida, Flora) and a second of enchantresses (Medea, Calipso, Circe).[7] Shortly thereafter the friend argues that when dealing with love, references to a particular Renaissance Neoplatonic writer should be made: "If it is loves, with the ounce or two of Tuscan that you know you may make the acquaintance of Leon the Hebrew, who will satisfy you to your heart's content" (1949, 14; 1978, 1:56). It should come as no surprise that in Hebreo's *Diálogos de amor* (*Dialogues on Love*), one of the mythological allegories described is that of the three Graces. Indeed, these figures, as Edgar Wind has pointed out, were used by Neoplatonists to define Platonic love: Love is a Desire for Beauty. Each one of the Graces represents one of these three terms, and for this reason they are seen as Venus's companions. It may well be that the three "country maids" in part 2 of *Don Quixote* reflect in grotesque fashion this definition of love. At a time when don Quixote struggles to understand what love is, Dulcinea/Venus is rendered as a homely peasant, exhibiting yet another key pagan mystery, the *discordia concors*, where mighty opposites come together to create beauty and harmony.

During the Renaissance, the best-known representation of the three Graces is found in Botticelli's *Primavera*. This painting, although located in Florence, seems to have been known either through prints or descriptions in Spain during the Spanish Golden Age. There is a scene in Calderón's play *Apolo y Climene* that clearly demonstrates his knowledge of the painting (de Armas 1986). As for Cervantes, his travels to Italy starting in 1569 allowed him to study many of the images and programs of Renaissance art, which he later incorporated in his works (de Armas 1996b). Indeed, George Camamis has shown that Cervantes was acquainted with the *Primavera* and "left us clear proof of his knowledge of this and other Venus paintings by Botticelli in two of his least read novels: *La Galatea* and *La Gitanilla*" (1988, 183). Given Calderón's and Cervantes's knowledge of the *Primavera*, I think it is entirely possible that the tenth chapter of part 2 of *Don Quixote* is also inspired by the painting. As Helena Percas de Ponseti states, "Cervantes can be seen to develop his fiction along two levels simultaneously: a narrative level . . . and a visual, *pictorial* level in which objects, form, textures, and colors sustain, refute, qualify, or transform what is said or intimated" (1988, 12). This is precisely what happens in chapter 10. A pictorial level that points to Botticelli's *Primavera* transforms the parodic narrative level and vice versa. By problematizing a painting with an underlying humanistic program, Cervantes takes on questions of *imitatio*, *ekphrasis*, and the uses of humanism in the arts.

Although most modern readings of the *Primavera* teach us to view the development of the *favola* by reading it from right to left (Dempsey 1992, 62), the Cervantine chapter unfolds the figures from left to right. On the extreme left-hand side of the painting stands Mercury. As Wind asserts: "The crux of any interpretation of the *Primavera* is to explain the part played by Mercury. By tradition he is 'the leader of the Graces'; but while that would seem to explain his place next to them, it is hard to reconcile with his disengaged—not to say, indifferent, attitude" (1968, 121).[8] When don Quixote sends Sancho to find and talk to Dulcinea in the village of El Toboso, he counsels him to look carefully at her actions and movements, since these will reveal her amorous attitude toward don Quixote: "exterior signs of this sort are the most reliable couriers that there are, bringing news of what goes on inside the heart" (1949, 566; 1978, 2.104). Gestures thus become messages or mail from the soul, revealing its inner movements. This is the message that Sancho is to bring back to don Quixote. Acknowledging his role as messenger, Sancho cites a ballad on Bernardo del Carpio that begins: "A messenger you are, my friend" (1949, 567; 1978, 2:106). Mercury's most obvious role is that of messenger of the gods. He is also a *psychopompos*, or leader of the souls to the beyond. In this Cervantine interpretation of Botticelli's program, Sancho/Mercury is just that messenger, who is to mediate between Dulcinea's soul and don Quixote's passion. Clearly, the image of Mercury in the painting, young and slender, pointing to the heavens with his caduceus, is very much the opposite of a portly Sancho, seated under a tree, conversing with himself (1949, 567; 1978, 2:105). But just as we are about to conclude that Sancho as messenger is a grotesque parody of the god, we begin to see in him a newly acquired perception and inventiveness. With his caduceus, Botticelli's Mercury turns away the clouds. Wind takes this to mean that this deity has the "power to dispel mental clouds" (1968, 213). The repeated questioning of his role as messenger represents Sancho's mental clouds. But these he eventually dispels with a new insight. As "patron of lettered inquiry" (Wind 1968, 122), Mercury provides his earthly counterpart with the means to resolve his dilemma. Sancho will create his greatest invention and deceive don Quixote into believing that whatever peasant woman arrives is actually the princess Dulcinea, hoping in this manner to shed his role as messenger ("he won't be sending me on any more such errands [*mensajerías*] as these" [1949, 568; 1978, 2:107]).

It is then that Sancho encounters the three peasant women riding their donkeys. Continuing in his role as Mercury, god of eloquence, the squire describes the recent arrivals to don Quixote in poetic terms: "She and her damsels are all one blaze of gold, pearls, diamonds, rubies, and brocade cloth" (1949, 569; 1978, 2:108). This brocade or rich design woven into the cloth of the imagined ladies is also found in the dresses of the dancing Graces of Botticelli. As for the pearls, diamonds, and rubies, they may be discovered in the jewels worn by the two Graces that face the spectator. The mercurial eloquence of Sancho goes on to describe their hair: "Their hair falling loose over their shoulders are so many sunbeams playing with the wind" (1949, 569; 1978, 2:108). The golden hair of the three imagined ladies derives from Botticelli's three Graces. As for the wind, it blows from the extreme right of the painting, where Zephyrus, god of the west wind, touches Chloris, thus recalling Sancho's eloquent comparison of the golden hair with the rays of the sun "playing with the wind."

One of the many levels of the humanistic program of the painting may be astrological. For Gombrich, Botticelli follows Marsilio Ficino, who conceives of three benefic planets (which he often refers to as the three Graces) with gifts to bestow on the initiate: Venus, Apollo, and Mercury (1972, 59). While Venus stands at the center and Mercury at the extreme left of the painting, the influence of Sol is pervasive. Having shown how Mercury's influence has transformed Sancho, granting him the power of eloquence and invention,

Cervantes's *Don Quixote* goes on to point to the luminescence of Sol/Apollo through the golden hair/rays of the Graces. When don Quixote fails to believe Sancho's argument that the peasant women are Dulcinea and her maids, the squire asks: "Are your Grace's eyes in the back of your head that you cannot see that those are the ones coming there, as bright and shining (*resplandecientes*) as the sun itself in midday?" (1949, 569; 1978, 2:109). This resplendence is certainly one of the attributes of the Graces. According to Pico della Mirandola: "The Poets say that Venus has as companions and as her maids, the Graces, whose names in the vulgar tongue are Verdure, Gladness and Splendour. These three Graces are nothing but the three properties appertaining to the Ideal Beauty" (Gombrich 1972, 56). These names, given to the Graces in the *Orphic Hymns* (60, 3) and included by Ficino in his *Commentary on Plato's Symposium*, can be considered both as representing ideal beauty and as impulses that become lively during the *primavera*. It is the vivifying sun that provides spring its qualities of *viriditas*, *laetitia* and *splendor*. Indeed the third grace or quality can be associated with the brightness of sunlight that comes about as Sol becomes more brilliant following the spring equinox.

Since Sol's benefic rays and warmth help to stimulate the growth of vegetation, it is surprising to observe the predominance of shadow in Botticelli's painting. Similar shadows appear in the Cervantine episode, since don Quixote has been waiting in a wood for Sancho's return. The squire, on the other hand, has waited under the shadows of a tree until late to search for the would-be Dulcinea, since he wants his master to believe that he has been to El Toboso and back. Both painting and prose text invoke the solar rays of spring but depict an action that takes place in the cool shadows at the edge of a forest.

In the *Primavera*, the light that defines the aureole of myrtle surrounding Venus's head can be regarded as the solar energies that are harnessed by the goddess. Astrologically, Venus is viewed as a humid planet (de Nájera 1632, 5). This quality combines with Sol's warmth to produce the spring, described by Nájera as warm, humid, and temperate (1632, 20). But the presence of Venus surrounded by light is not merely a representation of the forces that bring about spring. She is also the ideal beauty spoken of by Pico della Mirandola, and together with the three Graces, she embodies the definition of love found in Plato's *Symposium* (Wind 1968, 46), in

Ficino's *Commentary on Plato's "Symposium"* (1985, 40), in León Hebreo, and in other Neoplatonic writers, which states that *Amor* is a desire for beauty.[9]

In his search for the ideal conception of beauty as embodied in Dulcinea, don Quixote is not prepared to transform the vision of three peasant women into Dulcinea and her maids. Nor is he prepared to follow the humanistic program that has been set out for him through Botticelli's *Primavera*. Instead of Venus and the three Graces, the knight sees only three peasant women riding their asses. In addition to confronting don Quixote with the definition of love, the absence of Dulcinea/Venus may well reflect his refusal to follow humanistic teachings. According to Gombrich, the initial impulse for the *Primavera* stems from a letter sent by Ficino to Lorenzo di Pierfrancesco de Medici, who lived at the Villa di Castello where the painting was housed (1972, 33). Although recently Dempsey has shown that the painting was made for the *case vecchie de'Medici* in the Via Larga, this does not negate the possible importance of Ficino's letter as one of the possible models for the painting. The letter "culminates in an appeal to the young man that he should fix his eyes on Venus who stood for *Humanitas*" (1972, 33). It would be most appropriate that the *Primavera* should be interpreted, on one level, as a description of Venus-*Humanitas*. Describing Botticelli's frescoes in the Villa Lemmi outside of Florence, Gombrich explains that one shows "Venus and the three Graces," while a second shows Venus leading a young man "towards the personifications of Philosophy and the Liberal Arts" (75). Thus, these paintings would corroborate Botticelli's interest in Venus-*Humanitas* and in *Amor* as "teacher of all the arts."[10]

It is curious to note that the virtue of *Humanitas*, "which Ficino commends so passionately to the young man Lorenzo di Pierfrancesco, may have been precisely a virtue he conspicuously lacked. Throughout his life the younger Lorenzo was an irascible person. . . . How desirable it was to tame him and to teach him the value of *Humanitas*, which means not only culture but also affability" (Gombrich 1972, 33–4). Irascibility, the excess of a choleric disposition, is also a key trait in don Quixote. Throughout the novel, the would-be knight lets this choleric disposition propel him into inappropriate actions, which is one of the main aspects that lend humor to the work. It may be that the humanistic program of Botticelli's *Primavera* is inserted at this point in the novel to transform his

"Venus and the Graces Offering Gifts to a Young Girl" (c. 1430–33) by Sandro Botticelli (1444–1510). Louvre, Paris, France. Courtesy of Scala/Art Resource, NY.

character. His previous invention of Dulcinea has been based on romances of chivalry, a type of reading that led to his choleric and humorous behavior. By presenting an alternative model, Sancho, through the eloquence of Mercury, may be attempting to have the knight invent Dulcinea as Venus-*Humanitas*. After all, such a transformation in her representation would allow him to turn away from the chivalric, medieval, and choleric and move toward humanistic readings that would lead to affability, beauty, and goodness.

But don Quixote fails to view the peasant women in a painterly fashion. His invention resists this metamorphosis. He will argue instead that Dulcinea has been enchanted. This enchantment works through his perception of her: "The malign enchanter who doth persecute me hath placed clouds and cataracts upon my eyes, and for them alone hath transformed thy peerless beauty into the face of a lowly peasant maid" (1949, 571; 1978, 2:110). Let us recall that in Botticelli's painting, Mercury with his caduceus is attempting to remove the clouds from the sky. In *Don Quixote*, Sancho's mercurial ruse could have dispelled the clouds that blind the knight,

"Young Man Led toward the Seven Arts" by Sandro Botticelli (1444–1510). Fresco from Villa Lemmi. Louvre, Paris, France. Courtesy of Giraudon/Art Resource, NY.

but don Quixote admits instead that the clouds make him unable to properly see Dulcinea/Venus.

But Sancho's eloquence is not at an end. When the peasant woman, who has fallen from the ass, regains her seat and rapidly departs along with her companions, the squire uses figurative language to describe their flight: "and her damsels are not far behind, for they all of them go like the wind" (1949, 571; 1978, 2:111). The mention of the wind brings us again to the last section of the painting. At the extreme right, three figures recall Ovid's *Fasti*, since Zephyr, the west wind, impregnates Chloris. "However, he made amends by making her Queen of flowers." As Dempsey notes, "the meaning of the Ovidian model is transformed, for Ovid does not literally describe a transformation in the *Fasti*, but Botticelli has nevertheless imagined the event as an Ovidian metamorphosis and thereby rendered, in true Ovidian fashion, the meaning of the event in the actions themselves" (1992, 32–33). Cervantes had mentioned Flora in the prologue to part 1, where she formed part of one of two unholy trinities. Only one hint of her presence in chapter 10 is given by don Quixote. He bemoans the fact that the village maid is nothing like Dulcinea since the enchanter has robbed her "of that which is so characteristic of highborn ladies, namely their pleasing scent, which comes from always being among amber and flowers" (1949, 572; 1978, 2:112).

Now that the full painting is accounted for, with Sancho as Mercury, the three peasant women as the three Graces, the absent Dulcinea as Venus, Zephyr as the wind associated with the *labradoras*, and Chloris as Flora, queen of flowers, it may be pertinent to discuss why the Cervantine text debases the idealized images in Botticelli's painting to present a rustic atmosphere where don Quixote fails to perceive his Dulcinea. Such a rustification is actually in keeping with one level of the humanistic program followed by Botticelli. Dempsey explains that the gods depicted in the painting are, on one level, not the traditional Roman gods, but "archaic deities of nature's fertility" (1992, 49). The Zephyr-Chloris-Flora story is nothing more than "Ovid's account of the primitive origins of the feast of the Floralia"; while Venus is the archaic goddess of the garden, "an old-fashioned rustic deity" (44); and Mercury is "an archaic god of the springtime" (43). By infusing his text with rusticity, Cervantes reflects this primal era, before the gods moved to the Roman pantheon.

In spite of the arguments presented above, there are at least three elements that further problematize the representation of the *Primavera* within Cervantes's text. First, the rusticity of the deities depicted by Botticelli is by no means sufficient to account for the grotesque manner in which the would-be gods are portrayed in chapter 10. Second, the absence of Venus (the "enchantment" of Dulcinea), removes the central figure from the Cervantine representation of the painting. And third, the chapter "reads" the painting backwards—instead of proceeding from right to left, it begins with Mercury and ends with the Zephyr-Cloris-Flora triad.

Let us begin with this third problem. The two most contradictory readings of Botticelli's painting emphasize a narrative sequence that unfolds from right to left. The "rustic" reading shows the Zephyr-Chloris-Flora triad as the first flowering of spring: Venus as the "goddess of April," the fullness of *primavera*; and finally Mercury as May, the end of springtime (Dempsey 1992, 62). The Neoplatonic reading, on the other hand,[11] follows a similar pattern. From Proclus's *Elements of Theology* to Ficino's *Theologia Platonica*, there is a constant perception that "the bounty bestowed by the gods upon lower beings" began "as a kind of overflowing (*emanatio*) which produced a vivifying rapture or conversion (called by Ficino *conversio, raptio* or *vivificatio*) whereby the lower beings were drawn back to heaven and rejoined the gods (*remeatio*)" (Wind 1968, 37). The *Primavera* exhibits this Neoplatonic movement. Starting at the right hand side of the painting, Zephyr's downward flight is the *emanatio*, the overflowing from the heavens. Venus or ideal beauty leads to *raptio*, or the conversion of the lower beings, while Mercury as "mediator between mortals and gods bridging the distance between earth and heaven" (Wind 1968, 122) represents the process of *remeatio*. Why then does the Cervantine *ekphrasis* transgress against prevalent interpretations, reading the painting backward (from left to right)?

This backward reading may represent the knight's inability to read the signs of the world (or of the painting) correctly. Throughout part 1, don Quixote had chosen to read the world according to the chivalric authorities but was defeated in the end. In part 2, he no longer has the will to impose his vision on the world. Here, others will provide the chivalric backdrop in which he becomes merely an actor. In terms of the painting, the backward reading may well refer to the fact that he no longer has a vision of a Golden Age (the rustic gods of spring) and that he no longer has the Neoplatonic vision that leads to *raptio*. This allows us to comprehend the other two problems.

Venus, "who is the manifestation of the love and beauty that stirs the world to renewal" (Dempsey 1992, 62) cannot be envisioned by the knight. His idealized love, based on the romances of chivalry, cannot allow for a humanistic reading of his beloved as Venus, as the force that will lead him to harmony, affability, and culture. The knight will only accept a princess that will lead him into war and conflict. Her absence must mean that she has been enchanted. And yet this absence may point to the knight's struggle to metamorphose his own vision. Seldom in part 2 will he be the agent of warfare. Others, knowing his propensities, will create theatrical pieces in which the knight will act out his part. Venus-*Humanitas* has penetrated his being and is in the process of transforming don Quixote. As Henry Sullivan has noted, part 2 of the novel is very different. Here, "the theme of cruelty, the sufferings of Knight and Squire seemed invested with an arbitrary, even sadistic, dimension of excess" (Sullivan 1996, 2). For Sullivan, it connotes a desire for purification, which he relates to the notion of purgatory in this life.

I would argue that this desire for purification has to do with his encounter with Venus-*Humanitas*. As Petrarch has noted, humanism makes a man good. In abandoning his novels of chivalry and returning to civilization, don Quixote metamorphoses himself into Alonso Quijano "el bueno" ("the good"). In Botticelli's painting, both the rustic Venus and Flora abide in a land of eternal spring. This is don Quixote's goal from the start. His speech on the Golden Age shows his motivation—to bring back the perfection of beginnings. The novel's humanistic program emphasizes classical civilization's desire for this return to origins. Don Quixote's adventures in part 2 take him from an encounter with Venus, which he denies, through a series of purgatorial purifications so that he may become the ideal of the humanists. Sancho, under the influence of Mercury, or eloquence, will also grow in stature, becoming an ideal governor of the island of Barataria. Both knight and squire fulfill their destinies—the first in his vision of eternity (which is a return to origins) and the latter in the wisdom granted him by the god of speech.

Transformation, as Gombrich has noted, comes from the spell of the visual arts, leading to "lasting psychological effects" (1972, 34). Images were said to affect one's character in the same way as planets influenced those born under them: "If this belief existed it is natural that those who commissioned the painting of the Goddess would also be concerned with her authentic appearance. For just as an amulet is only effective if it has the right image so the picture destined to exert its beneficent spell would only work if it was correct." Although the effect of humanism in general was that of creating goodness, specific images would have limited effects: Venus would make one affable and harmonious while Mercury's gifts would be eloquence and wisdom. Such magical thinking may be at odds with modern conceptions and may marginalize humanism.[12] And yet some modern readers are coming to realize the power of literature, the worth of the image. If not "magical," it has a certain aura that rises beyond culture.

In a recent forum containing thirty-two letters on the relationship of cultural studies to the literary, Alan Powers spoke of the "bliss of reading" and of the humanist or literary scholar as a "teacher of pleasure" (Powers 1997, 264). For Renaissance Neoplatonists such as Ficino, *raptio* was key to the power of humanism. And it is represented as such in Botticelli's *Primavera* where, through Zephyr's emanations, the human spirit comes to envision the rapture of beauty (Venus). The power, the pleasure, and the rapture of reading is not merely a Renaissance phenomenon. In our time, Roland Barthes has conceived of *jouissance*, or the pleasure of the text, as the "body of bliss" (1975, 62); Haney claims it appeals "to a natural substratum beyond the transient forces of culture" (1993, 95). In Haney's interpretation, it is a "widening of consciousness" that serves to "peel away our sense of separateness and makes us participate in the process of History" (99). Frank Lentricchia has called for a return of the reader as rhapsode: "As Plato says in the *Ion*, rhapsodes are enthusiasts . . . I tell my students that in true recitation, we're possessed, we are the medium for the writer's voice" (1996, 65–66).

As rhapsodes or witnesses to the "primal numinous awe" (Otto 1973, 126) of "deep aesthetic experience,"[13] as believers that the word and the image can change our consciousness, we must also realize the complexities of these texts and images, their contradictions, which mirror the contradictions of humanity. Don Quixote's transformation is one based on *discordia concors*: when faced with Venus his choleric disposition begins to change. As in Botticelli's *Mars and Venus* the goddess can transform the warrior. So let us in our readings seek these metamorphoses and harness their transformative power. Literature and art can indeed lead to goodness when this concept is understood as the amazing harmony that can emerge from contrariety, as that self or consciousness that lies beyond the many political and theoretical controversies of our century. This is not to say that we ought to abandon the political and cultural contextualization of texts and images. There is no question that certain works weave in and out of the canon due to political imperatives (de Armas 1996a). We must continue to probe the limits of gender, power, and sexuality in the works of the early modern period. However, we may also want to foreground the forgotten *humanitas*. We may want to remember that aesthetic beauty and the rapture it produces can be one of the most subversive forces in the verbal and visual arts. After all, the possible laudatory or political

"Mars, Venus and Satyrs" by Sandro Botticelli (1444–1510). National Gallery, London, Great Britain. Courtesy of Alinari/Art Resource, NY.

program of the *Primavera* is momentarily forgotten when the viewer is enraptured by the mysterious beauty of the work.[14]

A move to the twenty-first century is a move to terra incognita, where knowledge becomes intimately associated with the knower, where the consciousness of the individual exposed to the *raptio* of "deep aesthetic experience" expands so as to understand the multiplicity and diversity of humanity as a union of contraries. It is this *raptio* that don Quixote first denies in viewing a rustic version of the *Primavera*. But Alonso Quijano "el bueno" learns in the end to go beyond oppositions, to subvert hierarchical thinking, transforming the Other, the *labradora*, into an image of Venus-*Humanitas*, into a vision of goodness.

NOTES

A version of this essay has appeared in the electronic journal *Laberinto*.

1. On this subject, see also Kristeller 1979, 22.

2. On *ekphrasis* during the Spanish Golden Age, see Bergmann 1979.

3. Dempsey has shown that the humanist program here is even more complex, based on Lucretius's *De Rurum Natura*, Ovid's *Fasti*, Horace's *Odes*, Seneca's *De Beneficis* and Hesiod's *Georgics* (1992, 36–37). Each is rethought and transformed. For example: "Botticelli has altered Lucretius's simple description of a rustic parade of springtime deities into his own invention, one that changes Lucretius's sequential listing into a manifestation of the growth and development of the season" (32).

4. "The search for Dulcinea with which Don Quixote begins the action of Part II forms the underlying motive for all he does throughout the rest of the work" (El Saffar 1984, 86).

5. The three parts of the sentence can be discerned in the Spanish text, the first beginning with *ya que*, the second with three "y's" and the third with *si ya* (1949, 571; 1978, 2:110).

6. In addition to the tripartite speech with three subsections within each part, the chapter includes three peasant women, three asses, and three mares whose colts would be given as a gift to Sancho (1949, 569; 1978, 2:108). Indeed, the number three is often repeated in the chapter: "tres yeguas," "tres aldeanas," "tres labradoras," "tres borricos," "tres hacaneas" (1978, 2:108–9).

7. For an analysis of the women cited in the prologue to *Don Quixote* and the way in which they are later incorporated into the first part of the work, see Nadeau (1994).

8. Both Panofsky (1960, 193) and Dempsey (1992, 37) agree with this assessment, but for very different reasons.

9. This definition became quite popular during the Spanish Golden Age and can be found, for example, in Lope de Vega's *Fuenteovejuna* (1990, vv. 409–10).

10. Citing these frescoes, Camamis relates Venus-*Humanitas* to Cervantes's *La Galatea* (1988, 187–88).

11. Dempsey reluctantly acknowledges that "it is obvious that the means exist to reintroduce a Neoplatonic interpretation of *Primavera*" (1992, 65).

12. One of the most influential Hispanic writers of this century has stressed the relationship between textuality and the magical nature of reality, which calls into question what is "real." This notion is found in an essay on *Don Quixote* by Jorge Luis Borges (1960, 69).

13. Etlin agrees with Otto in that the "primal numinous awe" is "analogous to deep aesthetic experience": "The nature and meaning of both experiences merit our utmost consideration if we wish to understand the question of value in art" (1996, 154).

14. Studying Sanskrit poetics, William S. Haney II offers a critique of modern and postmodern poetics, whose "emphasis on ambiguity and indeterminacy reflects the futile attempt on the part of the intellect to account for experiences that will always be enigmatic until grasped on the unifying level of consciousness" (1993, 60). He goes on to show how Sanskrit poetics opens texts "to the pure possibility of meaning, a function of the coexistence of opposites."

WORKS CITED

Auerbach, Erich. 1968. *Mimesis*. Trans. Willard R. Trask. Princeton: Princeton University Press.

Barthes, Roland. 1975. *The Pleasure of the Text*. Trans. Richard Miller. New York: Hill and Wang.

Bergmann, Emilie. 1979. *The Art Inscribed: Essays on Ekphrasis in Spanish Golden Age Poetry*. Cambridge: Harvard University Press.

Borges, Jorge Luis. 1960. "Magias parciales del Quixote." In *Ortas inquisiciones*. Buenos Aires: Emecé.

Camamis, George. 1988. "The Concept of Venus-*Humanitas* in Cervantes and Botticelli." *Cervantes* 8: 183–223.

Cervantes, Miguel de. 1949. *Don Quixote*. Trans. Samuel Putnam. New York: Random House.

———. 1978. *El ingenioso didalgo don Quijote de la Mancha*. Ed. Luis Murillo. Madrid: Castalia.

de Armas, Frederick A. 1986. "The Betrayal of a Mystery: Botticelli and Calderón's *Apolo y Climene*." *Romanische Forschungen* 98: 304–23.

———. 1992. "Interpolation and Invisibility: From Herodotus to Cervantes's Don Quixote." *Journal of the Fantastic in the Arts* 4: 8–28.

———. 1996a. "The Mysteries of Canonicity." In *Heavenly Bodies: The Realm of La estrella de Sevilla*, ed. Frederick A. de Armas. Lewisburg: Bucknell University Press.

———. 1996b. "Painting and Graffiti: (Sub)Versions of History in Golden Age Theater (Notes on Cervantes and Claramonte)." *Gestos* 11: 83–101.

Dempsey, Charles. 1992. *The Portrayal of Love. Botticelli's "Primavera" and Humanist Culture at the Time of Lorenzo the Magnificent*. Princeton: Princeton University Press.

de Nájera, Antonio. 1632. *Suma astrológica y arte para enseñar hazer pronos-ticos.* Lisbon: P. Alvares.

El Saffar, Ruth. 1984. *Beyond Fiction: The Recovery of the Feminine in the Novels of Cervantes.* Berkeley: University of California Press.

Etlin, Richard A. 1996. *In Defense of Humanism: Value in the Arts and Letters.* Cambridge: Cambridge University Press.

Ficino, Marsilio. 1985. *Commentary on Plato's "Symposium on Love."* Ed. Sears Jayne. Dallas: Spring Publications.

Gombrich, E. H. 1972. *Symbolic Images. Studies in the Art of the Renaissance II.* Chicago: University of Chicago Press.

Haney, William S., II. 1993. *Literary Theory and Sanskrit Poetics: Language, Consciousness and Meaning.* Lewiston, N.Y.: The Edwin Mellen Press.

Hope, Charles, and Elizabeth McGrath. 1996. "Artists and Humanists." In *The Cambridge Companion to Renaissance Humanism,* ed. Jill Kraye. Cambridge: Cambridge University Press.

Kraye, Jill, ed. 1996. *The Cambridge Companion to Renaissance Humanism.* Cambridge: Cambridge University Press.

Kristeller, Paul Oskar. 1979. *Renaissance Thought and Its Sources.* New York: Columbia University Press.

Lentricchia, Frank. 1996. "Last Will and Testament of an Ex-Literary Critic." *Lingua Franca.* (September/October): 59–67.

Lope de Vega, Félix. 1990. *Fuente Ovejuna.* 11th ed. Ed. Juan Maria Marin. Madrid: Cátedra.

Mann, Nicholas. 1996. "The Origins of Humanism." In *The Cambridge Companion to Renaissance Humanism,* ed. Jill Kraye. Cambridge: Cambridge University Press.

McGaha, Michael. 1980. "Cervantes and Virgil." In *Cervantes and the Renaissance,* ed. Michael McGaha. Newark, Del.: Juan de la Cuesta.

Murillo, L. A. 1980. "*Don Quixote* as Renaissance Epic." In *Cervantes and the Renaissance,* ed. Michael McGaha. Newark, Del.: Juan de la Cuesta.

Nadeau, Carolyn Amy. 1994. "Women of the Prologue: Writing the Female in *Don Quixote, I.* Ph.D. diss., Pennsylvania State University.

Otto, Rudolf. 1973. *The Idea of the Holy: An Inquiry into the Non-Rational Factor and the Idea of the Divine and Its Relation to the Rational.* 2d ed. Trans. John W. Harvey. Oxford: Oxford University Press.

Panofsky, Erwin. 1960. *Renaissance and Renescences in Western Art.* Stockholm: Amquist and Wiksell.

Percas de Ponseti, Helena. 1988. *Cervantes the Writer and the Painter of "Don Quixote."* Columbia: University of Missouri Press.

Powers, Alan. 1997. "Forum." *PMLA* 112: 164–65.

Sullivan, Henry W. 1996. *Grotesque Purgatory: A Study of Cervantes's "Don Quixote," Part II.* University Park: Pennsylvania State University Press.

Wind, Edgar. 1968. *Pagan Mysteries in the Renaissance.* 2d ed. New York: Norton.

Part III
Humanism and Human Concern

Signing the Frame, Framing the Sign: Multiculturalism, Canonicity, Pluralism, and the Ethics of Reading *Heart of Darkness*

DANIEL SCHWARZ

PLURALISTIC CRITICISM

ELIE WIESEL BEGINS *NIGHT*, HIS AUTOBIOGRAPHICAL NOVEL OF THE Holocaust, with a description of Moshe the Beadle, an insignificant figure in a small town in Transylvania who taught the narrator about the cabala: "They called him Moshe the Beadle, as though he had never had a surname in his life. He was a man of all work at a Hasidic synagogue. The Jews of Sighet—that little town in Transylvania where I spent my childhood—were very fond of him. He was very poor and lived humbly. . . . He was a past master in the art of making himself insignificant, of seeming invisible. . . . I loved his great, dreaming eyes, their gaze lost in the distance" (1960, 5). But Moshe is expelled in early 1942 because he is a foreign Jew, and is not heard of for several months. He unexpectedly returns to tell of his miraculous escape from the Gestapo slaughter of Jews in the Polish forests. But no one believes him. Moshe cries: "Jews, listen to me. . . . Only listen to me." But everyone assumes that he has gone mad. And the narrator—still a young boy—recalls asking him: "Why are you so anxious that people should believe what you say? In your place, I shouldn't care whether they believed me or not."

Let us consider the significance of Moshe the Beadle. For one thing, Wiesel is using him as a metonymy for himself in his present role as narrator who is, as he writes, calling on us to listen to his words as he tells his relentless tale of his own miraculous escape from Nazi terror. Implicitly, he is urging us that it is our ethical responsibility not to turn away from the Witnessing Voice—Moshe himself and indeed all those who have specifically seen the Holocaust or, metonymically, man's inhumanity to man—whether it occurs in Bosnia, Northern Ireland, or Somalia.

Why do I begin with *Night*? For one thing, it is a novel that depends upon and affirms the concept of individual agency, for the speaker tells a wondrous and horrible tale of saving his life and shaping his role as Witness—perhaps as our Daniel. We see dramatized the process of the narrator's developing into his role of Witness in the face of historical forces that would obliterate his humanity, his individuality, and his voice. Notwithstanding the efficiency of Nazi cultural production and technology of the death camps and gas chambers, the narrator re-creates himself through language. In the sense of the technological fulfillment of an ordered state that subordinated individual rights to the national purpose of the state, Nazi ideology has been thought of as a product of modernism. For those who have experienced, like Wiesel, the Holocaust firsthand—for whom Auschwitz is not a metaphor but a memory—language is more than the free play of signifiers. For these people and others on the political edge, their very telling—their very living—testifies to will, agency, and a desire to survive that resists and renders morally irrelevant simple positivistic explanations arguing that an author's language is completely culturally produced. In psychoanalytic linguistic terms, the narrator's telling is a *resistance* to the way in which the word "Jew" was culturally produced to mean inferior people who were progressively discounted, deprived of basic rights as citizens, labeled with a yellow Star of David, imprisoned, enslaved, and killed.

I select this spare, rough-hewn text because it is an eloquent testimony that depends on human agency and ethical commitment. *Night* reminds us, too, that the concept of author-function as a substitute for the creating intelligence does not do justice to the way in which language and art express the individual psyche. Readers will recall that the book's signification depends on its taut structure, which is the underpinning for an apparently primitive testimony, and depends, too, on its spare, even sparse, style. Its eloquence derives from its apparent ingenuousness. Yet *Night* speaks on behalf of meaning, on behalf of will—the will to survive, the will to witness—and on behalf of language's signification. *Night* eloquently reminds us of a grotesque historical irony—that with its use of modern technology and Enlightenment rationality, Western man's progress led to the efficiency of the Nazi transport system, Nazi work camps, and Nazi gas chambers. *Night* is a text that resists irony and deconstruction and cries out in its eloquence, pain, and anger as it enacts the *power of language*. The text traces the death of the narrator's mother, a sister, and, finally, father; it witnesses an encroaching horrible moral NIGHT, a night that includes the speaker's loss of religious belief in the face of historical events.

Assuming in its form—especially its prophetic voice—an ethical narratee, *Night* also demands an ethical response. By that I mean attention to issues that pertain to how life is lived within imagined worlds. Truth in novels takes place within the hypothesis "as if," which is another way of saying that as we think about our reading we are never completely unaware of the metaphoricity of literature. At one time, some critics may have naively ignored the metaphoricity of language and confused characterization with actual human character. But have not some theorists reached the other pole of willfully denying analogies to human life and naively repressing the possibilities of significance?

While I would be the first to acknowledge that the stakes are infinitely smaller, I think humanists and those interested in the ethical implications of writing, reading, and teaching have justifiably felt, like Moshe the Beadle, that their voices were for a while being ignored in the din of theoretical shouting. But in the wake of the de Man revelations and the insistence of many feminists, minorities, postcolonialists, and new historicists that we look at what literature represents, the voice of those who all along believed in the ethical and aesthetic dimensions of literature and culture are once again being heard.

By beginning my discourse with Wiesel's *Night*, I am enacting my view that each of us belongs to different interpretive communities at the same time, and that these communities are in a dialogic relationship with one another. For example, I am an American academic, an English professor at Cornell, a divorced father who for several years has been the primary parent of two young adult sons, and, despite three or four generations of assimilation, still a Jew for whom the Holocaust—and, indeed, the book of Daniel—has profound meaning. In my chapter on de Man's life and work in my book *The Case for a Humanistic Poetics* (1991), as well as in my work on *Ulysses* (1987), I write as a secular Jew who feels deep synchronic and diachronic ties to his heritage, and who tends to be drawn to the culturally marginalized—whether by nationality (Conrad and Joyce) or by gender (Woolf)—and to those in economically straitened circumstances (Lawrence). To situate ourselves and our interests is part of an ethics of reading.

A word more about Jewishness. Perhaps it is because the Jewish tradition—for me, at least, as a secular Jew who makes choices about how and what I believe—has always been open and exegetical that I resist theoretical dogma. When one looks at a page of the Talmud, one sees an unresolved dialogue among diverse commentators. In Judaism, there is no Nicene Creed, no attempt to resolve issues in a concluding statement. For example, in the Passover Haggadah, the various rabbis comment upon the meaning of the Exodus story and specifically the meaning of Passover customs, but again there is no attempt at resolution. Because historically Jews have lived on the margin, in ghettos and *shetls*, never sure of what pogroms tomorrow will bring, they have tended to be skeptical of sweeping universals and to dwell in the particular. Moreover, Jews have been concerned with relations between man and God and man and man, not simply the hereafter—in part because the hereafter was often a luxury while they eked out a living and awaited what seemed like arbitrary changes in the political winds. And the Jewish tradition is ethically based—think of the Talmud as a debate about law and ethics—with an emphasis on living in what Aristotle called the "ineluctable modality of the visible" (and Joyce redefined into "what you damn well have to see").

Because each of us is a nodal point where multiple major influences as well as secondary influences meet, each of us encounters the texts we read on the seam of reading—and by seam, I am playing with S-E-A-M, S-E-E-M, and S-E-M as in semiotics and dissemination. I stress how texts shape readers and readers shape texts. I am a pragmatic Aristotelian who stresses the relationship of the poem as a made object, the product of an author's conscious (and unconscious) art or craft, designed to achieve foreknown ends that result from the psyche, values, and idiosyncracies that differentiate her or him from others. Thus my version of cultural criticism would seek to create what Saul Rosensweig, speaking of his own "Freud, Jung and Hall the King-Maker," calls the "idioverse, the universe of events that constitutes the individual" as it is realized in the artists' works (Rosensweig 1993, 20). I am prone to ask, "What is your evidence?" to myself and to my students, and expect my and their answer to consist of passages from primary texts. I am conscious of how plot enacts values, and how plot is a structure of effects. I try to balance the structure of tropes with a sense that the plot represents an anterior reality. (I do not believe the citation by one theorist of one theorist constitutes an argument. Indeed, if current theory is a production of knowledge, not the reproduction, how is it that current theory relies so much on the argument from authority?)

Narrative is both the representation of external events and the telling of those events. My interest in narrative derives from my belief that we make sense of our life by ordering it and giving it shape. The stories we tell ourselves provide the continuity among the concatenation of diverse episodes in our lives, even if our stories inevitably distort and falsify. Each of us is continually writing and rewriting the text of our lives, revising our memories and hopes, proposing plans, filtering disappointments through our defenses and rationalizations, making adjustments in the way we present ourselves to ourselves and to others. To the degree that we are self-conscious, we live in our narratives—our discourse—about our actions, thoughts, and feelings. While there is always a gulf between imagined worlds and real ones, does not the continuity between reading lives and reading texts depend on understanding reading as a means of sharpening our perceptions, cultivating discriminations, and deepening our insights about ourselves? For reading is a process of cognition that depends on actively organizing the phenomena of language both in the moment of perception *and* on the fuller understanding that develops as our reading continues, as well as in our retrospective view of our completed reading.

Reading is a dialogic activity in which multiple ways of looking at a text contend with one another; each perspective implicitly suggests interrogatives to other approaches. I would like to suggest that as readers we can and should belong to multiple interpretive communities; rather than propose unitary stories of reading and choose between the either/or of possible readings, we can and should enjoy multiplicity and diversity in our readings. The kind of pluralistic criticism I imagine sees criticism as a series of hypotheses rather than as a final product. In its healthy and open pluralism, it is inclusive rather than exclusive. Even as we answer each question and pursue each line of inquiry, we become aware that each explanation is partial. It may be time to back off from the notion that the critic is *vates* and return to the more modest Socratic question-and-answer structure in order to leave rhetorical space for other explanations. Pluralism may at times define a position passionately but always in the mode of "This is true, or is it?" and always leaving space for a response. By contrast, dogmatism asserts its position without allowing for an alternative, while relativism accepts all positions as if they were equal.

The text itself, what it represents, what it signifies, and how it enacts a meaning should always be an important part of our pedagogy. Yet, as Stephen Greenblatt understands, all reading has an element of self-fashioning and we should be self-conscious about how self-fashioning creates angles of distortion. For example, how each of us responds to the narrative of Paul de Man's life and work depends on how we were personally situated, including the extent to which we invested in deconstruction. How we situate ourselves as individual readers and as members of interpretive communities is an important part of our reading and, as teachers, we need to make the students aware of how we and they might acknowledge *our differences*. We need to be careful about defining our own position because we do not always see ourselves as others see us. We can get lost in a welter of self-pity and can overestimate our own worth.

As I have argued elsewhere, finally, the largest interpretive community is one reader. Positioning oneself in relationship to a text is as important as positioning a text in relation to cultural contexts and our debates within the academic community about critical assumptions. Simply put, texts like Elie Wiesel's *Night* are different for those whose family disappeared in the concentration camps and different again for those fellow Jews who, like myself, by accident of place survived. Indeed, I believe that there is a place within literary studies for texts that reflect our own varied interests. Special interest has always been an engine that has driven literary studies—first as an offspring of classical study and philology, then of historicism and textual editing, later of New Criticism—and special interest has produced the wonderful revolution in feminist studies, postcolonial studies, and ethnic studies.

Where, let us ask, are theory, criticism, and the study of literature going? I have always doubted that theory was teleologically advancing in a kind of Manifest Destiny from the International Academic Datelines of Paris and New Haven. Why has theory evolved into *theology* and why do partisans of one or another approach form sects? Is it the power of theory's arguments or, for some acolytes, the importance of *belonging*—and excluding and scapegoating those who do not belong? Theories, including Marxism and deconstruction, are valuable as part of a pluralistic discourse but become oppressive and distorting when they become monolithic paradigms worshipped by monotheistic cults. At times literary studies have suffered from reductive rhetoric that has done intellectual violence to complex texts in the name of various monolithic theories.

I feel like someone who, with a small band of other surviving humanists, has created a little island outpost where we pursued our interests, and perhaps been grudgingly given a place in the General Assembly—certainly not the Security Council—of theory. Because while welcoming the destabilizing insights of much recent theory—including the idea that language does not signify absolutely and texts are historically and culturally produced, I am willing to be identified with such quaint ideas as humanism, pluralism, and canonicity, and use such terms as "ethics" and even "author." I am for a pluralism of readings, a pluralism of texts, and a pluralism of cultures. Because I assume human agency in writing and reading and believe that there is a space for a non-Marxist version of cultural studies, I am on occasion invited to play the role of academic dissenter—for some, read: dinosaur—in journals and at conferences.

Within any theory of cultural production—whether of texts or readers—we need to leave space for the creative intelligence of authors and readers who make choices that have ethical implications. My focus, my concern, is the act of reading specific texts. I have always been wary of extravagant readings that use the text as point of departure for flights of fancy and/or to make a political point. Indeed, for me, extravagant reading is an oxymoron.

As a way of anticipating my approach to *Heart of Darkness*, I want to provocatively propose two columns:

ingenuous or unsophisticated	rigorous, urbane, or sophisticated
essentialism	materialism
univocal, monistic	dialogic
positivistic logic and "A" causes "B"	affinities, playfulness
binary thinking	free play of signifiers as revealed to an imaginative, interesting and powerful reader

conservative	progressive
traditional	avant-garde
close-minded	open-minded
simple, facile, deductively consistent	complex, difficult, disruptive
static	destabilizing
subjective	objective
rational, detached, restrained	passionate, engaged, committed
old-fashioneden	lightened
dogmatic insistence on monolithic truth	belief that some readings are better and truer than others

While the column on the left is usually used to describe humanistic criticism and the column on the right to describe various advanced theories—including deconstruction and Marxism—I want to suggest that the categories on the right, which are thought to belong to advanced theory, at times more aptly describe humanistic pluralist criticism, and I want to subversively invite a questioning—a de-deconstruction—of these binary distinctions as they are now applied. Moreover, I want to suggest that the best of all criticism understands these supposedly binary concepts in terms of "both/and," not "neither/nor," and that well before deconstruction Kenneth Burke, William Empson, R. P. Blackmur, Dorothy Van Ghent, and M. H. Abrams demonstrated in their works how these supposedly binary concepts cross-fertilize one another, invade each other's borders, and form a continuum.[1]

In *Professing English: An Institutional History*, Gerald Graff calls literary theory "a discourse that treats literature as in some respects a problem and seeks to formulate that problem in general terms" (1987, 252). Some recent theory has claimed for itself a position as a master discourse rather than one of many discourses. Let us look for a moment at one of the most brilliant and influential theorists today, Fredric Jameson. When Jameson writes, "Only Marxism can give us an adequate account of the essential *mystery* of the cultural past . . . by arguing its ultimate philosophical and methodological priority over more specialized interpretive codes whose insights are strategically limited as much by their own situational origins as by the narrow or local ways in which they construe or construct their objects of study" (1981, 21), that is an ethical statement. It is also an example of how essentialism finds a home in the house of materialism. And his notion of history as an "absent cause," "inaccessible to us except in textual forms," is only paying homage to language's need to be understood—hypothetically and within its "as if" metaphoricity—as essential. Graff rightly urges us to "think of literary theory not as a set of systematic principles, necessarily, or a founding philosophy, but simply as an inquiry into assumptions, premises, and legitimate principles and concepts" (1987, 252). Yet all too often the energy and unruliness of a text disappear to the hegemonic claims made by followers of Marx, Lacan, and Foucault.

Jameson believes that if we can locate the master narrative of a particular age, we can get at the political unconscious. For him, "only Marxism can give us an adequate account of the essential *mystery* of the cultural past." He disdains the notion of freedom from the "omnipresence of history and the implacable influence of the social" (1981, 19–20). Is Jameson's claim for Marxism an *ethical* approach toward texts and the variety of lived life? Or is such a reductive and extravagant approach unethical in its distortion of the specificities and differences of human experience? As an Aristotelian and pluralist, I ask why rewrite, resolve, and homogenize the whole rich and random multiple realities of concrete everyday experience into a monolithic story of the political unconscious?

ETHICS OF READING

Let me state my credo. I believe that the close reading of texts—both from an authorial and resistant perspective—enables us to perceive more clearly; I believe in a continuity between reading texts and reading lives. I believe that the activity of critical thinking—not merely literary criticism—can be taught by the analysis of language. I believe in the place of the aesthetic. I believe that we can enter into imagined worlds and learn from them. Following Aristotle, I believe that the aesthetic, ethical, and political are inextricably linked.

In considering ethical reading, I want to differentiate between an ethics *of* reading and an ethics *in* reading. For me, an ethics *of* reading includes acknowledging who we are and what are our biases and interests. An ethics of reading speaks of our reading as if, no matter how brilliant, it were proposing some possibilities rather than providing Daniel's prophetic reading of handwriting on the wall; it means reading from multiple perspectives, or at least empathetically entering into the readings of those who are situated differently. For me, an ethics *in* reading would try to understand what the author was saying to his or her original imagined audience and why, as well as how the actual polyauditory audience might have responded and for what reasons. An ethics in reading is different from but, in its attention to a value-oriented epistemology, related to an ethics of reading. An ethics in reading implies attention to moral issues generated by the events described within an imagined world. It asks what ethical questions are involved in the act of transforming life into art, and notices such issues as Pound's anti-Semitism and the patronizing racism of some American nineteenth- and early-twentieth-century writers. What we choose to read and especially what to include on syllabi have an ethical dimension. Thus, I will choose to select other Conrad works for my undergraduate lecture course than the unfortunately titled *The Nigger of the Narcissus*.

Why did ethics disappear from the universe of literary studies? Was it in part the disillusionment of the Vietnam War that seemed to give the lie to the view after the Second World War that we could cultivate our minds and control our lives following the defeat of the Nazis and the Japanese? As critics, we once addressed the ethics of reading and the ethics in reading and that in part is what Arnold meant by "high seriousness" and Leavis by such phrases as "tangible realism" and "bracing moralism" and Trilling by "the hum and buzz of implication." All theory is in part disguised autobiography and the current emphasis on the meaningless of language and on the overwhelming power of history to produce cultural effects without allowing room for explanations that stress creative intelligence, as well as on the transformation of the author into author-function reflects a kind of skepticism about human agency; such skepticism at times approaches a harsh, abrasive ahumanistic cynicism.

Let me continue my credo: literary meaning depends on a trialogue among (1) authorial intention and interest; (2) the formal text produced by the author for a specific historical audience; and (3) the responses of a particular reader in a specific time. Texts mediate and condense anterior worlds and authors' psyches. The condensation is presented by words, words that are a web of signs but that signify something beyond themselves; within a text, words signify differently. Some words and phrases almost summon a visible presence, others are elusive or even may barely matter in the terms of representation—as in Joyce's encyclopedic catalogues in "Cyclops" (1922). The context of any discourse determines the meaning—or should we say the epistemological and semiological value of the word or sentence. And once we use the word *value*, are we not saying that words have an ethical quotient? Human agency—on the part of author, reader, or characters within real or imagined worlds—derives in part from will, from the idiosyncrasies of human psyche and, in part, on cultural forces beyond the control of the individual. That is another way of saying that language is constituted and constituting, although it gives subjective human agency to the act of constituting. While we need to be alert to the implications of racist, sexist, and anti-Semitic nuances, we also need to stress reading the words on the page in terms of the demands made by the text's context and form—in particular, by its structure of effects, or what I have called the *doesness* of the text.

If self-awareness of oneself and one's relationship to family and community—including one's responsibilities, commitments, and values—is part of the ethical life, then reading contributes to greater self-understanding. Reading complements one's experience by enabling us to live lives beyond those we live and experience emotions that are not ours; it heightens one's perspicacity by enabling us to watch *figures*—tropes, that is, personifications of our fellow humans—who are not ourselves, but like ourselves. For me, books are written about humans by humans for humans, and elaborate "theories" that ignore narrative and representational aspects of literature in favor of rhetorical, deconstructive, or politically correct readings are unsatisfactory.

Let us welcome the turn to considering the relation between literature and theory but insist with Aristotle on the interrelationship of the political, aesthetic, and ethical. In prior academic generations our insulation from politics was mirrored in the supposedly objective and hermetic world of art, and New Criticism (and in more recent times deconstruction) often encouraged the binary opposition between art and life. For me, the intentional fallacy has always been to ignore how art is self-expressive and the affective fallacy has always been to ignore real readers reading. We need to worry about authors: *the failure to do so* was, for me, another version of the intentional or biographical fallacy—or how real readers read—*the failure to do so* was, for me, the affective fallacy. For New Criticism, the text existed in a Platonic world of ideas and was resolved in a unity that provided an aesthetic alternative to the political chaos—the Depression, the world wars, the threat of nuclear war, the Vietnam War—that raged outside. Later, at the time of the totalizing vision of Reaganomics, accumulation of ostentatious wealth, and the patronizing bankruptcy of Bushery, texts were reexamined—sometimes by smug and patronizing deconstructive picaros—for their rhetorical subtext that undermined unity and order.

Humanists have also been attacked implicitly and explicitly for not opening up the canon or profession on their watch. Yet notwithstanding resistance from others in their generation, in the 1960s and 1970s it was often liberal humanists—espousing free speech, respect for others, the value of listening, tolerance to diversity of ideas—who opened the door to the theorists and pushed for inclusion of diverse perspectives, including feminism and Marxism, and who welcomed women and minorities. But we intellectuals differ from cannibals in that cannibals eat only their enemies and we eat our friends, particularly our elders, our predecessors, our teachers. For some, committing intellectual matricide and patricide has become a ritual of our profession. At times the younger turn on their own because we are not as zealous as they in pursuing imagined ancient enemies. Are not we like the Torajans of Sulawesi, who celebrate funerals by killing a member of a village that contains, as tradition has it, the weakest members of their tribe because, according to oral history, centuries ago that village didn't join the rest of the Torajans in a war against their ancient enemy, the Bugis? Do we not need to remember that all of us literary intellectuals belong to that odd collection of freemasons whose secret rituals consist of reading books, speaking about them to colleagues and students, and writing articles and books about them?

Why have concepts like objective truth, essence, nature, identity, and teleology—once progressive ideas that insisted on the separation of the aesthetic from the political—become labeled conservative and reactionary ideas? As Graff remarks: "If one wished, a plausible case could be made for the view that the interpretive *objectionists* are the real heirs of the radical tradition which has sought to secularize and demystify the concept of meaning, and that the deconstructionists are carrying on a rearguard attempt to preserve some element of linguistic mystery from secularization" (1983, 153).

How has the evidentiary test for testing our readings changed? Dominick La Capra has cautioned against overuse of "world-in-a-grain-of-sand anecdotes" as if these anecdotes imply universals; we should be as wary about finding the secret of a text in a few subversive lines. In the name of interesting or extravagant readings, have we strictly differentiated between logical argument and random association? Have we installed the critic/theorist as *vates* and substituted paralogic for logic? As La Capra writes, "Old historicism sometimes placed a premium on aimless exhaustiveness and contextualization. New historicism often opts for a rather precious play of analogies, anecdotes and associations" (1989, 7).

Graff has commendably argued that those of us who use contemporary theory need to defend the truth claims of our readings. In the act of doing so, do we not need to consider in our arguments issues such as narrative cohesion, agency, aesthetic achievement, and authorial intention? On the whole, feminist and postcolonial readings that draw upon the texture—I use that word deliberately—of lived experience more frequently meet the truth test than those extravagant readings that place being "interesting" before respect for what the text says. The glory of the best of resistant readings—gay, new historical, feminist—is that they often meet the test and provide logical, plausible readings based on evidence.

When we enter into an imagined world, we become involved with what Nadine Gordimer has called "the substance of living from which the artist draws his vision," and our criticism must speak to that "substance of living" (1981, n.p.). In Third World and postcolonial literature—and in politically engaged texts like *Night*—this involvement is much more intense. Thus the recent interest in postcolonial and Third World literature—accelerated by Soyinka's and Wolcott's Nobel prize—challenges the tenets of deconstruction. Literature written at the political edge reminds us what literature has always been about: urgency, commitment, tension, and feeling. Indeed, at times have we not transferred those emotions to parochial critical debate rather than to our responses to literature? While it may not be completely irrelevant to talk about gaps, fissures, and enigmas and about the free play of signifiers in the poetry of Wally Serote ("Death Survey") and Don Mattera ("Singing Fools"), we must focus, too, on their status as persecuted blacks in South Africa

and the pain and alienation that they feel in the face of that persecu-
tion. Nadine Gordimer has written—and Joyce might have said the
same thing about Ireland—"It is from the daily life of South Africa
that there have come the conditions of profound alienation which
prevail among South African artists." When discussing politically
engaged literature—be it Soyinka, Gordimer, or Wiesel—we need
to recuperate historical circumstances and understand the writer's
ordering of that history in his or her imagined world. We need to
know not merely what patterns of provisional representation are
created by language but the historical, political, and social ground
of that representation. We need to be open to hearing the often un-
sophisticated and unironical voice of pain, angst, and fear.

When we read literature we journey into an imagined land, while
at the same time remaining home. Reading is a kind of imaginative
traveling; unlike real traveling, it allows us to transport ourselves
immediately back "home." Travel is immersive; home is reflective.
How we take our imaginative journeys depends on how we are
trained to read: what we as readers do with the available data—how
we sort it out and make sense of it. Although the text has a kind of
stability because it cannot *change*, our ways of speaking about texts
are always somewhat metaphoric.

Aristotle, we recall, inextricably linked the ethical and the aesthetic—seemingly opposites. As he puts it in *The Poetics*,
"Poetry"—by which he means imaginative forms such as tragedy
and epic—"tends to express the universal, history the particular.
By the universal I mean how a person of a certain type will on occasion speak or act, according to the law of probability or necessity"
(1958, 205). His very stipulations about what constitutes a good
tragedy imply that the artist has an ethical responsibility to his audience to provide a certain kind of action within a set of conventions.
What interests Aristotle is what actions reveal about character:
"Character is that which reveals moral purpose, showing what
kinds of things a man chooses or avoids. . . . Any speech or action
that manifests moral purpose of any kind will be expressive of character." And this includes, I propose, any narrative, including narrative about the history of the profession or about a particular theory.

MULTICULTURALISM AND CANONICITY

With the welcome return to mimesis and representation, cultural
criticism has opened the door once again to historicizing. Culture is

dynamic, and at any given point culture is heteroglossic, a dialogue of diverse thoughts, feelings, goals, and values. According to Isaiah Berlin, "Cultures—the sense of what the world meant to societies, of men's and women's collective sense of themselves in relation to others and the environment, that which affects particular forms of thought, feeling, behavior, action—. . . cultures differ" (1992, 50). We need to honor cultural differences and respect the claims of cultural enclaves. Clifford Geertz has written, "The problem of integration of cultural life becomes one of making it possible for people inhabiting different worlds to have a genuine, and reciprocal, impact upon one another" (1983, 168). While I respect and welcome other stories of culture and understand that civilization has many components, I have been arguing for a cultural criticism that takes seriously the notion of canons, periods, and culture as the best that was thought and created during a period of civilization.

Let us turn to the concept of canon. Canon needs to be an evolving concept, a house with many windows and doors, rather than a mausoleum. Within my pluralistic concept of canon there is room for enclaves to establish their own subcanons. I still value the major Western texts—the plays of Shakespeare, the Homeric epic, *Paradise Lost*, the great metaphysical and romantic poems, the masterworks of the novel like *Emma*, *Wuthering Heights*, *Jane Eyre*, *Middlemarch*, *Bleak House*, *Lord Jim*, *Ulysses*, and *To the Lighthouse*—but can we not within a healthy pluralism teach some common texts and speak to each of our legitimate and multicultural interests in other texts? A curriculum, I suggest, can be something of a smorgasbord, and our courses—and maybe syllabi—need to have room for teachers and students to pursue their own interests.

The breakdown into enclaves and tribes—the effect, in part, of the end of the binary cold war struggle between two superpowers—in the latter part of the twentieth century takes the form of curricula battles between people who once thought that they had more in common than they had differences. If we are not careful, the Balkanization of English departments means we will talk to only those in our ethnic neighborhood. Often in a spirit of intolerance, political enclaves seek to *cleanse* the syllabi of objectionable texts—whether it be objectionable works by dead white males or humanistic theorists. Canonical texts become—as Clifford wrote of what the West had become for Edward Said—"a play of projections, doublings, idealizations, and rejections of a complex, shifting otherness" (Clifford 1988, 272). The debate about who owns the syllabi and who owns the curricula and canon parallels the debate about who owns the land, whether it be the land of Northern Ireland, Hawaii, Palestine, or Bosnia and Herzegovina. It is as if cultural stratification were akin to geological stratification. In nineteenth-century American studies, there is a black and female and Hispanic and Indian canon and cultural history that is at once part of and separate from the prevailing hegemonic cultural history. For while the same groups inhabited the same space at the same time, their cultural history is reflected and refracted, displaced, sublimated, and transposed in different texts.

HEART OF DARKNESS

Let us define lines of inquiry to pursue in our reading and teaching of *Heart of Darkness*. Of course, we should regard the questions that follow as only instances of the multiple possibilities of a pluralistic approach. Let us think of these questions as concentric circles of inquiry, circles that vary in their relevance from reading to reading by one reader, from reader to reader, and from passage to passage. Let me point out, too, that my questions stress the inseparability of ethical, aesthetic, political, and contextual issues, and that the order of the questions is not meant to indicate the relative importance of each question or questions.[2]

1. How is *Heart of Darkness* a personal story written out of moral urgency that reflects Conrad's Congo experience and his own epistemological and psychological inquiry at a time of personal crisis in 1898? How can we use the Congo diary and Conrad's letters to relate his life and work? How is Marlow a surrogate for Conrad? If we see Marlow as a fictional surrogate for Conrad, how does such an approach relate to the fiction making and masques of the late 1890s and the first decade of the twentieth century, as instanced in Wilde's *The Decay of Lying*, Yeats's poems, and Joyce's use of Stephen Dedalus?

2. How is *Heart of Darkness* a voyage of Marlow's self-discovery? Do we need to stress how that self-discovery takes place in a political frame and is a political reawakening? Conrad's narrative enacts the *value* that the Africans and Europeans share a common

humanity: the English too were once natives conquered by the Romans and England too was once one of the dark places of the earth. Moreover, Europeans not only require laws and rules to restrain their atavistic impulses, but they become more monstrous than those they profess to civilize. Finally, terms like "savage" and "barbarian" are arbitrary designations by imperialists who in fact deserve these epithets more than the natives.

3. How is *Heart of Darkness* a political novel concerned with the Belgian King Leopold's rapacious exploitation of the Congo? What attitudes do imperialists take to the natives and why? How is it, as Marxists would contend, a story about the "commodity fetishism" of later capitalism? Is it, as Chinua Achebe has claimed, a racist drama whose images reinforce white stereotypes about the dichotomy of black and white? Is *Heart of Darkness* an imperialistic romance about the conquest of Africa? Or is it more accurate to stress how it is an ironic inversion, a bathetic reification, of such a genre? Are black and white and light and dark always equated with the polarity of civilization and savagery, good and evil, corrupt and innocent, or is the dialectic of images more subtle than that?

Conrad plays on the clichés and shibboleths of his era, when Africa was the "dark continent"—the place of mystery and secrets—and the primitive continent where passions and emotions dominated reason and intellect. He asks us to consider whether we can cross cultural boundaries without transgressing them, for in situating himself in response to imperialistic exploitation, is Marlow able to separate himself from colonial domination? And can we as Westerners teach a story like *Heart of Darkness* in a non-Western setting without reenscribing ourselves as colonialists? When we teach *Heart of Darkness*, are we in the same position as Western museums displaying non-Western art, that is, are we invading a different culture with our texts about colonialism? *But not so fast.* For his time Conrad was avant-garde in acknowledging that at times Africans were more controlled and ethically advanced than Westerners; he, like Gauguin, knew that their cultural practices and their art—chants, dance, drumming—were alien to Western concepts of display, that their art was religious in function and linked daily experience to abstract beliefs, and that their art was used performatively in funerals, weddings, and initiation rites.

Heart of Darkness speaks with passion to the issues of colonialism and empire. Whether in Ireland, Malay, or Africa, Western colonialism in the name of civilization despoils the people and the land it touches. *Heart of Darkness* debunks the concept of the white man's burden and shows how the concept of empire is a sham. Conrad chooses to show Kurtz's "Exterminate the Brutes" as a stunning abandonment of the moral pretensions on which imperialism is based. Kurtz's radical transformation exposes his reductive perspective and that of Marlow, King Leopold of Belgium, other Europeans—indeed, all of us who would seek to adopt a position where one culture views another from an iconoclastic stance.

4. How is the disrupted narrative, the circumlocutious syntax, and the alternation between impressionistic and graphic language indicative of modernism? Should we also not think of *Heart of Darkness* as part of the awareness of modern artists that multiple perspectives are necessary? After all, in 1895 Conrad wrote, "Another man's truth is a dismal lie to me" (Jean-Aubrey 1927, 1: 184). We need to stress how it takes issue with Victorian assumptions about univocal truth and a divinely ordered world. Conrad's use of the dramatized consciousness of Marlow reflects his awareness that "we live as we dream—alone," and the concomitant awareness— seen in the development of cubism and Joyce's ventriloquy in *Ulysses*—that one perspective is not enough.

Picasso's and Braque's cubist experiments demonstrate how they, too, are trying to achieve multiple perspectives. Conrad, too, was freeing black and white from the traditional morphology of color, just as the fauvists and cubists were freeing traditional ideas of representation from the morphology of color. Conrad is also freeing his language from the morphology of representation—as in his use of adjectives for purely affective rather than descriptive reasons. Conrad's use of allegorized rather than nominalistic adjectives, such as "subtle" and "unspeakable," invites the frame narrator and Conrad's readers to respond in terms of their own experiences and to validate in their responses that they, too, dream alone. When creating his Congo, Conrad knew Gauguin's 1893 Tahitian journal *Noa, Noa* and was influenced by that and perhaps Gauguin's paintings. Gauguin anticipated Picasso and other modernists in seeing the elemental and magical aspects of primitive lives as well as their passion, simplicity, and naturalness.

5. How does *Heart of Darkness* relate to the intellectual history of modernism? How is Kurtz indicative of the Nietzschean will-to-power that was a major strand of the intellectual fabric of imperial-

ism and fascism? How does Conrad's text relate to his contemporary Freud's probing of the unconscious? How does *Heart of Darkness* speak to the breakdown of moral certainty, the sense that each of us lives in a closed circle, and the consequent fear of solipsism? Conrad feared that each of us is locked in his or her own perceptions and despaired in his letters that even language will not help us reach out to others. Thus, the fear that "we live as we dream—alone" is also an idea that recurs throughout the period of early modernism, a period in which humans felt, to quote F. H. Bradley, that "my experience is a closed circle; a circle closed on the outside. . . . In brief . . . the whole world for each is peculiar and private to that soul" (1893, 346). That the frame narrator can tell the story shows that Marlow has communicated with someone and offers a partial antidote to the terrifying fear of isolation and silence that haunted Conrad.

6. How is *Heart of Darkness* a comment on the idea of social Darwinism that mankind was evolving into something better and better? *Heart of Darkness* refutes the position that history was evolving historically upward. Recall Conrad's famous 1897 letter about the world as a knitting machine, where the ironic trope of the world as a machine is a rebuttal to Christianity: "It knits us in and it knits us out. It has knitted time, space, pain, death, corruption, despair and all the illusions—and nothing matters. I'll admit however that to look at the remorseless process is sometimes amusing" (Jean-Aubrey 1927, 1: 215–16). Conrad uses this elaborate ironic trope to speak to the late Victorian belief that the Industrial Revolution is part of an upwardly evolving teleology; this belief is really a kind of social Darwinism. According to Conrad, humankind would like to believe in a providentially ordered world vertically descending from a benevolent God—that is, to believe in an embroidered world. But, Conrad believed, we actually inhabit a temporally defined horizontal dimension within an amoral, indifferent universe—"the remorseless process."

7. How would a pluralistic approach address the meaning of "The horror! The horror!" as a part of an evolving agon that generates a structure of affects? Let us look at "The horror! The horror!" in the context of what precedes. That Kurtz has achieved a "moral victory" may very well be a necessary illusion for Marlow. But did Kurtz pronounce a verdict on his reversion to primitivism and achieve the "supreme moment of complete knowledge" (Conrad

1926, 149)? Or is this what Marlow desperately wants to believe? Coming from a man who "could get himself to believe anything," how credible is Marlow's interpretation that "The horror! The horror!" is "an affirmation, a moral victory paid for by innumerable defeats, by abominable terrors, by abominable satisfactions" (151)? When Kurtz had enigmatically muttered, "Live rightly, die, die . . . ," Marlow had wondered, "Was he rehearsing some speech in his sleep, or was it a fragment of a phrase from some newspaper article?" (148). Marlow had just remarked that Kurtz's voice "survived his strength to hide in the magnificent folds of eloquence the barren darkness of his heart" (147). If Kurtz had kicked himself loose of the earth, how can Kurtz pronounce a verdict on his ignominious return to civilization or an exclamation elicited from a vision of his own imminent death? For the reader—the reader responding to the inextricable relationship between the ethical and the aesthetic in Conrad's text—Kurtz remains a symbol of how the human ego can expand infinitely to the point where it tries to will its own apotheosis.

8. In what ways does *Heart of Darkness* reveal overt and covert sexist attitudes? Is *Heart of Darkness* a sexist document? Brantlinger writes, "The voices that come from the heart of darkness are almost exclusively white and male, as usual in imperialist texts" (1988, 271). In a situation where opportunities for heterosexuality are limited, what does *Heart of Darkness* say about male bonding among the whites and about miscegenation? Are we offended that one of Kurtz's supposedly "abominable practices" is the taking of a savage mistress? If we understand Marlow's patronizing attitude toward women as naive and simple, can we not use the text to show the difference between authorial and resistant readings, between how texts are read when they are written and how they are read now? Does the lie to the Intended reveal Marlow's sexism? Is Conrad aware of Marlow's sexual stereotyping, even if he means the lie to the Intended to be a crucial moment of self-definition for Marlow? We need to examine the assumptions about women that dominate this final episode, and to align them with the passage when he tells us that the women are always "out of touch with truth." But, of course, the tale dramatized that all of us live in a world of our own, and none of us is in a position to patronize the other, be it natives, women, or others who go to the Congo armed with ideals.

9. How is *Heart of Darkness* a heteroglossic text embodying di-

verse modes of discourse? Marlow's recurring nightmare begins not only to compete with his effort to use language discursively and mimetically, but to establish a separate, more powerful telling. The narrative includes the semiotics of a primitive culture: gestures of the savage mistress and the Intended; the beating of the drums, the shrill cry of the sorrowing savages; and the development of Kurtz into Marlow's own symbol of moral darkness and atavistic reversion. This more inclusive tale, not so much told as performed by Marlow as he strains for the signs and symbols that will make his experience intelligible, transcends his more conventional discourse. Conrad shows that these instinctive and passionate outbursts, taking the form of gestures, chants, and litany, represent a tradition, a core of experience, that civilized man has debased.

TEACHING CONRAD

Finally, why do we continue to teach and read Conrad? Does the concept of canon have value? Is it not the very kinds of urgent questions—and, yes, relevance to us and to our students' *minds*—that *Heart of Darkness* elicits that gives it value today? We need a criticism that, as Martha Nussbaum has put it, "talks of human lives and choices as if they matter to us all. . . . [Literature] speaks about *us*, about our lives and choices and emotions, about our social existence and the totality of our connections. As Aristotle observed, it is deep and conducive to our inquiry about how to live, because it does not simply (as history does) record that this event happened, it searches for patterns of possibility—of choice, and circumstance, and the interaction between choice and circumstance—that turn up in human lives with such a persistence that they must be regarded as *our* possibilities" (Nussbaum 1989, 61). A study of modernist culture and the colonial Congo, Conrad's *Heart of Darkness* also speaks to our culture and raises urgent issues for us. Is that not why we read it, even as we consign some former canonical texts to the margins? Because it is an urgent political drama, because it raises questions of racial and sexual identity, and because it is a wonderful story that probes our identity with our human antecedents, *Heart of Darkness* lives for us as surely as Kurtz lives for Marlow, and Marlow lives for the narrator.

What does Marlow's reading of Kurtz teach us about our reading of texts and lives? As an allegory of reading, *Heart of Darkness* resists easy simplifications and one-dimensional readings, resists attempts to explain in either/or terms. Even as *Heart of Darkness* remains a text that raises questions about the possibility of meaning, it suggests the plenitude of meaning. Just as Marlow gradually moves from seeing a drama of values to living a drama of character, so as readers do we. Like him, we make the journey from spectator to participant. Are we not trying to make sense of Marlow as he is trying to make sense of Kurtz? And are we not also trying to make sense of the frame narrator who is trying to make sense of Marlow making sense of Kurtz? Does not the tale's emphasis on choosing a sign for our systems of meaning call attention to the arbitrary nature of choosing a framing sign and make us aware of the need for multiple perspectives? Do we not learn how one invests with value something not seen or known in preference to the ugly reality that confronts us? Is not Conrad's ironic parable about belief itself, including the Christian belief in whose name much of imperialism was carried on? Thus, in essence, the tale urges us toward a pluralistic perspective. Finally, one-dimensional readings bend to the need for a pluralistic reading that takes account of Marlow's disillusionment and his magnetic attraction to Kurtz as the nightmare of his choice. For Conrad has turned a story about a present journey to Africa into a journey through Europe's past, as well as into each human being's primitive psyche. Our students remind us that narrative, story, and response in human and ethical terms triumph over excessively ideological readings. Our students remind us, too, of the need to link hermeneutics and rhetoricity; for them, "bits of absurd sentences" of their reading (Conrad 1926, 46)—to use Marlow's words to describe what he hears from the manager and the manager's uncle and tries to *read* in terms of his experience—need to be understood in terms of our most fundamental text: the story of our own lives.

CONCLUSION

I conclude with a scene from the book of Daniel when the Babylonian king Belshazzar is feasting and drinking from sacred vessels that his father Nebuchadnezzar plundered from the Holy Jewish Temple in Jerusalem; suddenly a hand unattached to a body appears and writes mysterious words on the wall: "Mene, Mene, Tekel, Upharsin." But neither Belshazzar nor his followers can understand the words, which seem to be written in an unknown tongue. So, desperate to know what has been written, Belshazzar summons Daniel, who has a reputation for wisdom. Daniel can read the words, which are in an early Semitic language, Aramaic, from which Hebrew is derived. Literally, Daniel explains, the words mean "numbered, numbered, weighed, and divided." But Daniel offers an ethical interpretation, foretelling the destruction of Belshazzar and his kingdom. Daniel's story of reading is a prophecy: "God hath numbered thy [Belshazzar's] kingdom, and brought it to an end; thou art weighed in the balances, and found wanting. Thy kingdom is divided, and given to the Medes and the Persians." In doing so, Daniel acts as a literary critic with an ethical bent and tells Belshazzar a story of reading.

Let us use the mysterious words that appear to Belshazzar and that require an interpretation as a parable of what readers must do. While Daniel's prophecy comes true, is it because Daniel knows and speaks God's will or because he is lucky? In any case, because most of us do not read texts with a sense that God has blessed our readings, we must draw upon our own intelligence, ethics, imagination, perspicacity, and experience. Whenever we read texts—or life experiences—we are a little bit like Daniel. Snippets of texts require that they be read, and yet they always remain partially understood or at least open to diverse interpretations. Texts—and our life experiences—cry out for understanding even as they resist our understanding. Since we cannot call upon Daniel, we have to be our own Daniels and do the work ourselves. To be sure, there are commentators and teachers—and theorists—who would be our Daniel, and we should make use of them. But, finally, we must interpret our words and experiences according to our own perspectives and believe in our intelligence, imagination, and ethics. Occasionally, we have works like Joyce's *Ulysses* or *Finnegans Wake* or difficult poems like Wallace Stevens's *Notes toward a Supreme Fiction* (or, for some of us, an organic chemistry textbook), which seem to require the presence of an external Daniel; but even these reveal their mysteries to an experienced reader. Words that we read may have never before appeared to us in the context in which we see them now; even if we have read them before, rereading puts them in a new context, for we have inevitably changed. As for Belshazzar, for us words may have no prior significance other than their own manifestation, or, more likely, they may refer to something with which we are familiar. But they must always be understood anew and brought within the ken of our experience and values.

NOTES

1. I have explored these distinctions in depth in my book *The Case for a Humanistic Poetics*, (1991). See also my "Culture, Canoncity and Pluralism: A Humanistic Perspective on Professing English" (1992a).

2. Because of space limitations, my responses need to be limited, but I refer readers to my "Teaching *Heart of Darkness*: Towards a Pluralistic Perspective" (1992b).

WORKS CITED

Achebe, Chinua. 1977. "An Image of Africa." *Massachusetts Review* 18(4): 782–94.

Aristotle. 1958. *Poetics*. Trans. S. H. Butcher, ed. Mark Schorer, Josephine Miles, and Gordon McKenzie. New York: Harcourt, Brace and World.

Berlin, Isaiah. 1992. "Philosophy and Life: An Interview." New York Review 39(10): 46–54.

Bradley, F. H. 1893. *Appearance and Reality: A Metaphysical Essay.* London.

Brantlinger, Patrick. 1988. *Rule of Darkness: British Literature and Imperialism, 1830–1914*. Ithaca: Cornell University Press.

Clifford, James. 1988. *The Predicament of Culture: Twentieth Century Ethnography, Literature, and Art.* Cambridge: Harvard University Press.

Conrad, Joseph. 1926. *Heart of Darkness*. Garden City, N.Y.: Doubleday.

Geertz, Clifford. 1983. *Local Knowledge: Further Essays in Interpretive Anthropology*. New York: Basic Books.

Gordimer, Nadine. 1981. "The Arts in Adversity: Apprentices of Freedom." *New Society* 24(31): n.p.

Graff, Gerald. 1983. "The Pseudo-Politics of Interpretation." *The Politics of Interpretation.* In *The Politics of Interpretation,* ed. W. J. T. Mitchell. Chicago: University of Chicago Press.

———. 1987. *Professing English: An Institutional History.* Chicago: University of Chicago Press.

Jameson, Fredric. 1981. *The Political Unconscious: Narrative as a Socially Symbolic Art.* Ithaca: Cornell University Press.

Jean-Aubrey, G. 1927. *Joseph Conrad: Life and Letters.* 2 vols. Garden City, N.Y.: Doubleday.

La Capra, Dominick. 1989. "On the Line: Between History and Criticism." *PMLA: Profession 89:* 4–9.

Nussbaum, Martha. 1989. "Perceptive Equilibrium: Literary Theory and Ethical Theory." In *The Future of Literary Theory*, ed. Ralph Cohen. New York: Routledge.

Rosensweig, Saul. 1993. "Freud, Jung and Hall the King-Maker." *New York Times Book Section*, 24 January 1, 20.

Schwarz, Daniel R. 1987. *Reading Joyce's "Ulysses."* New York: St. Martin's Press.

———. 1991. *The Case for a Humanistic Poetics*. London: Macmillan.

———. 1992a. "Culture, Canonocity and Pluralism: A Humanistic Perspective on Professing English." *Texas Studies in Language and Literature* 34(1): 149–75.

———. 1992b. "Teaching *Heart of Darkness*: Towards a Pluralistic Perspective." *Conradiana* 24(3): 190–206.

Wiesel, Elie. 1960. *Night*. Trans. Stella Rodway. New York: Hill and Wang.

The Radical Tradition of Humanistic Consciousness

ROBERT M. TORRANCE

Humanism is humiliated or dead. Consequence: *we must establish it anew.*

—Thomas Mann, 26 June 1930

The story is told—no doubt apocryphal to begin with, and distorted through many retellings and through the fallibility of memory; but such is the stuff of any good legend—that President Eliot of Harvard once asked Professor William James what he would suggest as an inscription to be placed above the main entrance to the newly constructed Emerson Hall; James promptly replied, "Man is the measure of all things." Imagine, then, his surprise, looking up at the finished building, to find the inscription that the dour President had chosen read (and still reads): "What is man, that thou art mindful of him?"

THOUGH *HUMANITAS*, IN THE EXTENDED SENSE OF "LIBERAL EDUcation," "general culture," or "human studies," goes back to the ancient Romans, for whom it was an equivalent of Greek *paideia*—especially for Cicero, who several times associates this cardinal quality of the educated human being with *studium* (*De Oratore* II.60256; *Pro Caelio* 10.24)—and although *humanista*, in the sense of a student and teacher of the newly revived Greek and Roman classics (the *studia humanitatis* or *litterae humaniores*) dates from the late fifteenth century and was retroactively applied to Petrarch and others in the century before, the noun *Humanismus* was not coined until 1808, by the German educator J. J. Niethammer, "to express the emphasis on the Greek and Latin classics in secondary education, as against the rising demands for a practical and more scientific education" (Kristeller 1961, 9). Since then, and especially in our own century, "humanism" has been used in such a variety of senses as to seem nearly senseless: for what can mean almost

anything—except, perhaps, the quaintly antiquated notion of studying the Greeks and Romans—soon threatens to mean nothing at all.

Thus humanism often connotes nothing more than a vague hu-
maneness or humanitarianism—the very target at which Irving
Babbitt and his fellow New Humanists of the early twentieth century fired their most irate missiles. A more understandable distortion is the shibboleth of "secular humanism"—the bugbear of
Christian fundamentalists—thought to depreciate religion by substituting the human for the (nonexistent) divine or, alternatively, by
exalting the human in place of the divine: more understandable,
since many writers of atheistic bent (from the young Karl Marx of
the 1844 manuscripts [1964] to the Jean-Paul Sartre of *L'Existenti-
alisme est un humanisme* [1948] to Corliss Lamont [1982], Paul
Kurtz [1994], and other spokesmen for the American Humanist Association and signatories of its humanist manifestos) are among
those who have been prominently declared, or have militantly declared themselves, humanists. Yet not only is the identification of
humanists with secular opponents of religion in general and Christianity in particular historically unjustified—though humanists of
the Renaissance may indeed have esteemed more highly than their
medieval predecessors "pagan" and this-worldly values associated
with antiquity, the most eminent of them, from Petrarch to More
and Erasmus (1957) to Milton, were explicitly Christian humanists—but twentieth-century religious thinkers such as Jacques Maritain have raised the standard of humanism no less than have their
atheistic counterparts. Psychoanalysts, including Erich Fromm
(1962) and Viktor Frankl (1978), have likewise espoused variants
of this pliable ism in a spectrum stretching from Communist to
Catholic. Toward religious supernaturalism as toward scientific naturalism, modern humanists have expressed attitudes from denuncia-
tion to exaltation, further blurring any sense of a shared identity.

And if humanism has seen its meanings expand beyond recognition, the "humanities"—amorphous residues of the once rigorous
and central *studia humanitatis*—have often become similarly disso-
ciated from any precise discipline. Just as branches of "natural philosophy" peeled away, one by one, to become natural sciences as
they became more exact, so the humanities today can not implausi-
bly seem the squishy remnant left over after the "soft" social and
the "hard" natural sciences have been stripped away: an impression
confirmed no less by conservatives who fulminate against science

as alien to the humanities than by radicals of the cultural studies
flank who no less absurdly assert that in the "social construction of
reality" there is no distinction between them.

Despite or because of its plasticity, however, throughout much
of the earlier twentieth century the situation of humanism differed
strikingly from that of recent decades in being a matter of intense
debate and discussion by prominent intellectuals, proponents and
opponents alike. The fact that so many thinkers of seemingly anti-
thetical views flocked to its colors was an indication of the high
esteem associated with a term of such distinguished pedigree, so
that even those generally hostile to its prevalent values, such as T. S.
Eliot, hastened, like Maritain, to proclaim their opposing views a
"true" or "pure" humanism (1950). Books and essays with "humanism" in their titles crowded the library shelves. In contrast, the
term has recently seemed a dead letter, if not a term of opprobrium,
and the books discussing it have gathered dust on the shelves: Irving Babbitt (1908, 1919), Paul Elmer More (1936), and many others of humanist persuasion, who once aroused articulate passions
pro and con, have melted away from current awareness like the
snows of yesteryear, leaving little evident trace. Humanism is now
threatened by the worst fates of all, disdain, neglect, and irrele-
vance. How has this come to be? And what role, if any, can some
form of humanism (if any can be salvaged) play in today's largely
indifferent intellectual world?

A brief chapter of this kind can of course offer no more than a
few tentative suggestions in answer to such large questions. To
begin with, the eclipse in the last three or four decades of humanism
as a term of widespread (though never universal) approbation and
high (though hotly disputed) honor, owes much to the depreciation
of the human itself, which has roots in the nihilisms of an earlier
age but which has greatly intensified since Auschwitz and Hiro-
shima. What can the muddled pieties of academic and literary humanism weigh against the massive testimony of man's inhumanity?
We "must not blur the possibility," George Steiner writes (1996,
345), "that the death-camps and the world's indifference to them
marked the failure of a crucial experiment: man's effort to become
fully human." Deeply rooted though these fundamental doubts and
revulsions may be, however, they are not unique to our time: the
unspeakable atrocities of war and extermination—by Hitler or Stalin, Mao or Pol Pot—differ in scope and ruthless efficiency but not

in kind (as the Book of Judges, Thucydides' Melian dialogue [*History* VII. 84–116], and Euripides' *Trojan Women* attest) from those of earlier ages, which were fully aware of the human capacity for inhumanity (*homo homini lupus*: "man to man is a wolf"), yet could affirm the enduring value of the human in the face of human depravity. And poetry has, after all, somehow been written since Auschwitz.

Knowledge and memory of horrors unprecedented in scope—accentuated, for Americans, by the bitter disillusionments of Vietnam—form an ineradicably dark background for the denigration of lofty humanistic claims in the late twentieth century. So too does the continuing reification of the human being under the impact of technology, of which war and genocide are the most terrible expressions, but which surrounds us in the inescapable daily manipulations of the mass media, advertising, political campaigns, voice synthesizers, telephone menus, health maintenance organizations, and countless other expressions of the ubiquitous dehumanization by which we are blatantly assaulted or subliminally subjected at nearly every moment of our lives. Again, it is the accelerating intensity and pervasiveness, not the fact (or perception) itself, of mechanization that is new, along with the increasing drumbeat of claims for the replacement of human intelligence by the "artificial intelligence" of our own creations, so that, like other machines before it in the ongoing industrial and technological revolutions of modern times, the computer darkly threatens to become a runaway sorcerer's apprentice or Frankenstein's monster to which the merely human being becomes a superfluous appendage.

Such claims, whether in sophisticated scientific or pseudo-scientific formulations or popularized distortions, are themselves expressions of the intellectual reductionisms that have dominated so much of modern discourse, portraying man in terms of some single determining function—economic, social, sexual, behavioral, genetic—by which he is inexorably defined. Against the self-assured assertions of a Marx, a Freud, or a Skinner, each arrogating to his doctrine the incontrovertibility and precision of science, what, after all, are the vague moralisms of a host of piously humanistic Babbitts? The humanist of whatever variety affirms the complexity of man as an integrated whole, embracing seeming contradictions in the singularity of his composite human being: but it is this very complexity that the brash reductionisms of modernity have most contemptuously repudiated. And if the early twentieth century witnessed an incessant competition among such partial visions, arraying the Marxist against the Freudian against the structuralist or behaviorist, or sometimes endeavoring to reconcile or synthesize them, the "postmodernism" of recent decades has further heightened the sense of human fragmentation by being content to string such visions side by side without coordination, treating any claim, it would seem, as equally valid or invalid (for what criterion might we have by which to discriminate?) in the ultimately dogmatic ideology of all-encompassing relativism. It is in this context that the acolytes of Barthes and Foucault, Derrida and de Man, have proclaimed the death of the author, the death of meaning, and the death of man, defining our era as not only post-structuralist and postmodernist, but post-humanist and indeed post-human. What place can there be for humanism when the very concept of the human is deemed an anachronism?

Eagerly responsive to such pronouncements, which make them seem more up-to-date and more relevant, those who profess the humanities at our universities have frequently cast off altogether traditional disciplines (which had tended toward sclerotic reaffirmation of a fixed past) in their enthusiastic embrace of fashionable but dubious theoretical constructs to which any form of humanism, or indeed humanity, appears utterly foreign. Openness to genuinely interdisciplinary studies is a sign of intellectual vitality in a university system hampered by the outdated rigidities of departmental divisions: but the "interdisciplinarity" paraded by many humanists easily becomes a mere magpie's collection of bits and pieces from various disciplines gathered at random—psychoanalytic, Marxist, sociological, sociobiological, feminist, or what have you—in a hodgepodge of jargon leavened with little understanding and little or no correlation of disparate components. Affirmation of the rich diversity of cultures in a multipolar world likewise signals a long overdue broadening of perspective in universities whose studies of literature, history, and philosophy—the core of the humanities curriculum—were long dominated by European tradition to the marginalization or exclusion of others: but the "multiculturalism" currently in vogue tends instead to a *narrowing* of perspective by militant fragmentation of ethnic and gender studies, effectively denying any human commonality in their exaltation of a cultural relativism, or cultural apartheid, that barely masks the politically strident claims of each fragment to superiority (in the name of an Orwellian equality) over each of the others. The lack of shared assumptions and values, or shared disciplinary standards, has often turned hirings and promotions in humanities departments of our universities into naked political scrambles. In my own experience at the University of California at Davis, lofty affirmations of interdisciplinarity yield in practice to parochially myopic penalizing of those who depart from current fashions and whose reputation is not affirmed (in the absence of other criteria) by the self-congratulatory conference circuit satirized in David Lodge's *Small World* (1984) and acerbically portrayed by Camille Paglia in "Junk Bonds and Corporate Raiders" (1992): is it so different at other "research universities"? Will the humanities departments of our universities soon be the least likely place a humanist can hope to find a home before this endangered species becomes extinct?

These observations are far from new and may indeed seem thoroughly hackneyed; yet only in such contexts can we understand the depreciation of humanism in our historical moment. Not that this devaluation is only recent, however: already in the early twentieth century the humanist could seem an antiquated remnant, nor had his standing been wholly secure in the past. Before returning to the question of whether the humanist has any meaningful role to play today or tomorrow, let us look back again at some of his previous permutations.

The fifteenth-century coinage *humanista* was formed, of course, on Latin *humanus*, "human," itself derived from *homo*, "human being"; the humanist's main pursuits, continuing those of his medieval predecessors, were grammar, rhetoric, history, and moral philosophy (natural philosophy, logic, and metaphysics or theology being left largely in the province of the continuators of the medieval Scholastic-Aristotelian tradition). The rediscovery, editing, translation, and commentary of ancient Greek and Latin manuscripts unknown for nearly a millennium in most of western Europe (including all of Homer, almost all of Plato and Plotinus, much of Cicero, and all of Lucretius, Livy, Catallus, and Tacitus that now survives) were the humanist's principal pursuits and sources of prestige, for he was a proud participant in the momentous "revival of learning" or "renaissance" (as it was already being called by the sixteenth century) that immeasurably expanded the scope of European knowledge not only in the "studies of humanity" but in the sciences that lay outside the humanist's domain, yet were themselves revitalized by his discoveries, as by those of his predecessors in the earlier "renaissance" of the twelfth century. Copernicus would have been impossible without Ptolemy, Vesalius without Galen, Kepler without Plato. In their fervor for antiquity and belief that they had renewed its glories, the humanists (like Jacob Burckhardt [1954]) greatly erred, no doubt, in demeaning the intervening "Middle Ages" as a time of benighted ignorance; yet their pride in their own achievement as a shaping force of the new age was not misplaced.

At their worst, the humanists could indeed, and often did, become arrogant pedants prideful with book learning and valuing above all else the ability to write pseudo-Ciceronian Latin prose and pseudo-Virgilian Latin hexameter—to the great detriment of Italian literature in the century after Dante, Petrarch (who rated his Latin epistles and epic far above his vernacular love lyrics), and Boccaccio. In the scornful words of Leonardo da Vinci (1954, 1: 57), "They strut about puffed up and pompous, decked out and adorned not with their own labors but by those of others, and they will not even allow me my own. And if they despise me who am an inventor, how much more should blame be given to themselves, who are not inventors but trumpeters and reciters of the works of others?" Yet not only did the greatest of the humanists, such as Erasmus and More, transcend these limitations in works that shaped the intellectual temper of their times, but Leonardo himself, in both his scientific pursuits (stimulated by Galen and Archimedes) and his painting—like Michelangelo in both poetry and sculpture, and like the foremost vernacular writers of the age, from Machiavelli and Tasso to Rabelais and Montaigne, Camões and Cervantes, Marlowe, and Shakespeare—was shaped in significant part by the humanists' rediscovery of lost works of classical art and manuscripts, as well as by the popular and medieval traditions on which these and many other great artists also drew. For both better and worse, there is no doubt of the humanists' central importance.

The revival of learning was much more than a resurrection of the past, for it involved reshaping of the present and incipient creation of the future, nor were humanists interested solely in the Greco-Roman inheritance: Pico della Mirandola in particular immersed himself in Arabic and Hebrew wisdom as well. Even those who most scorned the humanists and deprecated their overzealous devotion to the ancients—such as Paracelsus or Francis Bacon—were deeply indebted to them and would have been inconceivable without them. And although, in defining their central dedication, it is no doubt true, as Kristeller remarks (1961, 120–21), that interest in human values "was incidental to their major concern, which was the study and imitation of classical, Greek and Latin literature," this "emphasis on man" was nonetheless "inherent in the cultural and educational program of the Renaissance humanists" (124). The famous treatises of Giannozzo Manetti and Pico della Mirandola on the dignity and excellence of the human being were, and were intended to be, defining documents in a shift toward a more positive vision of both man and the natural world of which he is part than had been characteristic, in the humanists' view, of the medieval centuries. (In fact, the Middle Ages were by no means so negative toward either man or nature as the humanists believed, as selections in my anthology *Encompassing Nature* (1997) make clear; but the monastic attitude of *contemptus mundi*, as expressed in Pope Innocent III's treatise on the misery of humankind—and revived, in different forms, by Savonarola, Luther, and Calvin—was widespread and antipathetic to the humanist affirmation of the high value of life in this world.) It is this emphasis, after all, that has clung to the word humanist in its many permutations since the Renaissance.

And it was this emphasis that the humanists rightly found in their cherished ancients; all of them knew the watchword of Terence (*Heautontimoroumenos* 77): *homo sum: humani nil a me alienum puto* ("I am a human being; I count nothing human alien to me"). Antiquity, rather than the Middle Ages, provided the great models of virtue or *virtù* for humanists as different as Petrarch and Machiavelli—though for Petrarch, and many others, antiquity included St. Augustine no less than Cicero. By and large these figures appealed not only as emblematic embodiments of single qualities (as Cato of Utica or Julius Caesar had appealed to Dante) but as rounded human beings (like Dante's Virgil) exemplifying the highest capacities, intellectual and moral, to which men might aspire, even in their failings: hence the renewed interest in introspective autobiographical writing that begins with Petrarch and culminates in Montaigne. In reviving antiquity the humanists were fully aware (as the name they proudly claimed surely suggests) that they were also reasserting this prominence of the human being—the multisided *uomo universale*, henceforth known as "Renaissance man"—gloriously embodied by the Greeks and Romans.

Yet the human being so exalted was not seen in isolation: it was not the Sophist Protagoras, who declared man "the measure of all things," who was central to the humanist vision of classical humanity, but the Sophists' great opponent, Plato, whom Marsilio Ficino translated in the mid-fifteenth century, and who insisted that the measure of man could only be taken in relation to the divine. The pervasive influence of Plato's thought—directly known to most of the Middle Ages only in a partial Latin translation of his cosmological dialogue, the *Timaeus*—worked in many directions, notably in disseminating, above all through the *Symposium* and Ficino's commentaries on it, the doctrine of love of the human and natural world by which man may be raised by degrees to the divine, in which he finds his true fulfillment: a concept that permeates Renaissance literature, thought, and art. Almost equally important was the figure of Socrates as portrayed by Plato, who largely eclipsed the more imperfect Cicero for some later humanists—as for their successors in the Enlightenment—as the embodiment of classical humanity and ethical attainment at its finest. And again, the human dimension was not divorced from the religious: Socrates and other pagan thinkers, to the humanists, could be thought of as Christians *avant la lettre*. "And so, when I read such things of such men," one of Erasmus's interlocutors exclaims in "The Godly Feast" (1957, 158), "I can hardly help exclaiming, 'Saint Socrates, pray for us!' (*Sancte Socrate, ora pro nobis*)." To which another replies: "As for me, there are many times when I do not hesitate to hope confidently that the souls of Virgil and Horace are sanctified." In this regard, Erasmus's ecumenical Christianity—and embracing humanism—took a giant step beyond what even Dante's deep reverence for his ancient masters could allow.

Among the defining characteristics of the humanist to emerge from the Renaissance, then, were his deep dedication to a continually renovated and renovative literary and philosophical heritage (along with incipient openness to other traditions of a world united by its common humanity); a high evaluation of man's dignity and importance in the natural world of which he is part; and an affirmation of the transcendent or spiritual dimension of human life: of that dedication to some higher goal by which alone man can be measured. Equally important, and implicit in the others, is an avowal of human freedom that goes far beyond orthodox Roman Catholic affirmation of free will in its Augustinian or Thomistic version. To man, Pico proclaims in his famous oration, "it is granted to have whatever he chooses, to be whatever he wills" (1948, 225). Less intoxicated writers of the later Renaissance would painfully learn (as don Quixote de la Mancha repeatedly does) how many strict limits reality might place upon this precarious freedom, yet abiding faith in man's capacity to realize his own destiny remained a central article of the humanist creed. As much as anything else, it is what prevented Erasmus, despite deep sympathy with reformation of the Church of his time, from joining with Luther, who declared, in contemptuous rebuttal of his humanist foe, "that, for myself, even if it could be, I should not want 'free-will' to be given me, nor anything to be left in my own hands to enable me to endeavor after salvation" (1961, 199). No statement could have been more antipathetic to the humanist spirit.

Such were some of the principal, and most enduringly definitive, characteristics of the humanism that united the Renaissance with classical antiquity. Nor had there, of course, been the gaping hiatus in between that the humanists averred: though the word was unknown to the Middle Ages, much of what Renaissance humanists would later most value had been a reality, both in the narrower sense of repeated renewals of a living classical tradition and in the broader sense of affirmation of human capacities and human freedom. It is a stretch, no doubt, to proclaim with E. K. Rand (1957, 35) that "St. Paul laid the foundation of Christian humanism" (by quoting pagan Greek authors in his epistles), and if John the Scot (Johannes Scotus Eriugena), who in the ninth century translated Christian Platonist writers from the Greek and composed a complex philosophy of nature in relation to God, was indeed a humanist of distinction, as Charles Homer Haskins affirms (1927, 17), he was very nearly an isolated link in a fragile chain. But medievalists including E. R. Curtius and Haskins have persuasively argued the importance of a meaningful humanism, embodied especially by John of Salisbury, in the twelfth-century "Renaissance," which in its early stages was influenced as much by Plato (little though his actual writings were known) as by Aristotle—a humanism, Curtius writes (1963, 315), which, "like every true humanism, delights simultaneously in the world and in the book." And R. W. Southern (1970, 31–32) affirms his belief that "the period from about 1100

to about 1320" was "one of the greatest ages of humanism in the
history of Europe: perhaps the greatest of all," not only or primarily
because of the revival of Greek and Arabic science and philosophy
that revolutionized the intellectual map of Europe, but because of
the "strong sense of the dignity of human nature" and the nobility
of the natural order of which man is part, to which writers of the age
give expression, and the assumption that nature is intelligible as "an
orderly system, and man—in understanding the laws of nature—
understands himself as the main part, the key-stone of nature." The
humanist tradition descending from the ancients was far less dis-
continuous than its Renaissance exponents believed.

That tradition was both reaffirmed and called into question by
the seventeenth- and eighteenth-century Enlightenment. For if the
scientific revolution owed much, including its very existence, to re-
vivals of Greek learning, and if the *philosophes* of the French Enlightenment were by and large no less fervid admirers of the
ancients than their Renaissance humanist predecessors had been,
the science associated with Galileo, Descartes, and Newton tended
increasingly to make the human being a detached observer of the
external world of nature rather than a central participant in it, thus
suggesting to many a mechanistic and deterministic view of nature
and man wholly foreign to humanism. It was perhaps dissidents
within the eighteenth-century Enlightenment—as different as Samuel Johnson, with his tormented tension between humanity and religious faith; Denis Diderot, with his exploration of the irrational
foundation of reason; Jean-Jacques Rousseau, with his visceral re-
pudiation of the very sciences and arts on which the Enlightenment
was based; and Giambattista Vico, with his deep appreciation of
primitive mythical and poetic thought and his ardent conviction that
human history is the product of human beings themselves—who
most importantly continued and transformed the humanist legacy
that the romantics of the succeeding century both renewed through
affirmation of the importance of the imagination and of the human
connection with nature and threatened to overwhelm by the irratio-
nalism that would culminate in the madness of Nietzsche and Strindberg. Both self-proclaimed humanists of the twentieth century
such as Babbitt and More and their Christian opponents such as
T. E. Hulme and T. S. Eliot have significantly rejected the romanti-
cisms that elevate sentiment and irrationality over reason and reasoned faith.

Against one of the extreme spokesmen for such antihumanistic irrationality in the literature of our century—Herr Naphta, the revolutionary reactionary, the Jewish Jesuit Bolshevik in *The Magic Mountain*, partly modeled on the Hungarian Marxist Georg Lukács—Thomas Mann sets the earnestly sympathetic, but often comically ineffective, figure of the *homo humanus* Herr Settembrini, who repeatedly asserts the primacy of human reason and the inevitability (in the face of all evidence to the contrary) of human progress: a figure, largely modeled, with humorous irony, on aspects of Mann himself, who in both his appeal and limitations is emblematic of the bravely defiant—or absurdly obsolescent—humanist in a century where humanity itself, even more than in others, has seemed at risk of terminal devaluation. Whatever other causes there may be, as suggested above, for the depreciation of humanism in our time, the vagueness, even banality of its formulations by its own advocates has made it hard to credit as a meaningful presence: "to be a good humanist," Babbitt writes, for example (1919, 13), "is merely [!] to be moderate and sensible and decent." Against such formulations, Eliot—despite respect for his former teacher—devastatingly asserts (1950, 422, 433) that a humanism torn in this way "from contexts of race, place, and time" is "a by-product of Protestant theology in its last agonies," heavily depending "upon the tergiversations of the word 'human'; and in general, upon implying clear and distinct philosophic ideas which are never there." And when Corliss Lamont (1982, 13) defines twentieth-century humanism as "a philosophy of joyous service for the greater good of all humanity," it is not hard—much though we might sympathize with so estimable a goal—to understand the force of reaction against its platitudinous emptiness. The antihumanistic post-structuralist and postmodernist reaction finds antecedents in Rousseau and Nietzsche and Heidegger (whose "Letter on Humanism" rejects, in the name of a "truth of Being" divorced from reason, logic, and values, both traditional "metaphysical" humanism and Sartre's humanistic reaffirmation of existential human freedom) and culminates in the twisted assertion of Derrida's disciple Philippe Lacoue-Labarthe (1990, 95) that "Nazism is a humanism in so far as it rests upon a determination of *humanitas* which is, in its view, more powerful—i.e. more effective—than any other. . . . The fact that this subject lacks the universality which apparently defines the *humanitas* of humanism in the received sense, still does not make Nazism an antihumanism."

What more antihumanistic claim could be made than that Nazism was not antihumanistic?

In the face of the frequent vacuity of its own recent declarations and the repudiations of those who scorn them as hollow banalities or tolerate them as harmless truisms, is humanism in the twenty-first century obsolete or dead—a derelict bulwark futilely erected by sentimental liberals or hidebound conservatives against the inevitable change professed by hardheaded proponents of less anthropocentric, and less humane, views of the world? Or can it, instead, be a radical alternative to the narrow reductionisms and specializations and fragmentations—and the consequent derogation of human nature itself—to which it is intrinsically opposed?

For affirmation of some common (dare we say universal?) human nature, binding together peoples of different times and places, genders and races and classes, underlies humanism in any form, and thereby inherently challenges the politicized ideologies of today's postmodernisms, rooted not in Renaissance and Enlightenment but in the illiberal reactions against them, whose prophets have included Marx and Lenin, Nietzsche and Heidegger. "The whole concept of humanity and humanism," Fromm writes (1962, 29), "is based on the idea of a human nature which all men share. This was the premise of Buddhist as well as of Judaeo-Christian thought"—as it is of modern psychology, linguistics, and science in general. To the extent that contemporary multiculturalism promotes not openness to shared values of different cultures but, as it often does, balkanization or ghettoization of human beings into narrower categories, so that Afro-American studies are mainly pursued by African Americans, gay and lesbian studies by gays and lesbians, women's studies by women, and so on, the effect is to deny any human commonality that might transcend—without of course denying—these divisions. A meaningful contemporary humanism will begin by affirming the rich diversity of human cultures, but also the underlying human nature that allows us, despite deeply important differences, to communicate with one another as members of a common species.

The word "species" is itself a reminder of the biological dimension often neglected by those who emphasize cultural distinctions—as dominant traditions of cultural relativism and social construction in anthropology and other social sciences frequently do—to the point of losing sight of human commonalities. As a dissident force in this intellectual climate, humanism will affirm with

Isaiah Berlin that the diversity of ends and values pursued by different societies, groups, classes, and individuals "cannot be unlimited, for the nature of men, however various and subject to change, must possess some generic character if it is to be called human at all" (1991, 80) and with Martin Gardner that "what is urgently needed at the moment is a corrective of the corrective [of cultural relativism]—the boldness to affirm that there is a common human nature on the basis of which valuations can be made and in terms of which real progress can be measured" (1996, 158). Genders are dual, sexual preferences varied, ethnic groups and classes many, but the human species is one, and biology emphasizes, with humanism, that unity.

And here the subjects of humanism and consciousness converge, for consciousness, if "irreducibly subjective" in the experience of each individual, as Searle writes (1992, 98), is nonetheless a biological phenomenon common to all human beings—and to many non-human beings as well: "an emergent feature," in Searle's words, "of certain systems of neurons in the same way that solidity and liquidity are emergent features of systems of molecules" (112). Human consciousness is a human trait shared in some degree with fellow animals, but foreign—as Searle, along with Gerald Edelman, Roger Penrose, and others, has stressed—to the algorithmic calculations of Turing machines and digital computers—calculations most characteristic among human beings, as Oliver Sacks remarks (1995, 270), of the autistic. Not consciousness but the unconscious, Penrose suggests, normally operates in so mechanistic a fashion: "whereas unconscious actions of the brain are ones that proceed according to algorithmic processes, the action of consciousness is quite different, and it proceeds in a way that cannot be described by any algorithm" (1989, 411). It follows, Sacks observes, that "traditional neurology, by its mechanicalness, its emphasis on deficits, conceals from us the actual life which is instinct in all cerebral functions—at least higher functions such as those of imagination, memory and perception" (1990, 89). The capacity for consciousness is common to all human beings qua human, greatly though it may differ in intensity, to say nothing of content: it is not a static entity but a dynamic process—as I have emphasized (drawing on such thinkers as Peirce, Popper, and Ricoeur) in *The Spiritual Quest*—by which the human being continually surpasses the limitations of the given through transformative exploration of the new. In reaffirming this common substratum of humanity (*humani nil a me alienum puto*), the humanist of today, far from opposing naturalism and science, endorses the biological commonality and counteracts the extremes of cultural relativism.

And this dynamic process of consciousness is inherently transcendent, never satisfied with a final end point, a full stop of quietus; like her predecessors in antiquity and the Middle Ages, the Renaissance and Enlightenment, a contemporary humanist will acknowledge the spiritual or religious dimensions of human experience no less than the biological from which they derive, and will no more be dogmatically atheist than dogmatically theist: for a humanist will always acknowledge the complexity and contradictions of humanity, its fallibility and imperfection, its perversities, indignities, even its horrors, along with—and inseparably from—its dignity and its capacity for greatness. ("What is man, that thou art mindful of him?" the Psalmist asked [Psalm 8: 4–5], and answered: "a little lower than the angels, and . . . crowned with glory and honor.") In this very awareness of human complexity, the humanist of today, by contesting the sufficiency of all reductionist determinisms—Marxism or Freudianism, behaviorism or structuralism or their multiple progenies—will reassert, against academic orthodoxies of the moment, the fundamental belief in human freedom central to humanism. In our world of "radical contingency," Merleau-Ponty writes, humanism "is a view which like the most fragile object of perception—a soap bubble, or a wave—or like the most simple dialogue, embraces indivisibly all the order and all the disorder of the world" (1969, 188–89): in this refusal of closure or determinism is the glory and honor of the humanistic tradition.

For humanism is a tradition: not a fixed or immutable tradition and certainly never a closed one, but a tradition precisely because it recognizes continuities of human nature that allow the past to continue to speak to the present, the present to the past, and that thus enable the future, through this unending dialogue, to come perpetually into being. A humanist of today will be open to diverse traditions of a genuinely multicultural world, finding (as Goethe did in Hafiz, and Irving Babbitt did in Confucius and the Buddha, and as many have done in the sages and poets of India and China, Buddhism and Islam, and the richly varied tribal cultures of every continent on the globe) fellow spirits in the affirmation of human dignity that is the property not of any one culture but of humanity at large.

But the humanist must never be satisfied with pious affirmations: the "studies of humanity" have been and rightly remain disciplines as rigorous as mathematics or science, and the humanist of today, like her Renaissance predecessors, must go beyond glib mastery of contemporary theoretical clichés (the current equivalents of Sophistry or Scholasticism in their decline) to undertake anew the long and arduous task of studying the languages and histories and cultures of the diverse humanity that is our subject—by learning Chinese or Arabic, say, or Turkish or Japanese, Sanskrit or Swahili, as indispensable tools for further and deeper knowledge and understanding.

Indeed, in the intellectual climate of today's universities, the truly radical outsider, the humanist as pariah and provocateur of the Western world, flying in the teeth of all orthodoxy by recklessly reaffirming the vitality of a humane tradition that threatens to be as deeply buried now as it seemed to be in the Dark Ages, might even daringly begin, at great personal risk and with enormous labor, with the study of Greek and Latin.

WORKS CITED

Babbitt, Irving. 1908. "What Is Humanism?" In *Literature and the American College: Essays in Defense of the Humanities*. Cambridge, Mass.: Houghton Mifflin.

———. 1919. *Rousseau and Romanticism*. Boston: Houghton Mifflin.

Berlin, Isaiah. 1991. "Alleged Relativism in Eighteenth-Century European Thought." In *The Crooked Timber of Humanity: Chapters in the History of Ideas*, ed. Henry Hardy. New York: Vintage Books.

Burckhardt, Jacob. 1954. *The Civilization of the Renaissance in Italy*. Trans. S. G. C. Middlemore. New York: Modern Library.

Curtius, Ernst Robert. 1963. *European Literature and the Latin Middle Ages*. Trans. Willard R. Trask. New York: Harper and Row.

Eliot, T. S. 1950. "The Humanism of Irving Babbitt"; "Second Thoughts about Humanism." In *Selected Essays of T. S. Eliot*. New York: Harcourt Brace.

Erasmus. 1957. "The Godly Feast." In *Ten Colloquies of Erasmus*. Trans. Craig R. Thompson. New York: Liberal Arts Press.

Frankl, Viktor. 1978. *The Unheard Cry for Meaning: Psychotherapy and Humanism*. New York: Simon and Schuster.

Fromm, Erich. 1962. *Beyond the Chains of Illusion: My Encounter with Marx and Freud*. New York: Pocket Books.

Gardner, Martin. 1996. "Beyond Cultural Relativism." In *Collected Essays 1938–1995*. New York: St. Martin's Press.

Haskins, Charles Homer. 1927. *The Renaissance of the Twelfth Century.* Cambridge: Harvard University Press.

Heidegger, Martin. 1977. "Letter on Humanism." In *Basic Writings*, trans. Frank A. Capuzzi and J. Glenn Gray, ed. David Farrell Krell. New York: Harper and Row.

Hulme, T. E. 1994. "A Notebook." In *The Collected Writings of T. E. Hulme*, ed. Karen Csengeri. Oxford: Clarendon.

Kristeller, Paul Oskar. 1961. *Renaissance Thought: The Classic, Scholastic, and Humanist Strains.* New York: Harper Torchbooks.

Kurtz, Paul. 1994. *Toward a New Enlightenment: The Philosophy of Paul Kurtz.* Ed. Vern L. Bullough and Timothy J. Madigan. New Brunswick: Transaction Publishers.

Lacoue-Labarthe, Philippe. 1990. *Heidegger, Art and Politics: The Fiction of the Political.* Trans. Chris Turner. Oxford: Basil Blackwell.

Lamont, Corliss. 1982. *The Philosophy of Humanism.* 6th ed. New York: Frederick Ungar.

Leonardo da Vinci. 1954. *The Notebooks.* 2 vols. Trans. Edward MacCurdy. London: Reprint Society.

Lodge, David. 1984. *Small World: An Academic Romance.* New York: Warner Books.

Luther, Martin. 1961. "The Bondage of the Will." In *Martin Luther: Selections from His Writings*, ed. John Dillenberger. Garden City, N.Y.: Doubleday Anchor.

Manetti, Giannozzo. 1966. "On the Dignity of Man." In *Two Views of Man: Pope Innocent III On the Misery of Man, Giannozzo Manetti on the Dignity of Man*, trans. Bernard Murchland. New York: Frederick Ungar.

Mann, Thomas. 1930. 1927. *The Magic Mountain.* Trans. H. T. Lowe-Porter. New York: Knopf.

———. *Briefe 1889–1936.* Ed. Erika Mann. Frankfurt am Main: S. Fischer Verlag, 1961.

Maritain, Jacques. 1941. *True Humanism.* Trans. M. R. Adamson. London: Centenary Press.

Marx, Karl. 1964. *Economic and Philosophic Manuscripts of 1844.* Trans. Martin Milligan. Ed. Dirk J. Struik. New York: International Publishers.

Merleau-Ponty, Maurice. 1969. *Humanism and Terror: An Essay on the Communist Problem.* Trans. John O'Neill. Boston: Beacon Press.

More, Paul Elmer. 1936. *On Being Human.* New Shelburne Essays, vol. 3. Princeton: Princeton University Press.

Paglia, Camille. 1992. "Junk Bonds and Corporate Raiders: Academe in the Hour of the Wolf." In *Sex, Art, and American Culture: Essays.* New York: Vintage.

Penrose, Roger. 1989. *The Emperor's New Mind: Concerning Computers, Minds, and the Laws of Physics.* Oxford University Press.

Pico della Mirandola, Giovanni. 1948. "Oration on the Dignity of Man." In *The Renaissance Philosophy of Man*, trans. Elizabeth Livermore Forbes, ed. Ernst Cassirer et al. Chicago: University of Chicago Press.

Rand, Edward Kennard. 1957. *Founders of the Middle Ages.* New York: Dover.

Sacks, Oliver. 1990. *The Man Who Mistook His Wife for a Hat and Other Clinical Tales*. New York: HarperPerennial.

———. 1995. *An Anthropologist on Mars: Seven Paradoxical Tales*. New York: Knopf.

Sartre, Jean-Paul. 1948. *Existentialism and Humanism*. Trans. Philip Mairet. London: Methuen.

Searle, John R. 1992. *The Rediscovery of the Mind*. Cambridge: MIT Press.

Southern, R. W. 1970. *Medieval Humanism*. New York: Harper and Row.

Steiner, George. 1996. "Through That Glass Darkly." In *No Passion Spent: Essays 1978–1995*. New Haven: Yale University Press.

Torrance, Robert M. 1994. *The Spiritual Quest: Transcendence in Myth, Religion, and Science*. Berkeley: University of California Press.

———. 1997. *Encompassing Nature: A Sourcebook*. Washington, D. C.: Counterpoint.

Part IV
Our Future Is Now

APIUM
(Association for the Protection and Integrity of an Unspoiled Mars)
BRIAN W. ALDISS

PLANS ARE ALREADY AFOOT TO SEND HUMAN BEINGS TO MARS. Behind these exciting possibilities lies a less worthy objective: an assumption that the Red Planet can be turned into something resembling a colony, an inferior Earth. This operation would extend prevailing dystopian tendencies into the next century.

Planets are environments with their own integrity. Any vast engineering schemes would be invasive. The end result could only be to turn Mars into a dreary suburb, imitating the less attractive features of terrestrial cities. A military-industrial complex will rule over it.

APIUM stands for humanity's right to walk on Mars, and is against its rape and ruination. Mars must become a UN-protectorate and be treated as a "planet for science," much as the Antarctic has been preserved—at least to a great extent—as unspoiled white wilderness. We are for a *White Mars!*

Mars should remain as a kind of Ayers Rock in the sky. It must be made visitable to ordinary men and women (the travel costs to be met by community service at home). Its solitudes will be preserved for silence and meditation and honeymooning. From Mars, traditionally the god of war, *a myth of peace* will spread back to Earth, supplanting the myth of energy/power/exploitation that has so darkened the twentieth century.

APIUM believes that great good will come to both planets if we have the courage to sustain a White Mars.

Brian W. Aldiss, President, APIUM

White Mars

A Socratic Dialogue of Time to Come

SHE: We want to present a history of the development of Mars, and how we have progressed spiritually. It is a glorious and surprising story, a history of human society understanding and re-creating itself. While I am speaking to you from Mars, my Earthbound avatar is speaking to you from our old parent planet. Let us cast our minds back before everything changed, to the Age of Estrangement, when nobody had ever set foot on Earth's neighboring planet.

HE: So. Back to the twenty-first century and a barren planet. The first arrivals on Mars found an empty world, free of all the imaginary creatures that have been supposed to haunt the Earth, the ghosts and ghouls, the elves and fairies—all those fantasy creatures that beset human life, born of dark forests and old houses.

SHE: You've forgotten the gods and goddesses, the Greek gods who gave their names to the constellations, the Baals and Isises and Roman soldier gods, the vengeful Almighty of the Old Testament, Allah—all imaginary superbeings who supposedly controlled mankind's behavior before humanity could control itself.

HE: You're right, I forgot them. They were all creaking floorboards in the cellars of the brain, inheritance from eo-human days. Earth was overpopulated with both real and imaginary persons . . . Mars was blessedly free of all that. On Mars, you could start anew. It's true the men and women who arrived on Mars had a lot of conflicting Mars legends in their heads . . .

SHE: Oh, you mean that old stuff. Percival Lowell's Mars of the canals and the dying culture? I still have a kind of nostalgia for that grand sunset vision—wrong in reality, right as imagery. And Edgar Rice Burrough's Barsoom.

HE: And all the horrors that earlier humanity invented to populate Mars—H. G. Wells's invaders of Earth, rather than the gentle *Hrossa* and *pfifltriggi* of C. S. Lewis's Malacandra.

SHE: Life, you see—always this bizarre preoccupation with life, however fantastic. Tokens of the insufficiency of our own lives.

HE: But the first men who went to Mars came from a technological age. They harbored another idea in their heads. Certainly they were hoping to find life of some sort, archebacteria being reckoned most likely. They nourished the idea of terraforming the Red Planet and turning it into a sort of inferior second Earth.

SHE: Having at last managed to reach another planet, they desired to make it like Earth! It seems strange to us now.

HE: They had not acquired the habit of living away from Earth. "Terraforming" was an engineer's dream—a novelty. Their perceptions had to change. They stood there, gaping—aware for the first time of the magnitude of the task—and of its aggressive nature. Every planet has its own sanctity.

SHE: Even at the most impressive moment in life, a voice seems to speak within us, the mind communing with itself. Percy Bysshe Shelley was the first to recognize this duality. In a poem on Mont Blanc, he speaks of standing watching a waterfall:

> Dizzy ravine!—and when I gaze at thee
> I seem as in a trance sublime and strange
> To muse on my own separate phantasy,
> My own, my human mind, which passively
> Now renders and receives fast influencings,
> Holding an unremitting interchange
> With the clear universe of things around . . .

HE: Yes, the words strike to the very essence of human perceptions. As phenomenology declares, our inner discourse shapes our outward perception. I'll remind you that the great Martian expedition was not the first scientific excursion that set out to discover a new world. It too had trouble with its perceptions.

SHE: You're speaking of the way the West was won in the case of North America? The slaughter of the Indian nations, the killing of buffalo? Wasn't all that a primitive kind of terraforming?

HE: I mean the expedition of Captain James Cook in H.M.S. *Endeavour* to the South Seas. In this 366-ton wooden ship, Cook eventually circumnavigated the globe. The *Endeavour* was commissioned to observe the 1769 transit of Venus across the face of the Sun, among other objectives. The choice of Joseph Banks, then only twenty-three, as scientific observer, was a good one. Banks had a trained connoisseur's eye.

It was regarded by the enlightened Royal Society as vital that accurate drawings should accompany written descriptions of all new discoveries. Banks's artists had their problems. Scientific diagrams of landscapes and plants and animals were made, but artistry also crept in. Drawing faithful records of the native peoples of the Pacific was beggared by the preconceptions of the time. Alexander Buchan took an ethnographic view, drawing groups of natives free from the conventions of neoclassical style; whereas Sydney Parkinson disposed of them according to the dictates of composition. In Johann Zoffany's famous canvas of *The Death of Cook,* many of the participants in that picture assume classical postures, presumably to increase the air of Greek tragedy.

Thus the unfamiliar was made palatable for the folks back home, was made to bend to their preconceptions.

SHE: I see what you're getting at. Behind the difficulties of coming to terms with the unknown lay a philosophical problem, typical of that century. Were the misfortunes attendant on mankind owed to a departure from, a defiance of, natural law—or was it that mankind could raise itself above the brute beasts only by improving on and distancing himself from nature? The city-dwellers or the Noble Savage?

HE: Exactly. The discovery of the Society Islands favored the former idea, that of New Zealand and Australia the latter.

Australia and New Zealand, when their barren shores were first sighted, fostered the concept of improvement and progress. When Captain Arthur Phillip founded the first penal colony in Australia, at Port Jackson in 1788, he rejoiced in an eighteenth-century version of natives—the area was flattened, and, Phillip declared, "By degrees large spaces are opened, plans are formed, lines marked, and a prospect at least of future regularity is clearly discerned, and is made the more striking by the recollection of former confusion." Ah, the straight line!—the marker of civilization, of capitalism!

The overwhelming belief in *conquering nature*—in somehow distancing ourselves from nature, from something of which we are an inescapable part—prevailed for at least two centuries.

SHE: Possibly this dichotomy of perception was reinforced by Cartesian dualism, which made a sharp distinction between the mind and body—the sort of thing Shelley spoke against. A metaphorical beheading . . .

HE: I'm unsure about that. It may be as you say.

SHE: What we need to bear in mind is that a belief can take rather firm hold, once it circulates among the population. No matter if it's totally erroneous. Even in these days of interplanetary travel, half the population of Earth still believes that the Sun orbits the Earth, rather than vice versa. What conclusions do you draw from that—other than that ignorance has more gravitational weight than wisdom?

HE: Or that we are more hive-minded than we care to believe?

SHE: Well, let's get back to Mars and those first arrivals here.

HE: Try to recall what the situation was in those days. With the growth in economic power of the Pacrim countries in the twenty-first century, the international dateline had been removed to the center of the Atlantic, and American trade was locked into that of its Asian neighbors. The cost of all Martian expeditions was met by a consortium, formed by US, Pacrim, and EU space agencies. That was EUPACUS, a long-forgotten acronym. However, the UN, then under a powerful and farsighted general secretary, George Bligh, brought Mars under its own jurisdiction. Once you were on Mars, you came under Martian law, not under the laws of your own country.

SHE: It was a sensible provision. A lesson had been learned from the days when Antarctica had been a continent set aside for science. Just occasionally we manage to learn from history! We wanted the Red Planet to be a White Mars—a planet set aside for science.

HE: That's an ancient battle cry!

SHE: Old battle cries still retain their power. In the mid-twenty-first century, there was a movement on Earth called APIUM—the Association for the Protection and Integrity of an Unspoiled Mars. It was regarded as a raggle-taggle group of eccentrics and Greens at first. APIUM wanted to preserve Mars as it had been for millions of years, as a kind of memorial to early man's early dreams. Their claim was that every environment has its sanctity, and sufficient environments had been ruined on Earth without starting out at once to monkey with another planet—an entire planet.

However, the people who landed on Mars in that first expedition had to justify costs. They were going to prepare to terraform it. It was a foregone conclusion for them. They were bound by the pressures of their rather primitive societies.

HE: Ah, yes, *terraforming* . . . ! That word and concept coined by the SF writer Jack Williamson. How alluring and advanced it was, when first coined. It was another of those ideas that took root easily in the fertile soil of the human mind . . .

SHE: Yes. There was nothing sinister about it. The astronauts simply took the idea for granted. It was part of their mythology—meaning an old way of thought. They imagined they'd improve the planet and make it like Earth. They had glowing computer designs to seduce them, showing all of Mars looking like the Cotswolds on a sunny day.

HE: But they also carried in their minds opposing preconceptions. Mars as a rubbish dump of rock, "suitable for development," like something from a diagram of "nuclear winter," that old guilt-myth—or Mars as a heavenly body, formidable, aloof, enduring. Similar to the two opposed ideas that Captain Cook had held, three centuries earlier. And—

SHE: They left their ships and stood there, like stout Cortez, silent upon a peak in Darien in Keats's poem, with the whole vista of the planet confronting them, and—

HE: And?

SHE: And they knew—it was that discourse of Shelley's between the outer and inner world—they *knew* that terraforming was just a dream, a terrestrial city-dweller's computer phobia. It was undesirable. To use an old term, it was blasphemous, against nature. You know how city-dwellers fear nature. In a kind of vision, they saw that this environment must not be destroyed. That it carried a message, an austere message: *Rethink! You have achieved much—achieve more! Rethink!*

HE: Rethink—and refeel—because it was experience that brought a revolution in their understanding. They knew as they stood there they were at a turning point in history. Yet, you see, some people claim this vital decision not to terraform sprang from a powerful speech by UN Secretary George Bligh, who argued against it. His words were often quoted: "Terraforming is a clever idea that may or may not work. But cleverness is a lesser thing than reverence. We must have reverence for Mars as it has always existed. We cannot destroy the millions of years of its solitude merely for cleverness. Stay your hand!"

SHE: You believe those words of Bligh's were in the astronauts' minds when they landed?

HE: I partly believe so. I wish to believe so because staying the hand is often a better, if less popular, way to proceed than conquest. Anyhow, they did stay their hands. It proved the beginning of a tide in the affairs of men. Fortunately, you couldn't exploit Mars: there were no natural resources to exploit—no oil or fossil fuels, because there had never been forests. Limited underground reservoirs of water. Just—just that amazing empty world, so long the target of mankind's dreams and speculations, a desert rolling ever onward through space.

SHE: The old-fashioned word, "space," had been relegated to the etymological museum, by the way. That highway of teeming particles is now know as "matrix."

HE: Thousands on thousands of young people desired to visit Mars, just as two centuries earlier they had walked, rolled, or ridden westwards across the face of North America. The UN had to formulate rules for visitors. Two categories of people were permitted to go, traveling uncomfortably in EUPACUS ships, the YEAs and the DOPs. (*Laughs*)

SHE: It was a sensible arrangement. Or at least it worked, given the difficulties of the journey. The YEAs were Young Educated Adults. They had to pass an examination to qualify. The DOPs were Distinguished Older Persons. They were selected by their communities. The cost of the Earth-Mars round trip was high. DOPs were paid for by their communities. The YEAs paid in work, doing a year's community service before the journey.

HE: So the giant fish farms off Galapagos and Scapa Flow and the bird ranches of the Canadian north and the vineyards of the Gobi were developed. . . all by voluntary labor.

SHE: And the afforestation of most of the outback in Australia.

HE: And of the great flow of people who went to Mars, that wonderful new Ayers Rock in the sky, to meditate, to explore, to honeymoon, to realize themselves—all found themselves up against the reality of the cosmos. All stood there in awe, breathing in the laws of the universe.

SHE: And one of them said, marveling, "And that I have come here to experience all this means I am the most extraordinary thing in the entire galaxy."

HE: Then came the crash!

SHE: Oh yes, just when minds were changing everywhere! And the crash marked the end of a certain exploitive chain of thought. Pundits in 2085 called it the end of the Twentieth-Century Nightmare. The consortium EUPACUS collapsed. It was a case of internal corruption. Billions of dollars had been embezzled and, when the figures were examined, the whole company fell apart.

EUPACUS had a monopoly on interplanetary travel and on all travel arrangements. All that traffic stopped. Five thousand visitors were on Mars at the time, together with two thousand administrators, technicians, and scientists—Mars of course made an excellent observatory for studying Jupiter and its moons.

Seven thousand people—stranded there!

HE: But Mars is a big desert island. By this time, it was a complex community, lacking Wild West atmosphere, with serious business to do. There were no guns on Mars; no mind-destroying drugs; there was no currency, only limited credit.

SHE: Another important thing. No animals. Because there was no grazing or fodder to be had, no animals lived on Mars, except for a few cats. People raised crops and vegetarianism became a positive thing rather than a negative. The habit was emulated by terrestrials. In fact, renewed concern for animals by demonstrations and lobbying induced many governments to bring in animal rights laws. A revulsion to rearing animals for slaughter and human consumption was widespread. The human conscience was getting up off the couch!

HE: You must be mistaken about the animals. I remember seeing documentaries showing your Martian domes full of bright birds. And there were fish, too.

SHE: Oh, birds and fish, yes, but no animals. The birds were genetically manipulated macaws and parrots. Instead of squawking, they sang sweetly. They were allowed to fly free in limited areas of the main domes, the "tourist" domes. They were prized. No one attempted to kill or eat them during the period when Mars was isolated.

HE: So the Martians remained cut off, happily under wise leaders. During the period of isolation, water—the fossil water from underground reservoirs—was strictly rationed. It was needed for agriculture and went through electrolysis to provide necessary oxygen. The isolated community had reason to cohere. Without coherence there was no chance of survival. No one died . . .

SHE: The collapse of EUPACUS brought financial crisis to the business centers of Earth: L.A., Seoul, Beijing, London, and Frankfurt. The disillusion with laissez-faire capitalism was complete. So much so that "Stay your hand!" became a popular phrase. Stay your hand from grasping another ice cream, another beer, another car, another house! You stayed your hand out of pride.

It was five years before a limited flight schedule with Mars was reestablished. By then the idea of community service had sunk in, reinforcing the concept of the world's population as a unit and as part of the planet's necessary biota. Discovering that the Mars community had achieved a frugal utopia, that all there were lean but fit, was a cause for great rejoicing—most nationalities had a representative member on White Mars.

HE: The Martian example hastened the swing away from exploitive capitalism toward the managerialism that had already begun. Laissez-faire passed away in its sleep, as communism had done before it. The epoch of peaceful Earth opened, with leadership concentrating on integrating its component parts and a general tendency to behave more like parkkeepers than robber barons.

SHE: Ah, but with the increase in YEA and DOP pilgrims to the heroic White Mars, the planet ran out of water. The underground reservoirs, such as they were, had been drained dry. It looked like the end of a civilization on Mars.

HE: I'm not sure it was as bad as that, because already manned probes were forging further out into the system and the realm of the gas giants: mighty Jupiter, Saturn, Uranus, and Neptune. Unexplained activity had been sighted between Neptune and its large satellite, Triton. The base was established on Jupiter's moon, Ganymede—

SHE: I have visited Ganymede City. It's a pretty swinging place. People live for the day. I fear Mars gets bypassed now, because views of Jupiter from Ganymede and the other moons are so inexhaustibly wonder-making.

HE: From Ganymede, it was just a hop to the neighboring moon, Oceania—the rechristened Europa—where views of Jupiter are even more stunning.

There's a floating base on Oceania, built on top of a kilometer-deep ice floe. Under the ice crust, remarkably, is a fresh water ocean—pure fresh water, without life, or without life until we seeded some there.

That water gets despatched in bladdees to Mars. Mars now has a large lake slowly turning into a sea of fresh water. Its main problem is solved.

SHE: And so of course Mars is being terraformed at last. The human race has moved on and no longer needs a monument to old dreams and illusions.

HE: Mars's period of frugal utopia did not last. But the blackness of the twentieth century, with all its wars, genocides, killings, injustice, and greed had faded away. Somehow, we found the strength, in Bligh's words, to stay its hand. The human race is happier—less tormented—as it launches out toward the stars.

SHE: To meet with all those other species we don't yet know of . . . Maybe with God?

HE: Unlikely. God was one of those creaking floorboards in the brain we left behind when we got to Mars.

SHE: I cannot accept that. What would become of the human race if there were no God?

HE: What became of it during the twentieth century when supposedly there was a God? You believers might say, "He saved us from destroying ourselves with our nuclear weapons. That was His will." Equally, if we had destroyed ourselves—that would have been God's will too, according to you. There's no God—yet I hate him. I hate the way religious belief has caused us to waste our energies looking away from our own intractable problems. He stood in our way of enlightenment, like Jung's Shadow, barring us from accepting that we are made of the ashes fallen from the flanks of extinct suns. That we are universe-stuff.

SHE: You must allow me strongly to disagree. God has been our inspiration, lifting us from the material. Have you never listened to all the beautiful sacred music composed in His name, or seen all the great paintings faith has inspired?

HE: The paintings were painted by men. God didn't have half the musical genius of Johann Sebastian Bach, I can tell you. You must give up this illusion, comforting although it is. Giving it up is part of the process of becoming adult.

SHE: I don't understand you.

HE: You mean you don't understand evolution.

SHE: Don't be silly. Science and religion are not in conflict.

HE: No—it's experience and religion that are in conflict.

SHE: And what will we do without God?

HE: We must learn—as we are slowly learning—to judge ourselves and our own actions.

SHE: You won't shake my faith. I'm sorry you don't have it.

HE: Faith? Being unmoved by facts? Come, you must not pride yourself on such blindness. Think how the concept of God separated us from the rest of nature, set us above the animals, gave us the example of puissance and abasement. Made us self-preoccupied idiots . . .

SHE: That's blasphemous rubbish. You sound almost inhuman when you speak like that.

HE: We are almost becoming another species, we spacegoers. Physical and mental change is rapid now. We have developed from the gift of that tormented twentieth century, from the discovery of DNA code and the subsequent advance of genetic engineering. The bladdees shuttling to and fro across matrix between Oceania and Mars are living entities developed by bioengineering skills from the modest bladderwort.

SHE: You remember the excitement when Ganymede was made habitable by new plant-insect stock. The plantsects were despatched in unmanned probes. They soft-landed on Ganymede, dispersed, reproduced rapidly, and prepared the satellite for us when we arrived there. By that time, the plantsects had culminated, consuming themselves, leaving their bodies for compost. Such advances would have been impossible in the early days of Mars landings, with their mechanistic approach.

HE: And did God walk on Ganymede? No, He stood in our way! Was He not Carl Jung's monstrous Shadow, cutting us off from a realization of ourselves as intrinsically a part of the whole cosmos—ashes from the flanks of extinct suns?

SHE: Try to love God, whether or not you think He exists. Hatred is harmful to you. God was necessary—essential, perhaps—for some ages past, and the Savior represented a condition for us to aspire to in the long period of darkness.

HE: *(Laughs)* You're saying we have saved ourselves?

SHE: I'm saying that the concept of a loving Savior helped us, once upon a time. But certainly we've done away with hatred on the outer satellites, along with most forms of illness; genetic revision and improved immune systems have altogether clarified our minds.

HE: It was the understanding that we are an intrinsic part of nature that transformed our perceptions when we arrived on Mars. Much has followed. The bleak Martian globe cleared our perceptions. A prompting of our symbiotic relationship with plant life speeded the development of warm-blooded plants. That epiphyte growing on your head, much resembling an orchid, is now women's crowning glory! It permits you to carry with you a micro-atmosphere, a temperature gauge, and other perceptions, wherever you go.

SHE: As do the ferns sprouting round your venerable cranium. You are

right there. We're now true terrestrials, half-human, half-plant, creatures
of nature, well-equipped to venture throughout a waiting universe.

HE: Well, it's been pleasant to talk with you. You must go on your way. I
have to retire; I'm growing too old to travel. We shall not meet again.
Farewell, dear spirit!

Notes on Contributors

BRIAN ALDISS is doyen of science fiction authors, with many established classics in the genre to his credit, as well as several volumes of autobiography and poetry and a history of science fiction. His many honors include four Hugo and five Nebula awards. His science fiction works include *Hothouse* (1962), *Greybeard* (1964), *Earthworks* (1965), *Barefoot in the Head* (1969), which uses ideas from Ouspensky and Gurdieff, and *White Mars* (1999, co-authored with Roger Penrose). Volumes of autobiography include *The Twinkling of an Eye* (1998) and *When the Feast is Finished: Reflections on Terminal Illness* (1999, co-authored with Margaret Aldiss).

FREDERICK A. DE ARMAS, a University of North Carolina Ph.D., is Andrew W. Mellon Professor in the Humanities at the University of Chicago. He has taught at Pennsylvania State University where he was the Edwin Erle Sparks Professor of Spanish and Comparative Literature and at Louisiana State University. He has been visiting professor at Duke University and at the University of Missouri. His books and edited collections focus on Golden Age Spanish literature, often from a comparative perspective. They include: *The Invisible Mistress: Aspects of Feminism and Fantasy in the Golden Age* (1976); *The Return of Astraea: An Astral-Imperial Myth of Calderon* (1986); *The Prince in the Tower: Perceptions of "La vida es sueno"* (1993); *Heavenly Bodies: The Realms of "La estrella de Sevilla"* (1996); *Star-Crossed Golden Age: Myth and the Spanish Comedia* (1998). His most recent book is *Cervantes, Raphael, and the Classics* (Cambridge, 1998).

DANIEL MEYER DINKGRAFE received his Ph.D. in 1994 at the Department of Drama, Theater and Media Arts, Royal Holloway, University of London, with a thesis on "Consciousness and the Actor: A Reassessment of Western and Indian Approaches to the Actor's Emotional Involvement from the Perspective of Vedic Psychology." He is currently lecturer in the Department of Theater, Film, and Television Studies, University of Wales Aberystwyth; editor of *Who's Who in Contemporary World Theater* (Routledge, 2000); and founding editor of the web-based journal *Consciousness, Literature, and the Arts* (URL: hhtp://www.aber.ac.uk/tfts/journal).

WILLIAM S. HANEY II, a University of California, Davis, Ph.D., is Professor of English Literature and Humanities at Eastern Mediterranean University, North Cyprus. He has taught at the University of Maryland and the Johannes Gutenberg University in Mainz, Germany. His books and edited collections focus on contemporary British and American literature and culture, often from a consciousness studies perspective. They include *Literary Theory and Sanskrit Poetics* (1993); *The Changing Face of English Literary and Cultural Studies in a Transnational Environment*, co-edited with Nicholas Pagan (1999); and *Literary Theory: Beginnings and Ends*, co-edited with Nicholas Pagan (2001). His most recent book is *Culture and Consciousness: Literature Regained* (forthcoming, Bucknell University Press).

DAVID JASPER is Professor of Theology and Literature at the University of Glasgow. He studied at Cambridge, Oxford, and Durham. His works include *Coleridge as Poet and Religious Thinker* (1985), *New Testament and the Literary Imagination* (1987), and "Theology and Postmodernity: Poetry, Apocalypse, and the Future of God" (*Svensk Teologisk Kvartalskrift*, 1997). He founded the Centre for the Study of Literature, Theology, and the Arts in the University of Glasgow, a center embracing people of all religions and none who are willing to undertake open discussion of difficult issues and underlying assumptions. Central interests are religion and aesthetics, theology and culture, and theology and the visual arts. He is currently Dean of Theology.

PETER MALEKIN studied at Oxford, taught at the universities of Durham (England), Uppsala (Sweden), and Tübingen (Germany). Currently a visiting professor at Eastern Mediterranean University, he is also establishing the Rags of Time Center, an alternative center for education, the arts, and new ideas. With Ralph Yarrow of the University of East Anglia he is attempting to develop training methods for "pashyanti theater" and to found a new modern mythic theater. His publications include *Consciousness, Literature, and Theater: Theory and Beyond*, co-authored with Ralph Yarrow (1997).

DANIEL R. SCHWARZ is Professor of English and Stephen H. Weiss Presidential Fellow at Cornell University, where he has taught since 1968. He received Cornell's College of Arts and Sciences Russell Award for distinguished teaching. He is author of the widely read *Imagining the Holocaust* (1999). His most recent book is *Rereading Conrad* (2001). His prior books include *Reconfiguring Modernism: Explorations in the Relationship Between Modern Art and Modern Literature* (1997); *Narrative and Representation in Wallace Stevens* (1993); *The Case for a Humanistic Poetics* (1991); *The Transformation of the English Novel, 1890–1930* (1989; revised 1995); *Reading Joyce's "Ulysses"* (1987); *The Humanistic Heritage: Critical Theories of the English Novel from James to Hillis Miller* (1986); *Conrad: The Later Fiction* (1982); *Conrad: "Almayer's Folly" through "Under Western Eyes"* (1980); and *Disraeli's Fiction* (1979). He has edited *The Dead* (1994) and *The Secret Sharer* (1997) in the *Bedford Case Studies in Contemporary Criticism* Series, and is co-editor of *Narrative and Culture* (1994). He has directed nine NEH seminars, and has lectured widely in the United States and abroad.

ROBERT MITCHELL TORRANCE is Professor Emeritus of Comparative Literature, University of California, Davis. He received his Ph.D. in Comparative Literature from Harvard University, 1970. His books include Sophocles' *The Women of Trachis and Philoctetes*, a new translation, with introduction 1966); *The Comic Hero* (1978); *Ideal and Spleen: The Crisis of Transcendent Vision in Romantic, Symbolist, and Modern Poetry* (1987); *The Spiritual Quest: Transcendence in Myth, Religion, and Science* (1994); *Encompassing Nature: A Sourcebook*, ed. (1998). Under review is a translation of Dante's *Inferno*.

Index